CHAPTERS BOOKSTORE
BARRIE, ONTARIO
10-14-01

Notes on a Beermat

To the pub-minded women in my life: Kitty Pashley, who still likes a good pub in her tenth decade, and Anne Pashley, who has been to all these pubs and more. And in memory of the late Stanley Pashley, who propped up a bar or two in his time.

Ale, ale, glorious ale,
Served up in pewter, it tells its own tale,
Some folk like radishes, some curly kale,
But give I boiled parsnips,
And a great dish of taters,
And a lump of fatty bacon,
And a pint of good ale.

- Traditional English drinking song

Notes on a Beermat

Drinking
and
Why It's Necessary

by

Nicholas Pashley

Foreword by
BILL BRYSON

Polar Bear Press, Toronto

Polar
Bear
Press

Distributed by
North 49 Books
35 Prince Andrew Place
Toronto, Ontario
M3C 2H2
(416) 449-4000

National Library of Canada Canadian Cataloguing in Publication Data

Nicholas Pashley, 1946-
   Notes on a beermat: drinking and why it's necessary

ISBN 1-896757-17-0

1. Drinking of alcoholic beverages — Humour. 2. Bars (Drinking establishments) — Humour. I. Title
PN6178.C3P383 2001   C818'.5402   C2001-930674-1

2001 02 03 04 10 9 8 7 6 5 4 3 2 1
Printed in Canada

Book designed by Fortunato Design Inc.

Contents

PART TWO: DRINKING IN PARTICULAR

Foreword

Though it pains me to say it, I don't believe I have seen Nicholas Pashley sober on more than six or seven occasions. On the other hand, and to be scrupulously fair, that is also the number of occasions on which I have seen Mr. Pashley, and that is where the pain comes in.

Mr. Pashley, as this book joyously attests, is clearly the finest drinking companion anyone could ask for. Unfortunately for me, he lives in Toronto, where he sells books by day and spends his evenings (and, it seems, quite a lot of his days as well) having a grand and amusing time in the city's varied drinking establishments, while I live in New Hampshire where I spend nine months of the year shoveling snow and the other three months drying out my mittens. Thus, I am able to enjoy his company only on those infrequent occasions when I am on the right side of Lake Ontario.

Still, on the basis of a tragically finite number of such meetings, I can report that he is witty, kind, thoughtful, almost preposterously good-natured and even smarter than he looks. Now with this handsomely bound volume he has produced what is unquestionably the funniest and most enjoyable book on beer drinking written by an English-born Canadian bookseller yet this century.

I joke, of course. This is a truly wonderful book from beginning to end—hugely comic, delightfully acerbic, gloriously discursive and staggeringly well informed. In short, it is very like an evening with Mr. Pashley himself, but cheaper and with fewer trips to the men's room.

You are in for a singular treat and I envy you for that. Me, I've got some walks to shovel.

BILL BRYSON

Introduction

So this fellow walks into a bar, right? Then he walks into another bar. And yet another bar. Repeat this action for thirty-five years. And that's how this book got written.

I don't know if my mother coined the expression, but it was at her knee that I learned the expression "pub-minded", a pleasing turn of phrase that captures my world-view with an uncanny precision. How lucky I was, then, to marry a woman similarly inclined. We met in a pub, of course.

This is a book about drinking. Now, we've seen a number of books about drinking in recent years, most of them telling either sad or inspirational stories about the perils of alcohol and the overcoming thereof. This is not one of those books.

There's no question, of course, that drink is a terrible thing. If I'd never touched a drop I'd have saved myself a lot of money. I'd be driving a fancy car today. On the other hand, I'd know a good deal fewer people, including my wife, so all in all I'm just as happy drinking. Otherwise I'd be a lonely guy driving a fancy car. (I know—there is an argument that says that you never have to be lonely if you have a fancy car. I wouldn't know. I'm a happily married drinking man with an '87 K-Car.)

And it's not just about drinking. It's about drinking well and drinking in public. I heard the friend of a friend express bewilderment one evening about why we chose to hang out in pubs when it was much cheaper to drink at home. I suspect this guy's a bit of a piker. For the beer drinker, of course, the pub has draught beer, which you can't get at home unless you live in a frat house. The pub also has that quality of pubness that few of us can achieve at home. Nor would most of us want to, the prime quality of pubness being that anyone is likely to turn up unannounced for a drink.

In his book *The Great Good Place*, Ray Oldenburg writes of the Third Place, a place that is neither home nor work, a place where friends can gather informally, without anyone having to be the host or clean up afterwards, where you can stay for one quick drink or for an evening, depending on your mood or on the social chemistry. Such places can be any of a number of things—a café or a bookstore, for instance—but they are most likely to be a pub, or something like it.

Oldenburg argues that society needs its third places, and that the suburbanization of North America makes third places not only unlikely but practically impossible. The shopping mall does not count. As Stan Rogers sang in *Barrett's Privateers*, "God damn the mall!" I think I've got that right.

The need for a third place probably originated in Europe, where people lived multigenerationally in tiny apartments and needed somewhere else to go, if only to get away from the other thirteen people who shared their room. The modern North American, living in splendid suburban isolation in his monster home, has no such need for escape. If you want company, you can invite the people next door in for a drink. Except, of course, that you don't know the people next door. Small wonder we all turn into serial killers. Statistics show that very few pubgoers become serial killers. It's a known fact. They might turn into all sorts of unpleasant things—bores, cadgers, and mutterers, for instance—but seldom serial killers.

As you will discover if you persevere with this book, I live in Toronto. Well, we all have to live somewhere. You'd be surprised where some people live. Within Canada, for some reason, Toronto arouses strong feelings among people who live elsewhere, far stronger feelings than its actual residents ever experience. (Our mayor reckons we're living in the greatest city on Earth, but mayors are like that. I'm sure the mayor of Pocatello makes similar claims. It's Mayoral Hyperbole Syndrome, hereafter known as MHS.) Among non-Canadians Toronto arouses almost no feelings at all. "It's very clean and safe," visitors say, and we beam with pride.

The celebrated cleanliness of Toronto—gradually becoming a thing of the past, thanks to budget cuts—is best exemplified by the oft-told but possibly apocryphal story of the film crew working on a downtown street. Toronto has used tax breaks and an almost worthless dollar to attract American movie-makers to come up here and turn Toronto into New York or other American cities. I believe there has been talk of awarding a special Oscar to the cinematographer who most successfully manages to keep the very tall CN Tower out of shots. Anyway, this particular film crew had strewn garbage about in order to give the street an authentic American look but then made the mistake of going to lunch. They returned to find that the city had come along and cleaned it all up. Accurate or not, the story reveals a psychological truth about this city.

Toronto used to describe itself as The City That Works, but finally stopped when it had become palpably untrue. Peter Ustinov, of course, has famously described Toronto as New York run by the Swiss. What makes this line particularly funny is that Torontonians see it as a compliment. If New York is a nice place to visit but you wouldn't want to live there, Toronto's just the opposite. I'm never quite sure how visitors to Toronto fill their time. Actually, I do know, because I'm frequently called upon to give directions to Casa Loma, our authentic rococo castle (built 1914). I mention all of this because in the course of this book you will be subjected to references to Toronto. I feel you should know ahead of time; this book is nothing if not honest.

That said, this isn't a guide book to drinking in Toronto—or anywhere else, for that matter. It doesn't offer phone numbers, opening hours, or lunchtime specials. Still, if you find a bit of useful information about a pub you might not have discovered otherwise, you're welcome to it with my blessing.

As a young person, still fairly fresh off the boat from England, I was involuntarily relocated to a rugged western suburb called Etobicoke, an Indian name meaning We Planned This Community But We Forgot to Plan a Pub. Faced with the absence of a nearby Anglican church, my parents began attending an odd fundamentalist church that was run exclusively by people from South Bend, Indiana. This church was sound on baseball—Rocky Nelson, who went on to hit a home run in the seventh game of the 1960 World Series, was a parishioner—but death on most other forms of fun, which they called sin. One Sabbath morning a Sunday School teacher informed us —and these words have been etched in my brain ever since— that anybody who drank was a bum. That's what he said: "We know that anyone who drinks is a bum." Surely, I said to myself, he means "has a bum", not "is a bum", though even then I was sophisticated enough to suspect that we all had bums, drinkers and abstainers alike.

I was not a drinker myself at the time, being just a slip of a boy, but most of the adults I knew were drinkers, and they seemed altogether decent people, with not a serial killer among them. Already I was questioning doctrine and I was coming down on the side of fun. And possibly even sin. There I have remained.

People who think the fifties were a joyless period in which the pinnacle of pleasure was a new recipe for anything that included miniature marshmallows should have known my parents. There were no pubs in Etobicoke, so the denizens of that benighted borough drank at one another's homes. And did they drink! On at least one occasion my church organist father left a party in time to go home and shave, go to church and work his magic, then return to the party. An American writer has described my parents' ilk as The Greatest Generation and I'm tempted to agree, if only on the basis of the parties.

Under the terms of the international regulations that govern the global book trade, it is compulsory in any book about drinking in public to include the words of Doctor Johnson, so I thought I'd get them out of the way early. And here they come now: "There is nothing which has yet been contrived by man, by which so much happiness is produced as by a good tavern or inn." Now, I know that such man-made contrivances as indoor plumbing or the tenor saxophone have their supporters, but when it comes to the contriving of happiness I'm with Johnson all the way.

Not everyone agrees, I know. There are also people who think Kenny G. is a jazz musician, and people who think that artificial turf is an acceptable playing surface for sporting events. Such people—though I'm reluctant to say it—might not need this book. They may, however, have friends who do, people whose lives might be enriched by this meditation on pleasure. Feel the quality of the paper. Admire the excellent typeface. You don't see value like this every day.

Part I: Drinking in General

The Impossible Dream: Looking for the Perfect Pub

I was thinking about George Orwell one Saturday afternoon as I supped my ale in the Rose and Crown, a theoretically English pub in uptown Toronto. It wasn't that the bartender looked like Orwell or that there were copies of *Animal Farm* everywhere I looked (he didn't and there weren't). Perhaps it was something to do with the 1984-like sensation of seeking pleasure in a place that seemed designed for anything but. The Rose and Crown looked like an accountant's version of an English pub. It seemed more a business plan than a pub.

The notice by the door insisting that customers were not to bring in their own food and/or drink raised the obvious question: what was so bad about the Rose and Crown's food and drink that people were tempted to bring their own? The Rose and Crown is a big pub, a very big pub. And it was disturbingly dark. I'd estimate that two-thirds of the clientele the afternoon I was there were huddled together at the front near the windows, seeking the comfort of daylight.

A singer called Ian Robb wrote a song about the decline of the English pub that you really should get to know. (It can be ordered from www.magi.com/~ianrobb/). It asks the musical question, "What has become of the old Rose & Crown?" In the case of Toronto's Rose and Crown, unfortunately nothing has become of it. It's exactly as it always was.

In an essay called *The Moon Under Water*, George Orwell—and I knew I'd get back to him eventually—writes about his favourite pub. It has everything he wants in a pub, including draught stout, working fireplaces, and barmaids who call everyone "Dear" (and it has to be "Dear"; "Ducky" won't do at all). Toward the end of this tribute to the perfect pub, Orwell acknowledges that he's made it all up. There is no such place. The Moon

13

Under Water is the pub he dreams of but never finds. Of his ten ideal pub criteria, he knows of a place that offers eight.

Perhaps it's just as well we never find the perfect pub. It is the quest that keeps us going. And, in any case, if we found it someone would almost certainly wreck it, and what would be the likelihood of future happiness then?

No, it's best as it is, in an imperfect world. Here in Toronto we haven't been at it for long, so it isn't surprising we haven't created the perfect pub yet. The perfect pub, when it happens, will have taken time. They've had several centuries in England, so it's not surprising that they have more contenders than we have. In London alone, the Dove in Hammersmith and the Holly Bush in Hampstead are pretty darn close to perfect. The New Inn at Waterley Bottom—and I couldn't make up a name like Waterley Bottom even if I wanted to –is a rural gem, set in a lovely Cotswold valley. The Tan Hill Inn, said to be the highest pub in England, is alone worth the drive to North Yorkshire, but then so is just about everything else in North Yorkshire. The Blue Anchor, in Helston, Cornwall, is an old stone pub that serves its own beer, as it has done for several centuries. And if you haven't seen the Fleece in Bretforton, Worcestershire, please make plans to do so as quickly as possible. Your life to date is practically worthless.

The White Horse, near Priors Dean in Hampshire, is often known as the Pub With No Name, as its sign fell down some decades ago. It is also one of the most difficult pubs to find in all of England, located off a minor road, sheltered from view by a copse of trees. The first time I went there I spotted a local rustic, who was scything down some long vegetation growing by the side of the road. The more I think about it, he can't possibly have been wearing the traditional smock of the agricultural labourer, but that's the way I remember him. I rolled down the car window. "Excuse me," I said, "but would we be going the right direction to find the White Horse?" He looked up from his work and, with the rich, savoury tone of south/southwestern England, explained, "Well, if you're not thursty you might be. But if you're thursty—and by the looks of you you are—you'll want to turn around." He then gave us impeccable instructions, without which we would never have found the place. When we arrived a few minutes later, the pub's car park was packed. Inaccessibility should never impinge on one's quest for the perfect pub.

The reason I go on about English pubs is that when Toronto finally moved away from the traditional taproom we instinctively turned to the English pub model. There are, heaven knows, worse models. And we all know what an English pub looks like, which is what the people who brought us our first neo-crypto-quasi-English pubs gave us: flock wallpaper, tin ceilings, dark wood, frosted glass, and staff who said "Cheers" when they served us a drink. (They'd call us "Ducky" if they thought of it.) This model is based on the late Victorian gin palace, which is just one of many English pub styles. None of the above-mentioned great English pubs fits that model. Next time you're in London, check out the Lamb in Lamb's Conduit Street or the Red Lion in Duke of York Street to see the prototypes. It's a perfectly good pub style, but it's far from being the only one.

So what's the formula for a great pub? Obviously there is no formula. There are pubs built to a formula—and some are highly successful—but I don't know of a great one or even a very good one. It helps to have a good setting and an ancient building with lots of character. It's imperative to sell good beer that is well maintained.

The key to the great pub is that we feel comfortable in it, which has most to do with the people who run it. This may seem obvious, but there are still people who don't get it. An English novelist called Ian Cochrane once wrote of an unsatisfactory pub experience: "The landlord was a very unhelpful unhappy man and didn't agree with drinking in a pub." Some years ago a woman with a similar philosophy ran the Artful Dodger in Toronto.

All great pubs are the handiwork of someone who has a vision of the place he or she would ideally like to drink in. A great pub—like a great restaurant or bookstore—should give the impression that all the important decisions are being made on the premises, not by someone in a suit miles away.

So what would we find in the perfect pub? My perfect pub would almost certainly be different from your perfect pub, but then I'm the guy who's writing the book. (If you want *your* perfect pub, write your own damn book.) My pub, for starters, has no canned music. Orwell notes that, in the Moon Under Water, "it is always quiet enough to talk." He says he doesn't want a radio in the pub. Radio? Orwell died in 1950, long before the modern sound system was created. Lucky man.

And I'm not convinced that we need a television either. I remember in the early seventies when the old Morrissey Tavern in Toronto got its first television, expressly for the hockey playoffs. It was, we were told, to be used for no other purpose, but eventually, of course, it became part of the furniture. I don't mind bringing in a set for a major occasion. I was surprised in October 1970 to see a television in McSorley's Old Ale House in New York, but it was the World Series after all. Bushe's Bar in Baltimore, West Cork, one evening suddenly boasted a television so we could all watch Ireland's feisty Sonia O'Sullivan in the World Track and Field Championships; she finished fourth, alas, behind three almost certainly artificially stimulated Chinese women.

My wife and I watched the end of a France-Brazil blockbuster in the 1986 World Cup in a bar in Menton on the French Riviera. As extra time edged slowly toward a penalty kick conclusion, the staff quietly gathered up anything made of glass. When the Brazilians had the ball we aimed the hex sign at the screen. When the French had the ball we sang La Marseillaise. Finally the French won, and sixty men fled the bar and drove around honking their horns until they ran out of gas.

And it isn't just sports. At Christmas in 1967, not owning a TV in my little bedsit, I watched the Beatles' *Magical Mystery* Tour in a Camden Town pub. There's a big ugly television in a Toronto pub called the Munster Hall Pub that is there primarily to show *Coronation Street* reruns on Sunday afternoons. Normally, however, it sits unused and covered up. Television in a pub—except for special occasions—is anti-social and has no place in my perfect pub.

There is wide disagreement on cellphones in pubs. I admit that I own a cellphone. My wife bought it for me, as it seemed a friendlier way of keeping tabs on me than one of those electronic ankle bracelets they put on convicts on probation. Occasionally the damn thing has gone off while I've been in a pub, and I think I've had the good grace to apologize for it. There are pubs that ban cellphones. As far as I'm concerned, any pub that inflicts piped music on its customers has no place banning other noisemakers. Quiet pubs, on the other hand, have a point. The Lewes Arms in Sussex has a zero-tolerance policy on cellphones and warns that use of these devices warrants a penalty of a round of drinks for the house. I haven't seen that extreme sentence inflicted, but I have watched a terrier-like barman bustle customers out into the street with their cellphones. The Digby Tap in Sherborne, Dorset, levies a 50p fine for cellphone use, proceeds to charity, which seems not unfair. There is a cellphone for at least every other resident of the UK, so the English are more sensitive to this problem than we are. The otherwise excellent White Horse in west London can sound like a convention of arcade games when it gets busy.

The perfect pub has attentive, friendly bar staff. After I left the Rose and Crown that afternoon I stopped in at the Duke of Kent, just to the south. A woman whose name appeared to be Mia was playing the bar like a violin. Serving drinks, chatting with regulars, bestowing a million-dollar smile on all and sundry, she was worth her weight in hops. She might even have been able to brighten up the Rose and Crown, which would be no mean achievement. My wife has accused me of falling in love with any woman who brings me a beer, which is not an unreasonable accusation, but I had a feeling the whole bar—man, woman, and undecided—was in love with Mia. I almost went back to the Rose and Crown to encourage the long-suffering inmates to pay up and move a few doors down, but only a few of them could have got into the crowded Duke of Kent.

Like Orwell, I like a fire on a cold day, and God knows we get enough of those. Presumably because we have central heating here, we have very few fireplaces in our pubs, and we're poorer for that. Dora Keogh on the Danforth has a fireplace, if you're interested.

Orwell likes a pub with a garden. We don't go in much for pub gardens here, but we do have patios. I like a patio, but not just any patio. Drinking beer on a city sidewalk holds limited appeal for me, though it's better than not drinking beer at all. My favourite Toronto patio is the rooftop bar at Paupers on Bloor Street. It's a hell of a climb on a hot day, especially as some of us get older, but you're up above the hubbub when you get there. So I might put that rooftop patio on my list.

Now, here's something I resent, as a fellow who goes to pubs on an almost daily basis. I resent not being able to go to a pub on St. Patrick's Day or New Year's Eve just to have a pint or two as I like to do. No, suddenly the pub is filled with galoots who have their minds—if that isn't too strong a word—set on getting pie-eyed and making as much noise as possible. A pub-minded Irish friend of mine refuses to go into a pub on St. Patrick's Day, citing the unpleasantness of drinking in the aggressive company of so many amateurs.

The pub of my dreams will discourage ritualized drunkenness of this nature, and the bar staff will look askance at customers who dress oddly on October 31. They will not necessarily refuse to serve such people—I'm not an unreasonable man—but they will make it apparent to unduly festive persons that other pubs are more welcoming to their sort. My ideal pub might recognize more offbeat festivals: Stephen Sondheim's birthday (March 22), for instance, or the anniversary of plucky young Marilyn Bell's swim across Lake Ontario (September 9). Such occasions will be marked by the striking of a small bell at the bar and a quiet chorus of "Well done"s from the patrons. If New Year's Eve is your sort of thing, every other bar in town will be catering to your needs. There's nothing wrong with one pub that regards December 31 as John Denver's birthday and nothing more. At midnight, the locals will quietly raise a glass and murmur, "West Virginia, mountain mama, country roads, take me home." It'll be very tasteful, and it's not as if we'll actually play the song.

I like to be able to get something to eat in a pub, though usually I don't need a full meal. Too many English pubs—the current term is gastropubs—have been ruined by being turned into restaurants that also, grudgingly, serve beer as well. There are still lots of English pubs that will sell you a sandwich. Just a sandwich. Not with fries, not on a kaiser, just a sandwich: decent cheese on honest bread. The Duke of York in midtown Toronto used to offer a basket of sausage rolls, and I don't think it's an exaggeration to say that those sausage rolls saved lives. Sometimes a few sausage rolls among a small group of people can keep an evening going, especially with a bit of sharp English mustard on the side. Those sausage rolls are gone from the Duke's menu now, which is yet more evidence of a declining quality of life. Sausage rolls would always be available in my perfect pub. And not microwaved either.

Good beer, of course, is essential. Many great pubs offer only a few draught beer choices, but they're all interesting. Real ale—unpasteurized, cask-conditioned ale served without artificial carbonation—always cheers me up. Here in Toronto, I can think of seven pubs that serve real ale. The greatest city in the world, if our mayor is to be believed, and we can boast only seven pubs with real ale. The drawback of real ale is that the pub needs someone who knows how to take proper care of beer, but that's what pubs are for. (Just as a bookstore should have someone on the premises who knows something about books.) There is plenty of good beer being made these days throughout the western world, little of which is served in your local pub or mine either. Feel free to ask your local publican why not.

The consumption of beer, it goes without saying, leads to the act of micturition—peeing to you or me—and publicans are required by law to provide facilities to accommodate this all-too-human need. I know English pubs from which the drinker has to go out in the rain to reach the toilets. During the colder months—which can include the period from January through December—these are not places you want to linger. For that reason, I prefer paper towels to those infernal hand-drying machines that take roughly ten minutes per hand to work. I don't know what goes on in women's washrooms, but my observation is that far fewer men wash their hands before they leave if they have to use the machines.

For reasons of human physiology, women are inclined to come into more personal contact with the facilities so should be able to expect certain levels of comfort and hygiene. The woman with whom I do much of my drinking has been known to judge a pub by the quality of its ladies' rooms. The first time we visited the aforementioned New Inn at Waterley Bottom, Anne just about squealed with pleasure at the state of the ladies'.

There are, I know, men who feel that clean toilets only encourage women to go to pubs. The next thing you know the place is serving salads and you're finding lipstick stains on your glass. McSorley's Old Ale House in New York barred women from the premises for decades, relenting only when forced to by a court of law. Even then the pub drew the line at providing separate micturition facilities for its female customers, which led to some surprised faces in the gents', or what had been the gents'. McSorley's finally got over it and put in a ladies', and nowadays the sexes co-exist cheerfully. Though I'm still not sure you can get a decent salad to this day.

My perfect pub is a female-friendly pub and has freshly laundered gingham hand towels in the ladies' loo, or whatever it is women like in there. I'd be kind of grateful, however, if they didn't wear lipstick. It's hell to get off a glass and it's inclined to kill the head on a pint of beer. Perhaps women with lipstick could be asked to use a straw. If they'll agree to that, they can have as much salad as they like.

And how about children? Traditionally the English-speaking world has, by and large, banished the tykes from licensed premises on the grounds that drinking is a sin and should not, therefore, be witnessed by the young. This way of thinking is similar to the belief that if we don't tell children about sex it'll never cross their minds. If children were barred so as to give grownups a break from their company, I could understand it.

One reason that Europeans are more mature about drinking—or so we are told—is that they're exposed to it from infancy and don't regard it as some forbidden fruit. If you believe everything I've read, Portugal doesn't even have a minimum drinking age. Yet it is the English who are feared across Europe for their out-of-control drinking, and not just the football supporters either.

I have mixed feelings about children in pubs. The cigarette smoke can't be good for them, but it does make sense to socialize them early on, to integrate them into the company of adults. If nothing else, watching their elders behave like fools might de-glamourize alcohol for them. If they're going to run around and shout, however, I'd like them to do that outside, and that goes for their parents too.

A non-smoker myself, I'd certainly like a pub that's free of the abominable weed, but I'd be reluctant to tell my friends Alison Owen and Robbie Brown they're not welcome in my pub. The perfect pub offers a forceful yet silent air cleaner, something which may yet be uninvented. I write about smoking elsewhere in this book.

I drink once a week at the aforementioned Duke of York with people of education and breeding, or at least that's what they tell me. When we can hear each other over the unnecessary music, we frequently have lively discussions on any number of subjects. There are often issues that remain unsettled at the end of the evening because we have no way of looking things up. My perfect pub will have a variety of reference materials: a good dictionary, an all-purpose almanac of some sort, an encyclopedia, a decent anthology of poetry, at least one dictionary of quotations, an atlas, perhaps a film guide, a copy of Strunk and White and a vintage Fowler's, an English-French dictionary, some sort of sports encyclopedia, a fairly recent edition of *Canadian Who's Who*, and a *Brewer's Dictionary of Phrase and Fable*. For the price of a good sound system—which, of course, will not be needed—a pub could offer an arsenal of debate-settling books.

And one last thing: animals. Studies show that the proximity of animals actually lowers human blood pressure and makes people feel better. The best English pubs are filled with dogs and cats. I once knew a pub in West Hampstead in London that held almost as many dogs as people of an evening. The dogs were happy, the customers were happy. This, of course, is strictly forbidden in my jurisdiction, on the grounds that people might actually attain some degree of happiness. Technically animals are barred from pubs for health reasons, which seems pretty bogus to me if you look at some of the people who get in. I went to a west end Toronto pub recently which at one point in the afternoon boasted four dogs, all cheerfully present with the people who had walked them there. I won't mention the pub in question for fear of attracting the local anti-dog activists at the licensing authorities, but I for one will go back to this pub because of its animal friendliness. If I come back as a border collie in my next life, I'll want somewhere congenial to go.

What a Good Idea: The History of Beer

There is an old English music hall song that credits the invention of beer to a man named Charlie Mopp: God bless Charlie Mopp, the man who invented beer. Although the song makes a fairly convincing case, beer historians remain skeptical. They reckon beer predates Mr. Mopp. They figure beer goes back to early man, or possibly early woman.

Early man was a rough sort of brute, and early woman wasn't much better, that memorable Raquel Welch movie notwithstanding. They lived nomadically, without any of what we would consider the necessities: air conditioning, reality television, or the Canadian Alliance. (One of the reasons early man didn't have the Canadian Alliance, incidentally, is that the planet didn't exist at that point, according to the Canadian Alliance.) Their lives were short and mostly bereft of pleasure.

Every now and then, however, something nice happened. Bits of soggy wild barley accidentally came into contact with wind-borne yeasts, and fermented. Primitive, or unnecessarily fastidious, early man might then have said, "Darn, this barley's gone rotten. Better throw it out. Don't want to get sick."

More advanced early man might have replied, "Not so fast, Ogg. Let's have a look at it." The next morning, head pounding, early man might just have decided he had had a good time the night before, what he could remember of it. He might even have woken up with early woman next to him (see the chapter on Drinking and Sex).

Somewhere along the way a bright spark among early man (and it might well have been early woman) began to think that this fermented barley was a good thing, and that just possibly there might be a way to induce it deliberately rather than wait for one of nature's little accidents. Like fire, fermentation might be created and harnessed. Alas, we don't know the name of the early person who figured this out—it is unlikely to have been Charlie Mopp—but this is very probably a good time to open a beer and drink a toast to the unknown brewer. Cheers.

The era of which we speak is an estimated 8,000 to 13,000 years ago, long before the designated hitter rule and other annoying modern devices. To ensure a steady and regular supply of beer, it was necessary to cultivate grain. This in turn transformed early man (and the early woman he was now shacked up with after the accidental brewing incident of a couple of paragraphs ago) from the hunter-gatherer to the agriculturalist. Even then, beer was making people smarter.

Another bright spark of prehistory wondered if there was anything else we could make out of grain and yeast, thus inventing bread. Hence the sandwich, the drinker's best friend. Bread, of course, led to variations like cake—which was good—and the kaiser bun, that tasteless, doughy piece of stodge named as revenge upon the Germans for WWI and served in many pubs to this day to diminish the pleasure of an honest hamburger. (The kaiser bun is mandatory in Ontario bars as a pivotal part of the legislation aimed at curtailing pleasure among the citizenry. Citizens who became accustomed to pleasure might start to see it as their due, which would be inconvenient for the authorities.)

It was beer that gave civilization its kick-start. Without beer, there would have been no agriculture, no science, no Renaissance, no Shakespeare, no Jane Austen, no Mozart, no Charlie Parker, no—well, you get the picture. That said, we might not have liked early beer as much as early man did. When you've never had any beer at all, you're not terribly picky. (Look at the stuff teenagers drink.) The Mesopotamians took germinated barley and made it into partly-baked cakes, which were then dumped into a jar of water and left to ferment. (What they almost certainly didn't understand was the role of yeast in the process, but at some point a bit of rogue yeast got into the mixture and turned soggy barley cakes into something wonderful.) The result was a lumpy brew which might, in the classier taverns of the day, be strained through a cloth to make it less chewy. To this day Egyptians make something similar called "bouza"; oddly enough, they have not found a big export market for this product. Equally oddly, "bouza" is not the source for our word "booze", which entered Middle English from early Dutch.

Apart from being lumpy, early beer lacked the distinctive hops we're used to. We're not quite sure when hops became widely used in the making of beer. Brewers throughout history have used flavouring agents like herbs, fruit, berries, spices, or honey, and some historians suspect the Hebrews learned to use hops during the Babylonian captivity, in which case the experience wasn't a complete write-off. Their version of beer was said to alleviate leprosy, which I find altogether plausible. To this day I have yet to see a leper in a pub; perhaps you hang out in different places. The ancient Greeks grew hops, but there's not much evidence they used them in beer, which seems uncharacteristically wasteful.

We know that hops were being grown in Bohemia and Bavaria in about the eighth century. Hildegard of Bingen—everyone's favourite medieval baebe—wrote about brewing with hops in the twelfth century, and certainly Flemish brewers were exporting hopped beer into Britain in the early 1400s, to the horror of English traditionalists. Hops, of course, add the bitterness we have come to expect in beer (except drinkers of Molson Golden, who have come to expect almost no taste at all), and they also act as a preservative.

Risk-taking microbreweries these days are known to replace or supplement hops with such oddities as heather, bog myrtle, ginseng, and hemp. As hops are related (by marriage) to cannabis—that other great medicinal herb—we shouldn't be surprised to encounter hemp beer, and indeed you can usually find it on tap in Toronto at C'Est What down on Front Street. It's not bad either, once you get it lit, which is the hard part.

Brewing, until very recently, has always been a local enterprise. Inns brewed their own beer, as did many private homes. Early commercial breweries sprang up to make beer for local customers, and in parts of Europe that model still works. The Young brewery in southwest London still makes its local deliveries by horse-drawn dray. It's cheaper and—given the state of London traffic—no slower than using trucks. It's also good marketing, except when a member of your target demographic steps in a bit of horse exhaust. Pasteurization made beer easier to keep, hence easier to transport, and it led to the rise of mega-brewing. Now, wherever you are in the world, you can enjoy a perfectly bland Carlsberg. No longer need you risk tasting a local beer made for local palates. It's progress, so it must be good.

In any event, over the centuries beer has become less lumpy and more scientific and, until the recent boom of microbreweries, seemed to have reached the end of its evolutionary trail. Companies that had once been run by brewers were now run by accountants and marketing guys. Focus groups were more likely to influence the flavour of beer than the brewmaster. Beer was being dumbed down, brewed to fit an advertising campaign, its flavour downplayed so as not to give offence to a larger market. It almost makes one nostalgic for Mesopotamia.

Don't Rule Out Miracles: How Beer is Made

Those of us blessed to live in Toronto find it easy to forget that there are other people out there living in other places. I know it seems odd, but it's true. I've seen some of these other places. In the mid-seventies I once undertook a walking tour of Ontario cottage country, thinking I'd throw myself in a body of water if I got hot and stop in at local hostelries for refreshments when I got thirsty. A good plan, if a trifle naïve.

What I hadn't counted on was there being virtually no bars in cottage country in those days. I had a beer with friends in Orillia, then set off on my walk. I walked to Bobcaygeon, and I found exactly one bar along the way. Hail to thee, blithe Coboconk! I spent some time in that bar, talking to an older guy who had worked on the Avro Arrow and who was still bitter about that ill-fated plane. When I hit Bobcaygeon a day or two later and found yet again a town without a bar, I hitchhiked to Lindsay, had a beer, and caught a bus home. On top of there not being any bars, most of the water along the way seemed privately owned, so I managed one swim between Orillia and Bobcaygeon. All of which taught me to stay close to home. Toronto's not the best drinking town in the world, but at least I know where the bars are.

That said, I'm happy to see that we can learn from others. There's a pair of brothers who opened a brewpub in Halifax back in 1985 and saw it prosper. In 1991 Ron Keefe, one of these brothers, then decided to bring his brewing and pubbing prowess to the Big Smoke and try his luck. And I'm glad he did. The Granite Brewery, on Mount Pleasant south of Eglinton, is the home of one of our best beers. In 2000, when provincial legislation permitted brewpubs to open a second, non-brewing location, Keefe opened Beer Street on the Danforth at Pape. Beer Street, I reckon, is close to four miles from the actual brewery, but I hereby report that the beer travels well. The new location takes its name from the Hogarth prints that chronicle life on Gin Lane and Beer Street. Gin Lane is filled with vice, depravity, and poverty, and only the pawnbroker prospers. The residents of Beer Street, on the other hand, enjoy happiness, health, and prosperity.

The pawnbroker alone suffers from a want of trade.

The Granite Brewery brews several beers that range from a lightish ale to a fairly hearty stout, with an entertaining raspberry-flavoured ale, an India Pale Ale, and a noteworthy Peculiar, modelled on Theakston's celebrated Old Peculier. But the star of the show is the Best Bitter Special— I would have called it Special Best Bitter myself, but it's not my brewery— which is their Best Bitter dry-hopped and served as a real ale. Dry-hopping is a process whereby extra hops are added to the cask at the last minute to add aroma and flavour. The first time I had one of these I thought I'd died and gone to Heaven, or at least to England. I've been guilty of overlooking Keefe's other beers because, well, who needs anything else?

The forces that for so many years fought any sort of liberalized sale of beer in this province also worked to keep the little guy out of the beer market. Microbreweries were tacitly outlawed, as were brewpubs. The big breweries—which, coincidentally, contributed generously to the local ruling party—succeeded in keeping outsiders outside, where they belonged. Gradual changes in legislation have allowed people who aspire to brew good beer to do so, within limited boundaries. To be fair, this is not just an Ontario problem. Across North America, beer lovers have campaigned to make good beer more readily available, but they have had to fight for that right. If you want to see guns handed out on street corners, Charlton Heston will be delighted to speak on your behalf. In fact, try to shut him up. There is no Charlton Heston equivalent to speak out for beer. Guns good, beer bad.

There have been other, less interesting problems in brewing. Malt, for instance. For years, virtually the only source of malt in these parts was a company called Canada Malting, which produced the malted barley it wanted to produce. If you wanted to use something else in your beer you had to find your own barley and malt it yourself, which is tougher for a small brewery.

Well, here we go. At some point in any book about beer it is essential to discuss the process of brewing. There is no way around it. Frankly, I wish there were. The sad fact is that any description of the brewing process is dull, and I mean gruesomely, gut-wrenchingly dull. Most people will skip over this section, and they're right to do so, although they'll miss the racy bit about the sex life of hops. The handful of people who actually read it all the way through are people who brew their own beer and they're checking to see if I've got it right.

The mandatory chapter about brewing beer uses a lot of words like "wort", "ullage", "grist", and "sparging". These are the sort of words you might use if you were writing a cheap knock-off of The Hobbit: Wort came upon Grist in the forest, sparging his ullage.

Very few people understand the brewing process. People think they will understand it better if they go on a brewery tour. There is nothing wrong with going on a brewery tour—indeed, I encourage it—but please do not think that you will understand brewing at the end of it. I've been on brewery tours in all sorts of places, from Munich to Los Angeles, Dublin to Vancouver. I've toured huge monster beer factories (Anheuser-Busch, L. A.) and small local breweries (Black Sheep in Masham, Yorkshire). I've even made beer myself, which is probably the only way to begin to understand how it works. Even then you'll understand it properly only if you grow your own barley and hops, but not many home brewers are prepared to wait that long for their first batch.

What you will see if you tour a brewery is one or two people standing around in rubber boots, looking suspiciously at large copper or stainless steel kettles. The bigger the brewery, the more people standing around. If this is an English brewery, one of the people will almost certainly be called Roger and, if you're lucky, you might hear him say something technical like "Oh arr." If you stay long enough—and there's no reason you should—Roger might draw a small amount of murky fluid from a tap into a glass tube and look at it discouragingly. He will then go for his tea break. This is your cue to move immediately to the tasting room and get as much of the free local product as they're willing to give you.

What you need to know about the brewing process—and honestly, I'm getting to the crunch here—is that rather a lot of malted barley gets boiled up with a smaller amount of hops and even less yeast in quite a fair bit of water. Depending on how much money the brewer hopes to make from this concoction, you might see less malted barley and more rice and corn starch. This all gets put into a big container, then transferred to another container, and left for a while. Then—and this is the crucial bit—a miracle takes place. Oh, I know, in this secular age we hate to talk about miracles, but sometimes there's no other word for it. At some hard-to-define point this vat of goop becomes beer.

Yes, there are different sorts of hops, some of which have lovely old names like Fuggles and the Hallertau Mittelfrüh, and there are different sorts of barley. The real experts can possibly take a sip of beer and spot whether the brewer used a two-row or a six-row barley, but I can't and you probably can't either. Sometimes, depending on your luck, there are things like bog myrtle in your beer, and some brewers even make beer with chili peppers, which makes you thirsty even while you're drinking.

If, on your brewery tour, you see the wort in action it might put you off beer forever. It's not pretty. The foamy stuff on the average wort looks more like a rash than a head, but somehow it turns into something quite wonderful. If you have a better word than "miracle" for what transforms something raw and ugly into Fuller's London Pride or Samuel Adams Trippelbock, you let me know. The only other word I'll countenance is "alchemy", which I'll accept happily.

So what's in your beer? If you're in Germany—and chances are you're not—your beer contains only water, yeast, hops, and malted grains (usually barley, although wheat, rye, and oats are certainly possible). This is because of the Reinheitsgebot, or the beer purity law, of 1516, which decreed what was permissable in Bavarian beer. Interestingly enough, the original Reinheitsgebot—contrary to popular opinion—makes no reference to yeast, as understanding of what yeast does for beer was still three hundred years away. The Reinheitsgebot also set price ceilings for Bavarian beer; defenders of the edict conveniently ignore this part of it. Try to get a Kopf of beer in Munich for a pfennig these days.

There is some suggestion that the Reinheitsgebot was a self-serving boondoggle passed by Duke Wilhelm IV, who coincidentally held a monopoly on the supply of malt (he was the Canada Malting of his day), but what's the point of being a duke if you can't make people do what you want them to? When the German republic was formed in 1919, the Bavarians refused to join unless the rest of the German states accepted their purity law, which they did, although the law did not apply in East Germany during that interesting era. Given what they pumped into their athletes over the years, it would have been unrealistic to expect the East Germans to quibble over impurities in their beer. Breweries in the former East Germany are now required to hew to the purity laws.

At first glance, this legislation might seem to guarantee a fairly homogeneous beer across the land, which is clearly not the case. There is huge variety in the taste and colour of German beers. On the plus side, the German beer laws keep brewers from cutting corners by using sugar, corn starch, rice, and other such beer cheapeners, not to mention the sinister batch of chemicals routinely used by modern non-German brewers to add sparkle and clarity and lengthen the shelf life. On the other hand, making hops the only allowable flavouring agent bars all manner of interesting beer flavours that the Belgians and Scandinavians enjoy. Other European countries have argued that the Reinheitsgebot exists only to serve as a protection racket for German beers, keeping all sorts of other beers out of the German market.

If you were still awake at this point, I could mention the European debate over the sex life of hops. As you're almost certainly aware, only the female hop is useful in the brewing process. The male hop is charming and witty, but not of much practical use. Nowhere else in nature is this the case. The lager producers of the world use a bottom-fermenting process (you don't have to know this for the exam) in which fertilized female hops create a problem with the clarification of the beer. This problem does not arise with top-fermented beers like the ale family. Lager makers like an unsullied, virginal lady hop, while the brewers of ale are just as happy with a jolly female hop that's been around a bit and has some stories to tell. On the continent the wild male hop has been eradicated, while in sexually permissive England the wild male hop continues to roam free, doing his nasty little deeds wherever he may. And, for my money, long may he do so, though no doubt the commissars of the European Community are plotting ways as we speak to stifle the plucky English male hop.

Some time in the seventies, North Americans began to realize that it was not in fact compulsory to drink beers from huge beer factories, and small breweries started to sprout up. Even in Canada, for heaven's sake. The Granville Island Brewery in Vancouver got the Canadian microbrewery movement going in 1984, and a man called Jim Brickman started the first small Ontario brewery in a good long time with the Brick brewery, just a few months later. Leo Heaps followed along soon after with the Upper Canada Brewery, which got away from the lagers of Granville Island and Brick and into some decent ales.

In the intervening years, microbreweries have come and gone, and the quality of their beers has fluctuated as well. Some of the micros have transcended their micro status, becoming in the process larger regional breweries. Sleeman, for instance, is the brainchild of one John Sleeman, who took his grandfather's brewing recipe and a very good bottle design and built a company that is taking on national proportions. Unfortunately, like many ambitious brewers, Sleeman seems to feel that the way to the masses' hearts is through bland and inoffensive beers. If the beer lived up to the bottle, we'd be on to something.

In the late nineties Sleeman bought Upper Canada, closed down the brewery on Atlantic Avenue, and started brewing the Upper Canada beers at its Guelph plant. Beer lovers fear the worst. More recently Sleeman has bought La Brasserie Seigneuriale in Boucherville, the Shaftebury Brewing Company in B.C., and the Maritime Beer Company in Halifax. This is how E.P. Taylor got started on his campaign to take over brewing.

Canada's first brewpub was the Troller Pub in Horseshoe Bay, outside Vancouver. It remained a brewpub only a short time, and its founder John Mitchell left to help set up Spinnakers in Victoria in 1984, a pub that survives and thrives to this day. (If you want to be technical about it, the Troller's brewery was located in a separate building, hence the Spinnakers claim to be Canada's first actual brewpub. And how many brewmasters can dance on the head of a pin?)

Toronto lagged behind Vancouver in the brewpub revolution, and indeed Canada generally continues to lag behind its southern neighbour. Hell, even Buffalo has almost as many brewpubs as Toronto, and Vancouver offers nothing like the number of brewpubs you'll find in West Coast American cities, especially Portland, Oregon. Portland claims to have something like thirty-four brewpubs and microbreweries, which is not bad for a city of half a million people. Is it legislation or our entrepreneurial timidity? And how can we get over it?

The Best Time of Day to Drink

While studies show that most drinking takes place in the evening, the recreational drinker knows that the best time of all is the afternoon, particularly a weekday afternoon. There's something almost blissful about sitting quietly in a pub by daylight, knowing that everyone else in the world is at work. The lunchtime bustle has ended, and the dinnertime bustle far in the future. The bar manager has not yet turned the lights down to prevent you from reading, and the large groups of people who gather in pubs for the purpose of shouting at each other over the music have not yet arrived.

It was on such an afternoon, many years ago, that I settled in at a barroom table, spreading out my pleasures before me. I had a book, a newspaper, some writing paper. I was what my old auntie used to call "happy as a sandboy", whatever that means. (Extremely happy or carefree, Brother Oxford tells me, suggesting that sandboy probably derives from a "boy hawking sand for sale." Why such a boy should be so cheerful beats me, but I was certainly in that ballpark, happiness-wise.)

It couldn't last, of course, although I expected a little more time than I got. I could see—though I was not about to make eye contact—a fellow drinker arising from his table. It was the days of little draught beer glasses, and he clutched three or four of these glasses and brought them over to my table, carefully setting them down in front of him. He gestured toward my book, my newspaper, my writing paper. "You might as well put all that away," he said, "I've got plenty to talk about." And he did. It was, as I recall, a conspiracy theory that had something to do with the automotive industry. People have called me a good listener. If so, this was my finest hour.

It's not always like that, afternoon drinking. Usually it's better. In England, of course, afternoon drinking was until recently actually illegal, at least in pubs. In 1916, David Lloyd George, prime minister of the day, was worried that munitions workers might not get back to work after lunch. So he decreed that pubs should shut during the afternoon. Like income tax, this was intended to be a temporary measure, and so it proved. A mere seventy-five years later, the law was changed. Now publicans may, if they like, open during the afternoon. They are, of course, under no obligation to do so. Shortly after the rules had been abolished, my wife and I found ourselves in one of our favourite London pubs, the Surprise in Chelsea, getting there moments before three o'clock, the old witching hour. With a drink safely in front of me I asked the barman if the Surprise now stayed open all day. "Naah, guv," he replied, deftly ignoring the fact that his pub was two-thirds filled with people he would soon be evicting, "there's no call for it." (I can report that the Surprise now stays open throughout the afternoon.)

The Walk to the Ballpark, described elsewhere in these pages, generally takes place on a Friday. Workaholics of my acquaintance complain that it would be easier for them to take part if it happened on a Saturday instead, to which I reply that the whole point of it is to be hanging out in bars while the rest of the world is doing whatever it is it does during the daylight hours. A pub crawl on the weekend is better than no pub crawl at all, but that's about all you can say for it. On a weekday it is heaven itself.

Urban pubs don't always make it easy for the afternoon drinker. I have found a number of bars in Chicago that don't open until four p.m., and Chumley's in New York suffers from a similar affliction. In Toronto, Smokeless Joe and the Paddock are also unfriendly to the daytime tippler.

I bring the subject up because many of the pub encounters I discuss in this book took place during the day. Many of those were Saturdays and Sundays, so not really proper daytime drinking, but in daylight hours nonetheless. There are very few bad bars in the afternoon. Needless to say, in the course of one's life one has seen many of these places by evening as well. Still, if you want to know what all these places are like at midnight, you'll need to find a book written by a younger person. I'm assuming they're filled with packs of young people who have nowhere to be in the morning, and that's good enough for me.

Is Drinking Strictly Necessary?

Strictly speaking, the consumption of alcohol is not essential to the maintenance of human life, although studies reveal that non-drinkers live shorter lives than moderate drinkers. It is possible—with the help of exercise and a sensible diet—to lead (or possibly endure) a long, fruitful life without as much as a sip of alcohol, and there are in fact recorded instances of people doing just that. We can only guess at the motivation of such people, but this book takes a live-and-let-live position. This book is open-minded enough to recognize that it takes all sorts to make a world, that one man's meat is another man's poison, and that we should not stand in judgement of others until we've walked 1.609344 kilometres in their shoes. This book has a platitude for all occasions.

If you can believe the figures, fifty-eight per cent of Canadian women and thirty-five per cent of Canadian men don't touch the stuff at all, which raises the question of why the rest of us can't get into a midtown pub on a Friday night. It also raises the question of whether this is simply what Canadians tell their doctors. "Drink? Oh no, never touch it." I once read in one of those expensive wine magazines that eighty per cent of American homes don't possess a corkscrew. This doesn't mean, of course, that they're not drinking. It doesn't even mean they're not drinking wine. All it means is that they're not drinking wine from corked bottles, unless they're opening these bottles with their teeth.

There are, in fact, many reasons for not drinking, and I've been looking them up. Many people around the world abstain for religious reasons. Islam, of course, is notoriously anti-booze. There are Muslim countries in which drinkers face public lashings, presumably getting in a bit of punishment here on Earth just in case Allah missed it. There are also Christians who disregard—at their peril, I would have thought—the words of St. Paul: "Drink no longer water, but use a little wine for thy stomach's sake." Such heretical Christians regard drinking as a sin. Mormons are dead set against the hooch, as anyone who's ever tried to conduct a pub crawl in Salt Lake City can testify.

Other people say they just don't like the taste, which has always seemed an evasive answer to me. I can name several well-known brands of beer, for instance, that have virtually no taste at all. Don't tell me you don't like the taste of beer until you've had a Kokanee. Some people don't drink because they're afraid of losing control. That's what they say. To my mind they've never been able to make a particularly convincing case for control, but it's their life.

Some people belong to racial or ethnic groups that genetically have trouble processing alcohol; for such people the pleasure of drinking is outweighed by the hazards. Some people have specific medical conditions that would be worsened by alcohol.

There are, of course, many non-drinkers who used to be drinkers. These people have quit for any number of reasons. They might have developed worrisome medical conditions from drinking, or their drinking might have become a behavioural problem. Some drinkers become a hazard to themselves and others. Some people go from being sweet-natured sober individuals to quarrelsome monsters when they drink. Once started, some people can't stop until they have consumed everything in sight plus a few bottles that had been carefully hidden away. Clearly such people should not drink, and we are doing no one any favours by encouraging them to.

As I tried to make clear at the beginning, I'm a tolerant guy, full of love for my fellow creatures (especially when I've had a couple of pints), drinkers and non-drinkers alike. But the people who really bug the bejeezus out of me are the people who don't drink and don't think I should either. I'm slow to anger, but you start taking an axe to my saloon and I'm likely to forget I'm a gentleman. There's a limit to my tolerance, damn it.

The other people I could live without are the cheerful people who plaster a big stupid smile on their faces and say things like, "Oh, I don't need silly old alcohol to be happy!" Just because they're able to disregard the inherent painfulness of life doesn't mean the rest of us can. Don't these people read the newspapers?

This, it seems to me, is the issue. We drinkers are perhaps more sensitive souls, or possibly just better informed. Or maybe we live in worse climates. We need a bit of help to get through it all. A non-user of caffeine, I am married to a woman for whom the fancy-pants coffee revolution was a boon. She uses words to describe a cup of coffee that were never before in her vocabulary or mine. She has been known to mock me in the morning, saying, "Just think that this is as good as you're going to feel all day." To her I can say only one word, and that word is "lunchtime".

The world is fraught with peril, as is obvious to most people. Some people drink to forget. Others forget to drink. I don't recommend either extreme. I just think that the occasional tincture of something soothing takes the edge off the planet, cuts the angst just a bit, tones down the *Weltschmerz* a degree or two. I believe that we're justified in softening the blows a tad in a world that contains the following:

Sweeping global climate change.

Devastation of the natural environment.

Widespread poverty.

Plagues and epidemics, including AIDS, tuberculosis, malaria, Ebola, and much more.

Celine Dion's career.

The end of meaningful democracy in the wake of corporate globalization.

The merchandising deal between the New York Yankees and Manchester United.

Millions of people who wear the Nike logo without even being paid to do so.

The decline in accessible health care.

The utterly inexplicable popularity of Bud and Bud Light.

Celine Dion's husband and child.

Hatred and intolerance, except where aimed at pop stars.

Drug cartels (cartels are a bad thing).

Celine Dion's houses.

Political corruption.

Movies starring Arnold Schwarzenegger or Bruce Willis.

Movies with soundtracks that feature Celine Dion.

Violence of the strong against the weak.

The growing toxicity of our food and water.

The designated hitter rule.

A so far unused frozen Celine Dion embryo.

I could go on, but you see what I mean. Tough people can live in this world, somehow, without the buffering qualities of alcohol. We more sensitive folk cannot. If alcohol had not existed, the international drug companies would have come up with something even more expensive. To paraphrase A.E. Housman:

"And beer does more than Prozac can
To justify God's ways to man."

Beer and I: A Match Made In Heaven

Winston Churchill once said, "Most people hate the taste of beer—to begin with. It is, however, a prejudice that many have been able to overcome." I managed it. In fact, I managed it fairly early on. If there was any resistance at the beginning, I don't actually remember it. I had the occasional glass of beer at home, and from time to time the more roguish friends of my parents laid one on for me.

My first beer in a public place happened on October 1, 1965, and it was John Diefenbaker's fault. Younger readers may not recall our thirteenth prime minister, the Man from Prince Albert, but he cut quite a figure in his day. Dief the Chief took the rap for a lot of things—occasionally unfairly—but there is no letting him off on this one. He is on the hook for my life of squalor. To paraphrase W.C. Fields, it was John Diefenbaker who drove me to drink, and I forgot to thank him for it.

I was a fresh-faced young university student at the time, a pup of nineteen. If this seems rather old to be enjoying one's first public drink, please remember that in those days one was required to be at least forty to drink legally in the province of Ontario, on top of having a letter from one's mother and a form authorized by a doctor and a clergyperson. Even then a Toronto taproom waiter could still refuse to serve you on the slightest whim. It is difficult now to comprehend the kind of power a beverage room waiter wielded in those dark times. A tall friend of mine came close to eviction from the Embassy Tavern one afternoon for slouching. This is absolutely true.

In any case, on October 1, 1965, I left Hart House Theatre at the University of Toronto and strolled northward up Philosopher's Walk on my way to the subway. I had been rehearsing a production of Shaw's Heartbreak House, directed by the wonderful Robert Gill, who had directed the likes of Kate Reid and Donald Sutherland so was used to better actors than I. I had never seen a man use a cigarette holder before, so society's taboos were tumbling all around me. For what it's worth, Herbert Whittaker in *The Globe and Mail* thought I showed promise in the small role of the craven yet pragmatic burglar, but this was only October 1 and we were still a week or so from opening.

There is a parking lot in front of Varsity Arena through which I had to pass on my way home, and this particular evening people were gathered. Inside the arena John Diefenbaker was addressing a crowd of cheering Tories. It was the former prime minister's last hurrah in his final election as Tory leader, and he was spitting fire inside. Loudspeakers carried his message to an overflow crowd outside.

Passing through, I encountered a young fellow of my age in debate with an older man, a Tory. I don't recall the specifics of their discussion, but I joined in on the side of my contemporary, until finally the older man, clearly giving up on my generation, went back to listening to the Chief. The young guy turned to me and suggested a celebratory beer. There seemed no good reason not to, and I followed him to the Embassy Tavern. It was everything I hoped it would be—noisy, smoky, and as decadent as Toronto was likely to be in 1965. A waiter in white shirt and black pants dropped four glasses of draught beer on our table at fifteen cents per, and no questions were asked about our age. I felt a long way from Etobicoke. Even as I left I couldn't wait to come back.

Where the Embassy once stood, rich guys now come to buy suits from Harry Rosen. I wept the night the Embassy closed down. A year later I sat in the Morrissey Tavern drinking with John, one of the long-time Embassy waiters. He had come downtown that day and found himself walking past the old place. As he stood there, a group of men—U of T grads, as it turned out—came along, looking for their old haunt. It was gone, but there was John, one of the great waiters of the era. By the time I ran into him at the Morrissey, he'd had a few with these guys and he was feeling nostalgic.

I remember three waiters from the Embassy Tavern. Mike and Cliff were biggish guys. You didn't mess around with Mike or Cliff because they could tear you apart. You didn't mess around with John because you didn't want to disappoint him. He was a taproom philosopher with plenty to say, almost all of it worth listening to. Even in retirement.

The beer we drank in the Embassy was swill, and there was no choice, not on draught. They regularly changed brands, but it all tasted pretty much the same. We were young and drinking beer; we didn't care what it was. By 1969 I was living in England and working behind the bar at the Argyll Arms, one of the prettiest pubs in London. To this day there is still not a plaque outside, even though I tack one up every time I'm in the area. By this time I was drinking English ale and enjoying it, but I was still missing out on the good stuff. I was drinking Double Diamond, for Pete's sake. It was better than the Canadian swill I was used to, but that's not saying a lot. My cats pee better than that.

Young people drink lousy beer. It's just one of those facts of life. If they get through youth without killing themselves, some of them will go on to develop a bit of taste. Now I like a good hearty ale, something with a nice balance of malt and hops, something with a surprising aftertaste. Nowadays I don't often drink with the intention of getting drunk; that's for kids. If nothing else, grownups don't have time for hangovers. Give me a good conversation and a nice beery buzz, and I'm happy as a clam.

I like the taste of good beer, and I like the way it feels in my mouth. I like the way you can feel the first swallow of the day slide down the gullet. I wish every day could be the first time again—you never forget the first time—and that old John Diefenbaker was back again, ranting in a losing cause at Varsity Arena.

The More I Drink The Better I Look: Drinking and Sex

Yes, I might have known you'd head directly to this chapter, you mucky reader, you. I'll try to make it worth your while.

I think I've made it clear that I enjoy reading in pubs. Other people, on the other hand, go to licensed premises with darker, more basic drives in mind. The seventies, of course, were famous for singles bars, places people went to with no higher purpose than to find sexual partners. I didn't have the clothes for singles bars, and I was always too shy in any case. While North Americans from coast to coast were out there having it off, I was sitting in Toronto's Morrissey Tavern, reading a book.

Not that chances didn't crop up. One night, in the early seventies, I found myself at the El Mocambo with a glass of beer in front of me. (Funny, isn't it, the way we talk about "finding ourselves" in bars, as if we'd had no intention whatever of actually stepping inside such a place). This particular evening I had in fact gone to a party, which led to a group of people going to the El Mocambo to hear some band or other. I found myself (here we go again) sitting next to a young woman I had not previously met, a woman with a reputation of being formidable. During a quiet spell, she leaned toward me and said, "I only came out tonight because I thought I might find a good lay. [Pinteresque pause.] I guess I didn't."

In the intervening years, I have thought of many amusing responses to this line, some of which might have led to heaven-knows-what. I might not have been a good lay, but she wouldn't have found that out until it was too late, would she? They do say that sex is like golf, in that you can enjoy it without necessarily being very good at it.

At the time, I didn't know quite what to say. The girls I had known in high school were notable precisely for not saying things like that, so I was out of my depth. You can see what's coming. I blew it. Sex is like Jeopardy:

you've got to be quick on the buzzer. I didn't have my hand on the buzzer, or anything else.

When you think of it, I probably didn't have to say much. "Oh yeah?" might have done the trick. Practically any form of human speech might have done it. "That's what you think," for instance. I would not have been the first guy to get lucky as a result of a chance encounter at the El Mocambo, or the last—just look at the Rolling Stones—and who knows where it might have led? Mutual disappointment, outbreaks of lying, and that overall funk of shabbiness, in all likelihood, but that's what makes the world go round.

Early humans lived short, arduous lives, leaving little behind them for their time on the planet. Keeping the species going was touch-and-go. As discussed elsewhere in this book, the Mesopotamians invented beer, whereupon civilization really got going. After a couple of beers, other Mesopotamians started to look pretty good, and procreation really took off. You could argue (and I know how you get after a couple of pints) that humanity might not even be here at all if not for beer.

The bond between alcohol and sex is historic. People who drink are more likely to multiply. Look at the Irish. There's never been a shortage of Irish people. (This may be a Catholic issue. Historically the Catholic countries have managed to keep their populations up without having to evangelize. It's the non-drinking Protestants who need converts to maintain their numbers. Fair enough, the Inquisition wasn't Catholicism's finest hour, but these days they're fairly well behaved.)

Teetotallers, on the other hand, are usually too busy making sure that other people don't have fun to have any themselves. One teetotaller is never going to look suddenly wonderful to another teetotaller. And there are teetotallers who don't approve of dancing either. How that gene has survived down the centuries is a mystery to the evolutionists. If Darwin was right, non-dancing teetotallers should have been bred out of the species some time around the Phoenicians.

In 1969 I met a woman at a Bavarian brewery, and we wound up living together for two years. A few years later in a Toronto bar I met the woman who was to become my wife. We courted at another Toronto bar, and our first destination after tying the knot at City Hall was yet another Toronto bar. Interestingly enough, our marriage has outlasted all three bars, although two of them now exist in other forms.

The second of those three bars—the Morrissey Tavern on Yonge Street—was not an obviously romantic haunt. There were no cosy little tables with candles. One of the long-time waiters was so slow and desultory in his duties that sometimes people fell in love just for something to do while they waited for another beer. I know of at least four other long-term couples whose relationships gestated at the Morrissey, and I'll draw a discreet veil over some of the shorter-term alliances that sprang up as well. There are people alive today who wouldn't have existed if not for the Morrissey Tavern.

That the Morrissey could be destroyed to build yet another tiresome condominium block is an indictment on us all. It should have been treated as a sacred place, rather like a hospital. Oh, hang on—they're shutting down hospitals too, aren't they?

Mind you, it's a fine line we walk when we drink, if we have sex on our minds. Not that this has ever happened to any of us, but the medical professionals warn of the danger of diminished performance, particularly in the male of the species. To be blunt about this, by the time you've got her drunk enough to find you palatable, you may be too far gone to deliver the goods. The porter in *Macbeth* speaks of drink: "… it provokes the desire but it takes away the performance. Therefore much drink may be said to be an equivocator with lechery: it makes him and mars him; it sets him on and it takes him off; it persuades him and disheartens him, makes him stand to and not stand to…"

Aristotle, of course, thought the problem might arise (or not) because the "lower parts" need to be heated, while wine naturally travels upwards, producing heat higher up and withdrawing it further down. All right, do you have a better explanation? If caught in this predicament, you might try saying, "Hang on, I think I'm having an Aristotelian moment." I can't imagine what good that could possibly do you, but she might be impressed with the classical reference.

The only other advice I can think of comes from the cad in the Michael Flanders/Donald Swann song *Have Some Madeira, M'dear*. (Now there's a song you don't hear played in pubs; it might be a useful warning for maidens whose natural defences collapse a bit after a couple of tequila sunrises.) The cad, in attempting to seduce a sweet young thing by plying her with fortified wine, warns her against the evils of gin, adding as an afterthought, "Besides, it's inclined to affect me prowess."

Nevertheless, as long as intoxicating beverages are served, the preservation of humankind seems guaranteed, and I'll drink to that.

Play That Funky Music, Barkeep

I have friends who feel that researching a book of this sort is a doddle, a piece of cake, a walk in the park. Going about town, sitting in pubs—what's so tough about that? Still, I am reminded of the words of whichever member of the Thesiger family it was who, when asked about his experiences in the trenches of World War I, replied, "My dear, the noise… and the people!" In my case the people weren't so bad, but, my dear, the noise!

In *McCarthy's Bar*, Pete McCarthy notes that Van Morrison music always appears to be playing in every pub in Ireland, as if there were some sort of government quota in effect. My legal advisors have been working around the clock on our behalf, and they have concluded—to my shock—that there is no actual legislation that requires licensed premises to play every song you've ever heard by Sting over their sound systems much of the day. Bizarre as it may seem, they do this of their own accord. The government inspector who comes around to check for mouse fewmets in the kitchen does not then slap a health warning on a bar for the insufficient playing time of *Every Breath You Take*. "You've been warned before," this inspector does not say to a trembling publican. "You've got five minutes to make those guys at the bar listen to *Roxanne* or I'm shutting this joint down."

My crack legal team assures me that, not only do bar owners not have to play *Sting's Greatest Hits* several times a day, but they are under no legal requirement to play any music at all. I'm going to give you a moment to absorb that bit of news. No legal requirement: they're doing it to annoy you.

The main bar of Paupers Pub on Bloor Street occasionally sneaks a bit of piped-in noise but, for the most part, relies on the traditional sounds of human conversation to create a convivial ambience. And guess what—it works! Part of the second floor of the Madison offers a quiet but full smoking environment. If you want non-smoking you are subjected to the jukebox from hell. The basement bar at the Madison—like its counterpart at the Duke of York on Prince Arthur—was once a music-free zone, but around the same time—as if responding to a government directive—both rooms installed speakers and started making their customers listen to music they had not asked for.

Pub owners all seem to be worried that we will think we're not enjoying ourselves if we're not tapping our toes to idiotic music, much of it pitched at people who are too young to be in pubs anyway. (These same pub owners also believe it's important to dim the lights soon after six o'clock, whether or not there are paying customers reading books at the time. There is a fear that a young person or two will look in and recoil with horror at the sight of some old geezer quietly reading. "Look out, Jason—this place isn't for us! And let's make sure we tell all our friends as well!") There is also the question of whether the music in pubs is there for the entertainment of the staff or the customers. Well, it's not much of a question really, is it?

It's no accident that it is for the most part music lovers who hate enforced music in pubs (or indeed other public places). I used to drink with Tom Monohan, then principal bassist of the Toronto Symphony, a large man who kept the Duke of York quiet for years. He's dead now, unfortunately, and the music has crept in. Music lovers can't help listening to music, even if it's music they hate. Ironically the music is there for the people who are more or less indifferent to music, people who don't really notice what's being played. (Which is why pubs sometimes forget to turn the damn stuff on; the only people who have noticed are the least likely to complain.) Anyone who has ever played piano in a lounge or restaurant will testify that most nights someone will come up to request a song you've just played. They didn't really hear it while you were playing it, but they absorbed just enough to remind them that they like the song and wouldn't mind hearing it some time. Let's get the piano player to play it for us.

The relegation of music to background din is offensive to music lovers, as is the notion of inflicting unwelcome music upon others. A subway station near my home plays loud classical music through its halls with the clear intention of discouraging troublesome teenagers from lingering. And it seems to work. I have to conclude that pubs that make me listen to Sting or any number of other pop stars are actively trying to discourage me from spending my time and money with them, and it also works. I like reading in pubs, but I'd get cranky very quickly if a member of the staff handed me the latest Danielle Steel when I arrived and told me this is what I'd be reading today.

There are two principal reasons I spend so much time in pubs, apart from the draught beer. As mentioned, I like reading in pubs, and I like talking to friends in pubs. Neither of these activities is enhanced by the presence in the air of the Eagles singing *Hotel California*. Indeed, both are hampered. I can't imagine any form of human endeavour that is improved by listening to *Hotel California*. Defenders of canned music argue that it enables pubgoers to converse without being overheard, which is obvious nonsense. Everyone simply talks louder to be heard over the bloody Eagles, at which point some bright young spark on the bar staff usually cranks the music up higher because they can no longer hear it.

According to the director of music at Eton College (not to be confused with the venerable downmarket Eton House on the Danforth), George Bernard Shaw once arrived at a restaurant and was asked by the manager what he would like the band to play. "Dominoes," said the music-loving Shaw. This story comes from a fine guide to English pubs, called *The Quiet Pint*. The editors of this excellent book have located a host of pubs that— apart from any other distinguishing features—don't have piped music. Many of the great pubs of Britain, including a number of personal favourites, are in this guide, which clocks in at over 550 pages in length. It is sad that a corresponding guide for Toronto might occupy one photocopied page. Even the bar at the hoity-toity Four Seasons Hotel makes its clientele listen to dopey pop music.

The guide to quiet British pubs (heartily endorsed by an organization called Pipedown, a campaign to rid Britain of unwanted music) was necessary because most pubs play enforced music. I can date some of my trips to England by which songs were being played in practically every pub in the country. One trip was the *Bette Davis Eyes* trip, while another belonged to *Baker Street*. *Baker Street*, you may recall, was the song that became popular because it had a recurring saxophone solo. It was played exactly the same way each time it recurred—that's what Top Forty pop music is all about—but it gave an otherwise dull song a touch of sophistication. I wanted to cry out, "Are you people aware that you can buy whole records of saxophone music, all of them more interesting than this?" It would have been true at the time: Kenny G. had yet to burst on the scene.

Would it make a difference if pubs played the sort of music I like? Hard to say, because it's never been tried. I've spent a chunk of my life in pubs and bars, and I don't think I've ever heard a John Dowland lute piece, or a William Byrd mass, or a Stephen Sondheim show tune. (All right, I sat on a pub patio outside London in 1999 and heard bits of *Sweeney Todd* being played from a nearby house, but that doesn't count.) Once, in a Chicago brewpub, I heard a song by Wesla Whitfield—one of my favourite singers—but that's a total of once in a whole lot of man-pub-hours. There's a bar called Tosca in San Francisco that includes opera arias on its jukebox, but it's a long commute from my place. There's a pub called the Hand in Hand in Brighton on England's south coast that was playing Mozart horn concerti the last time I was there. You get occasional jazz if you know where to look (see below), and sporadic blues (see Smokeless Joe's), but for the most part it's the Eagles, Sting, Whitney Houston, Sheryl Crow, Rod Stewart, and the rest of them. You've heard it all a thousand times, and here it comes again. Have people no boredom threshold at all?

I'm a pro-choice kind of guy, especially when it comes to listening to the whiney boys and keening girls of the contemporary pop scene. My choice would be no thanks. In fact, the musicians we drinking folk have to listen to make me feel very pro-abortion, retroactively if necessary. I have a piano-playing cousin who feels strongly about music in pubs, and I have spent many hours with him in New York helping him in his quest to find the perfect Gotham drinking spot. Well, that's what family's for. There are no quiet bars in New York—even the lobby of the august Algonquin Hotel inflicts easy listening on its customers—but many of them have jukeboxes. And many of those jukeboxes actually offer a few jazz selections. So our standard procedure now is to head straight for the jukebox, feed it a few bucks so that we get at least our choice of music, and only then get the bartender pouring Michael's Guinness. One of the pleasant by-products of this practice is that it really annoys the staff to have to listen to grownup music. Michael reckons it's good for them, and maybe it is.

Cousin Michael, being a jazz guy, claims that he never liked rock and roll, even in the sixties. I did. I was not always squaresville, daddio. I saw the Beatles live. I saw Hendrix live, on a bill with Pink Floyd. I saw the Stones in London, in their first gig after they got home from Altamont. I saw the Grateful Dead in a Lower East Side theatre, doing a benefit for the Hell's Angels. I was out there, man. I've met Mike Lieber, who co-wrote *You Ain't Nothin' But a Hound Dog*. I even have an interesting theory about Little Eva, which I will tell you about some time after a few pints. So I have some credentials. (Admittedly, I've kind of lost track. I've never been able to tell Peter Frampton from Peter Gabriel, for instance, nor do I give a hoot.)

But there comes a time when you've heard it all. The rock music era has now lasted almost as long as the Classical era of Mozart and Haydn. In an age with no way of broadcasting music, an age when in order to hear music you either had to make it yourself or be in the same room as a musician, people wearied of the Classical sound in about fifty years. No one would have given rock 'n' roll five decades. One of the early practitioners of rock suggested the sound had a good six months left; after all, it had already outlasted the mambo. Can we not put it painlessly to sleep?

So which songs do I particularly not want to hear in a pub? It's a very long list, but there are a few clear choices. I've mentioned *Hotel California*. How about *Horse With No Name*, arguably the worst pop song since *Sugar Shack*? One way to guarantee that your songs don't get turned into elevator music is to make sure they have no discernible tune at all, and that nameless horse managed it. In recent years I've been extremely annoyed by a Sheryl Crow song that I assume—because the words get repeated far too often—is called *If It Makes You Happy*. This song does not make me happy, not in the least. It asks the question: Why the hell are you so sad? I am sad because I am being made to listen to Sheryl Crow for what must be the thousandth time. Sheryl Crow is to my mind a guarantee of lifetime employment for Dr. Kervorkian.

There's also a famous song, presumably by some famous band, probably called *More Than a Feeling*. This is a song I hear in pubs all the time and wonder why. Likewise *Play That Funky Music White Boy*, another Dr. Kervorkian favourite. How about *Witchy Woman*, which might be by the Eagles again? *What a Fool Believes. Rikki Don't Lose That Number. I Can't Go For That (No Can Do). Whoa Ho Ho Listen to the Music. Doan Chew Wan Me Baybay, Doan Chew Wan Me Oh-oh-oh-oh*. The list is endless. This is all stuff that saps the will to live, and few of us need more will sapping in our lives.

I recognize that my selection of the worst songs will not be the same as yours. A late friend of mine had in his younger years enjoyed some sort of romantic encounter—and I'm putting the best possible light on "romantic"—against the backdrop of *McArthur Park*, and would never hear a word against what was possibly the worst song ever recorded. The only good thing I can think of about *McArthur Park* is that it is so bad that no bar in North America would dream of playing it today, and as I write these words I imagine some vindictive publican reaching for his Greatest Hits of Richard Harris CD.

And even as I write these words I remember that I heard very recently a song I hoped had been buried along with so much other dross of the sixties. There is almost nothing I disliked about the sixties, but I'll make a very big exception in the case of a song that annoyed the hell out me then and did so again last week. It was the one and only hit for a guy called Peter Sarstedt, and I assume it was called *Where Do You Go To, My Lovely*. Remember that one? I want to see inside your head, yes I do, yes I do. Your loveliness goes on and on, yes it does, yes it does. Do I ever want to hear that song again? No I don't, no I don't. I'm not a violent man but even today I think I'd cheerfully punch Peter Sarstedt. I expect it's been done a time or two already.

The one piece of music I would unreservedly encourage the publicans of the world to play is a solo piano work by John Cage, a 1952 composition called *4:33*. In this work a pianist, armed with a stopwatch, very pointedly does not play the piano for exactly four minutes and thirty-three seconds. I see no reason why this piece could not be played (or not be not played, if you see my point) on other instruments. I picture a two-CD set of *4:33* arranged for horns, strings, electric guitar, the Javanese gamelan, and mixed-voice choir. The pop divas—Barbra Streisand, Celine Dion, Whitney Houston, and their awful like—could perform *4:33* without taking a breath. Roberta Flack could perform *4:33* very very slowly, so it would take about twelve minutes. And when the young person in a pub asks why there's no music playing, the bartender will shush him. "We're listening to John Cage, man," he will say. "It's the eighth cut on the second CD—*4:33* arranged for Hawaiian guitar. Amazing, man."

In 1950 a man named Jack Newman bought a Toronto bar on Dundas Street East. He also bought a jukebox and filled it with his own jazz records. All these years later, you can drink in that same bar—though it was touch-and-go for a while when the city decided it needed the land for its Yonge-Dundas redevelopment—and play that same jukebox at practically 1950 prices: two plays for a quarter, five for fifty cents, and ten for a buck. The drinking's a bit pricier than in 1950, but there isn't much Mr. Newman can do about that.

The Imperial Public Library is the upstairs bar of the two Imperial pubs, and that's where you'll find the jukebox. Photographs of jazz greats and somewhat undressed (yet tasteful) women of the jazz era decorate the walls, and old books sit on shelves, hence the name of the bar. Occasionally the bar is quiet, which is nice, and the rest of the time you're listening to altogether decent jazz, which is also nice. Mr. Newman—helped by his sons—is still rotating the choices from time to time, and long may he do so.

The Imperial is at the edge of the Ryerson campus, so you may be surrounded by irrepressible college students, and sometimes the pub hosts literary readings when the jazz will be replaced by the tones of poets and novelists. It still beats the hell out of the Doobie Brothers. Or Peter Bloody Sarstedt.

Losing the will to live: Surviving the Hangover

For a population of a titch over five million, the Finns make a fair impact on the planet. They produce hockey players, orchestra conductors, opera singers, and Formula One racing car drivers way out of proportion to their size. Given that there are so few of them, it's not surprising that we don't meet more Finns.

In the summer of 1968 I met Finns for the first time. It helped that I was in northern Europe, which brought me closer to the source. Studies have revealed that in the summer of 1968, some twenty-three per cent of the world's population was hitchhiking in Europe, and I was one of those people. We were all pretty dusty from spending our days at the sides of roads watching cars zip by (European drivers drive as quickly as they can), and we hauled great heavy knapsacks around. There was one exception, and I hitchhiked with her one day from Frankfurt to Hannover. She was a lovely young woman in a flimsy summer dress, carrying only a tiny purse. She was a Finn.

The number one male hitchhiker's fantasy entails being picked up by an oversexed blonde in a convertible, but meeting up with a vision of Finnish loveliness in a summer dress is not a bad second. I will draw a discreet veil over what happened between us, only because nothing at all happened between us. Are you kidding? If something had happened I'd be writing a chapter about it. Anyway, she had nothing at all to do with hangovers, but I thought it would be nice to let her make a cameo appearance in the book. And she did make me think about how little I knew of Finland.

I met my second Finn two or three days later. I had by now arrived in Lübeck, a handsome old town that had been painstakingly restored after the war. Lübeck, it turns out, is the marzipan capital of the world, which I didn't know at the time. It is also now home to what is apparently the best Irish pub in Germany, which shows you how crazy the world is. I'm fairly sure there were no Irish pubs in Lübeck in 1968, but nevertheless it looked very nice that morning, and I thought I'd get to know it a bit better by tasting the local beer. As I quietly drank my beer I listened in on a political discussion between the bartender and the bar's only other customer. It stinks now, but for a spell in the late sixties my German wasn't at all bad, especially when I was drinking beer. More evidence that beer makes you smarter.

Pashley's Third Rule of Drinking (and don't ask me what the first two are) is: never argue with the bartender. But it was 1968 and we young people were convinced we had the right to our opinions, so I joined in on the side of the other customer. Who turned out to be another Finn. He had spent the summer working in Germany but was now on his way back to Finland, where beer at the time was practically illegal. He had enjoyed a jolly summer of drinking German beer and was embarking on a full day of the same before he caught his ferry back to Helsinki.

(Had I known then what I know now I'd have asked him about Sahti, the great beer of Finland, beloved of home brewers. According to Michael Jackson, Sahti is generally made from equal parts rye and barley and seasoned with juniper berries. It gets fermented with baker's yeast for a week in wooden pails and is filtered through juniper twigs and straw. Apparently it is frequently brewed in the sauna and often gets consumed there, which doesn't surprise me a bit. At last word there was one commercial brewer of Sahti and, to buy the stuff, you have to purchase a voucher at a government liquor store then take said voucher to a producer, the only one of which is located some 200 miles northwest of Helskinki. No wonder many Finns simply make their own. Or just drink vodka.)

Despite their government's stand on alcohol—which makes Canada look at least like Gomorrah—the Finns like their beer. The early Finns even had a god of beer and barley, who went by the name of Pekko. The Finn I met in Lübeck was clearly a worshipper, possibly even a Pekko-head. He asked me—and all this went on in German, so if I seem a bit sketchy on the details, that's why—if I was familiar with the concept of *Ein Stiefel Bier*. *Ein Stiefel* is a boot, not be confused with *Das Boot*, which is a movie about a submarine. *Ein Stiefel Bier* is a practice whereby a large quantity of beer is poured into a big glass boot and then consumed. Well, you can see where this is going. I blame the Finn.

My new friend and I made it our project to have *Ein Stiefel Bier*, the most important component of which involved finding a bar that had the requisite glass boot. Lübeck, I can tell you, has a number of bars, but not many of them—in 1968, at least—boasted the *Stiefel*. "*Güten Tag,*" we greeted any number of Prussian barkeeps, "*Haben Sie ein Stiefel Bier?*" "*Ach, nein,*" they replied sadly. It seemed impolite—especially since they were all so nice—simply to walk on, so we stopped for a beer or two anyway.

By the time we found what we were looking for, we no longer needed it. But have it we did anyway. My, those big glass boots hold a lot of beer. And at what point my Finnish friend thought schnapps chasers were in order I cannot say. I know that at some point he set out for his ferry to Finland, and I somehow hitchhiked up to another ferry terminal at Puttgarden.

The other end of my ferry ride was a place called Rødbyhaven, which is Danish for Nowheresville, Denmark. It was a ferry terminal and nothing else, so another troupe of dusty hitchhikers stood about waiting for the next ferry to arrive. By chance, I met up with a pair of young Irish women. By now it was dark and chilly, and the Irish women offered me some of their native whiskey as a warming agent. It seemed to work, though in retrospect I recall the age-old wisdom: Beer on whiskey makes you feel frisky; Whiskey on beer makes you feel queer. And queer—queer in the old-fashioned sense, at any rate—is what I quite distinctly felt some hours later as I rode with the Irish women in someone's truck through the landscape of southern Denmark.

I awoke the next morning in a Danish field. I assume it was morning. It certainly felt like it. No part of me was functioning in anything like a normal way. Standing up was an adventure, and I didn't achieve it in my first few attempts. My normal aversion to death was suspended. I had had hangovers before and I've had them since, but this was the sort of life-sapping experience that has turned strong men into abstainers, if only temporarily. I felt like the hero of Kingsley Amis's *Lucky Jim*: "His mouth had been used as a latrine by some small creature of the night, and then as a mausoleum." Alas, there was no running water in this field to combat the dehydration, no raw eggs to do whatever raw eggs are supposed to do for you. Nothing, in short, to promote the will to live.

Fifteen yards away, up a short incline, lay the road to somewhere else in Denmark. It had to be better than the place I was. To its credit, wherever I was was a quiet part of Denmark, but in the long term I required somewhere a trifle more sophisticated, at least to the point of offering large quantities of water. It was several hours before I had recovered sufficiently to make my way to the road and be able to stand long enough to hitch a ride to Copenhagen. Once there, I holed up in the youth hostel for a couple of abstemious days, cursing the Finn who had brought me to this state. Oddly enough, I have never attached much blame to the Irish women who had put me over the edge with their grain tea, but then I wouldn't, would I?

There are many theories about hangovers, most of them not worth much. The ancient Greeks apparently believed that if you wore a garland of parsley on your head while you were out on the razzle you wouldn't get a hangover the next morning. That seems highly unlikely, but—like you, I imagine—I haven't tried it. Many of the places I frequent would almost certainly refuse to serve a customer with a garland of parsley on his head, even a regular.

One medieval hangover cure entailed consuming a raw eel and bitter almonds, but I can't imagine what sort of ethnic neighbourhood you'd have to live in to have easy access to raw eels. The Assyrians of yesteryear made a paste of ground swallow's beak and myrrh, and I've seen somewhere a recipe for fried canary that's supposed to be useful. Hungover cowboys, I am told, used to fix up a brew of dried rabbit droppings, which was probably about as pleasant as it sounds.

The hangover can be prevented, of course, by just saying no to intoxicating beverages. Many people do it every day. But not me, and probably not you either. And most of us drinking folk are smart enough to call it an evening before it comes to destruction on that scale. Every now and then, however, circumstances seem to dictate just the teensiest bit of excess. Where did I recently encounter the following exchange? Q. Do you ever drink to excess? A. I'll drink to anything.

The hangover might possibly be prevented by avoiding Finns, but I can recall hangovers after evenings that included no known Finns at all. Drinking lots of water or fruit juice along with the alcohol will definitely help, though you'll pee all night. A couple of Aspirin before retiring might help, unless it attacks your stomach lining, in which case you'll wake up with a sore gut instead of a sore head. Depends which you prefer, really. Cheap red wine is the surest guarantee of a hangover, as is widespread mixing of alcohols. And those alcohol-sugar-coffee concoctions can do untold damage: the alcohol makes you drunk, the sugar makes you sick, and the coffee makes sure you stay awake to enjoy every moment of it.

Vitamin B1 is said to be a good preventive measure, and no less authoritative a source than the *Quarterly Journal of Alcohol Studies*—and I hope your subscription's up to date—recommends taking Vitamin B6 before, during, and after a drinking session. The alternative health people, who tend not to drink much in my observation, swear by something called milk thistle. For best results, unfortunately, you need to take this stuff daily for a week before you go out on the bender. Most of us aren't that well prepared.

If the hangover has caught you by surprise and it's too late for milk thistle, what then? Plenty of fluids. Water, fruit juice, or sports drinks.

You're dehydrated, buster, and you've got to replace them fluids. A professor at the University of Sunderland says that when we drink a pint of beer we pee a pint and a third of fluid. I know it feels that way, but this guy says it's true. So if you drink six pints you lose two whole pints of bodily fluid; no wonder you feel rotten afterwards. Coffee, like alcohol, is a diuretic, so it should be avoided in the treatment of your hangover.

Modern science leans away from the old greasy breakfast cure. (The time for oily food is before you start drinking; it lines your stomach.) A mixture of lemon juice, maple syrup, and cayenne pepper in hot water is supposed to help. Pineapple juice is apparently good for the stomach. A doctor in the UK has recently sung the praises of artichokes for the morning after. The Russians—who should know something about hangovers—swear by cabbage juice with something fizzy in it. For the Ukrainian there's nothing like a cup of chilled sauerkraut, which is rich in potassium, natural salts, and magnesium. Northern Europeans recommend a breakfast of marinated fish, while a New England bar called Friendly's boasts a hangover cure that comprises a bowl of clam chowder, followed by a beefburger, then a chocolate pancake. I think I'd rather take the pledge and be done with it.

The list of hangover cures is practically endless: cucumber juice, orange pop with a chocolate milk chaser, bananas, pickle juice, coconut, hot baths, tomatoes, or a quail's egg in a cup of warm sake. Paul McCartney apparently blends a mixture of carrot, beet, celery, and parsley juices, and he's a billionaire so he should know.

There are those who practice even harsher measures than pickle juice for hangovers. The Scandinavians, for instance, are likely to jump into an icy lake, but it's worth remembering the allegedly high Scandinavian suicide rate. I suspect this method leads to hungover Swedes who are now also extremely cold. I don't see it myself.

Another traditional cure is the drinking of a glass of bitters. There are a number of such herbal concoctions, all of which combine an unspeakable taste with a strong alcohol content. Fernet Branca is probably the best known, though Kingsley Amis favoured Underburg. He said that the effect on the system was "like that of throwing a cricket ball into an empty bath"; in North America we can substitute a baseball. The bad taste is the gastric equivalent of the Swedish icy lake, as well as making you feel that it must be good for you, while the alcohol actually does the job.

Because of the alcohol, drinking bitters is really no different from taking a hair (or, as Cyril Connolly preferred, a tuft) of the dog that bit you.

Amis points out that the breed is not important; it doesn't have to be the same form of alcohol that brought you to this dire state. The danger here is what a friend has called the compound-complex hangover. By taking on another drink you ease the current pain, but you may be setting yourself up for something even bigger. One drink should suffice. Then consider going back to bed, if that's an option.

The American drug companies, needless to say, are working round the clock to develop an anti-hangover pill. There are fortunes to be made here. It is said that America loses $US148 billion a year in poor performance and days missed owing to hangovers. I don't know how they come up with numbers like this, but I read it in a respectable newspaper so it must be true. A team of researchers from the University of California, San Francisco, believes that a cure to the hangover lies in creating a pill that blocks the release of something called cytokines. These are molecules that are released by white blood cells to fight viruses and the like. As I understand it, the body gets hit by all this alcohol (strictly speaking, the congeners in the alcohol, but there won't be a quiz at the end of this chapter) and thinks it's getting flu, so it sends out these cytokines to fight it. Knowing the drug companies, we won't be able to afford this pill when they finally invent it, so keep drinking water and taking the milk thistle. And avoid Finns.

The Silliest Conversation
I've Ever Had in a Bar

Those who know me might quibble with my choice of Silliest Conversation in a Bar, choosing instead any number of conversations that I myself have initiated or even serious conversations that I have turned silly. Let them quibble. They weren't present for this one, and anyway it's my book.

And I'm not talking about the time a bunch of us were gathered in the Embassy Tavern some time in the mid-1970s. We knew from the newspapers that Elton John was in town recording, and there was, at a nearby table, a man who looked a lot like Elton John. This was just before Toronto had proper drinking places, but even so the Embassy seemed an unlikely spot to encounter a major recording artist. But still.

We were intrigued. Was it or was it not Elton John? The realists among us insisted that Elton John would not be drinking in a place like the Embassy, while others were reluctant to disbelieve the evidence of their eyes. This was before Mr. John had adopted the really bizarre attire that would have made him readily recognizable anywhere. At any rate, our group was unsure. Finally one of us—Patrick Lee, by name—volunteered to go over and ask. We did not discourage him. Patrick approached the table of the solitary drinker and exchanged a few words. He returned, poker-faced, to our table.

Well, we said, what did he say?
No, said Patrick, it's not him.
How do you know, we asked.
He said so, said Patrick.
He said he's not Elton John?
That's right.
Did he say it in an English accent?
Patrick paused. Yes, he admitted.

To this day we have no idea if we were drinking in close proximity to Elton John. Nor do we really care, if the truth be told. But you'd like to know.

Anyway, that's not the conversation I had in mind This one is.

It was an afternoon, I remember that much. A day of the week, very possibly ending in 'y'. Very likely in or about 1974, and almost certainly in Toronto. I found myself at a bar called the Young Station, no longer with us, in the building that is now the Brass Rail. I am given to understand that if you go into this place today young women will undress in front of you, which never in my experience happened when it was the Young Station. I don't get to the Brass Rail much, my limited knowledge of this sort of place informing me that the beer selection is invariably very poor, and overpriced too. And those young women can be very distracting if you're trying to read.

The Young Station was an odd sort of bar. By night it offered very loud rock bands, while by day it served up very cheap beer. The Young Station brought a new twist to drinking in those distant days. Most bars of that era served beer in tiny glasses cleverly designed to look bigger than they were. The Young Station served beer in glasses designed to look smaller than they actually were. This had the interesting effect of encouraging consumption on an industrial scale, and it worked. If getting people very drunk indeed was its goal, the Young Station succeeded brilliantly. Its motto might have been: A buzz for a buck, drunk for two bucks, falling down for three.

The cheap beer attracted a mixed clientele, with only a desire to get drunk cheap in common. Most of its daytime customers were obviously people with only a passing familiarity with the work ethic, though others did much of their work within its walls. A dealer in illicit substances I knew from high school (I knew the dealer, you understand, not the illicit substances) kept regular office hours at the Young Station. There was an older man, always well turned out, who I was absolutely sure was a remittance man of some sort. And it was in the Young Station one characteristic winter day that my friend Russ Hughes referred to Toronto as "this snow-soaked shithole of a city", a splendidly alliterative characterization I quote frequently.

As I then lived around the corner, I got to the Young Station more frequently perhaps than I should. You never knew what was going to happen. One day I sat next to four university boys who had just finished for the year and who celebrated by ordering 100 glasses of beer. The ringleader told me he had always wanted to order 100 draught beers, and he did it. They arrived in some splendour, four trays full of beer. Eventually, of course, I had to help them out, and I did my best.

I have every confidence that there was some fairly silly conversation that afternoon, but I don't remember any of it. No, the conversation I had in mind was a different afternoon, albeit in the same bar. I was sitting by myself at a Formica-topped table, quietly reading. At the next table sat a man I didn't know. Like many men who sit alone in bars, he had nothing to read, apparently happy to stare ahead and think his thoughts. Me, I don't have enough thoughts to see me through a whole afternoon in the pub, so I like to bring along a book. We had not spoken or acknowledged each other's existence.

Two men in turbans came in. They walked past us, paused while they considered sitting in our section of the bar, then moved on. When these men were out of earshot, the fellow at the next table leaned toward me.

"Them Pakis bug you?" he asked.

I hesitated, considering the implications of my answer. Was I willing to get into a fight about this? "No," I replied.

He paused slightly, apparently having decided we had both stepped out of a Harold Pinter play, then he said, "Yeah, me neither."

I returned to my book, we both took a sip from our beers, and never exchanged another word.

Who Owns Your Pub?

By law, English pubs have to sport a notice over the entrance advising the public of the identity of the licensee. While this is interesting information, it is seldom that the licensee of a pub is also the owner. Until quite recently most English pubs were owned by breweries, most of them regional. Driving through England in 1980 you would be aware of travelling through an area dominated by Morland's pubs, then Morrell's pubs, then, as you approached Wiltshire, Wadworth's pubs. If you wanted to drink Donnington's beers, you went to northern Gloucestershire and kept your eyes open.

The breweries essentially leased their pubs out to tenants, most of whom stayed for many years and stamped their own personalities on the pubs. They bought their beer from the breweries to which they were tied and—for the most part—lived in relative harmony with both their brewery and their customers. It was a system that worked for a very long time. There were also pubs that were independently owned, with no tie to any brewery, free to sell whatever beer they chose. These were called free houses and were generally seen as a good thing. They were such a good thing that many pubs lied and called themselves free houses when they were not. I know: imagine that.

In the 1990s the British government—in a well-intentioned move that was intended to protect the smaller breweries that were getting slammed by the big guys—passed legislation that limited the number of pubs a brewery could own, and also forced pub owners to allow their tenants to sell guest beers. The bigger companies had either to divest themselves of some of their pubs or get out of brewing. It is the nature of big companies that they don't like becoming smaller companies, and the new legislation guaranteed full employment for a number of corporate lawyers. The upshot is that a lot of English pubs are now owned by what is called "pubcos", companies that don't make beer but own lots of pubs. These companies are constantly buying and selling pubs and generally making drinkers nervous. While they are not owned by breweries, most of these pubcos have deals with big brewers, so the beer selection is likely to be unsurprising.

One of the most interesting of these companies is the rapidly expanding J.D. Wetherspoon chain, which predictably has nothing to do with anybody called Wetherspoon. Most of its pubs have been placed in buildings that were not originally pubs, some quite imaginatively. There is no music in these pubs, they all offer a no-smoking area (usually quite small), and they offer food all day—all pretty radical concepts in the UK.

Other chains have come and gone. Back in the late seventies, a fellow called David Bruce, laid off by one of the big breweries, got the idea of opening his own pubs. He started with a pub in Southwark that was being closed down as uneconomically feasible by one of the big guys. Bruce installed brewing equipment, redecorated, and gave the place a cute new name: the Goose and Firkin. Soon he was opening more brewpubs in slightly unfashionable areas—the Frog and Firkin, the Pheasant and Firkin, and—in a fire-damaged railway station—the Phoenix and Firkin. Eventually, of course, he sold the company and his concept got watered down and finally disappeared altogether.

The Firkin name has been adopted by a Toronto company that at last count boasts a couple of dozen pubs in southern Ontario. God knows the Firkin pubs have been a godsend for people in out-of-the-way places and for thirsty people just passing through those places, though there is something formulaic about the pubs. There are few surprises at the Firkin pubs (though it can sometimes be surprising how loud the music is at the Ferret and Firkin in Toronto); on the plus side, Anne swears by their hamburgers, despite the kaiser buns.

Perhaps the biggest success in Toronto's pub scene is that of David and Isabel Manore, proprietors of the Madison and Paupers, two midtown pubs that cater both to students and to residents of the hip Annex area. The Madison started life as a basement pub in an old house on Madison Avenue, inspired by the success of the nearby Duke of York. Eventually the Manores took over the ground floor, then the second and third floors of the house. By the 1990s they had bought the house next door and made their no longer little pub even bigger. At full tilt, when they have everything open, including three levels of patios in the back, the Manores can accommodate exactly 1,576 people. That's the full roster of all the teams in major league baseball and the National Hockey League, plus the original Broadway cast of Sondheim's *Follies*. Given the proximity of several frat houses, they frequently accomplish this goal.

In the mid-eighties the Manores took over what had been a bank on Bloor Street and turned it into Pauper's, complete with a quiet little room in what had been the vault. In 1999 they opened a 22-room "boutique hotel" just north of the Madison, possibly to be convenient for those people who meet other people at the Madison and feel a sudden need to become closer, and in 2000 they opened a villa in Puerta Vallarta, Mexico. Something tells me that David and Isabel have done well.

They didn't succeed by being dopey businesspeople, of course. From the start, they have been on the premises, keeping an eye on things, though presumably they have to spend more of their time in Mexico these days. To their credit, their staff includes a number of people who have been there forever, which suggests that the Manores are not dreadful to work for; bartenders and waiters are inclined to be nomadic.

That said, however, one could possibly take issue with the small notice in the menu that observes that, just in case you were tempted to be stroppy about this, a pint of beer is deemed to comprise approximately eighteen ounces of beer in a twenty-ounce glass. Readers of *The Globe and Mail* will be familiar with the injunction of Junius, who reminds us every day: The subject who is truly loyal to the Chief Magistrate will neither advise nor submit to arbitrary measures. As my friend Robbie Brown has noted, if an eighteen-ounce pint is not an arbitrary measure, I don't know what is. Mind you, it's only a ten per cent ripoff, and who could bicker with that? Oops, I think I just did. And one could argue that a pub capable of housing 1,576 people could afford to be a tad more adventurous in its choice of beers.

(And it's not just the Madison, by any means. The world is full of pubs that boast eighteen taps, twenty taps, twenty-two taps. But you go inside and it's always the same beer. Now I know that in supermarkets and big chain bookstores [or big chain anything], suppliers pay to have their products available. The more they pay, the better the placement. This practice is legal in most retail endeavours, and it may be legal in bars and pubs in some jurisdictions. It's not legal in the province of Ontario, where I live, and I'm not suggesting that any under-the-table payments are being made. Who'd be crazy enough to jeopardize their licence? No, I have to assume that a lot of Ontario publicans simply lack the imagination to offer their customers a meaningful variety.)

Still, all things considered, I'm just as happy that the Madison is there. I've had some good times within those walls. One night Anne and I met up with a guy who claimed to have worked with Neil Young. We drank far too much and sang along as he played the Madison's old piano. You can't put a price tag on that. Well, you probably can, but I've long since lost the Visa receipt. And I've gone there a time or two on Christmas Day. The Manores were the ones who broke the old taboo on serving drinks at Christmas.

English themselves, they knew about pubs being open on Christmas Eve and the day itself. In Toronto, pubs historically closed early on Christmas Eve and never dreamed of opening on the big day. But this is a biggish town and there are people without friends or family to go to—not to mention a few people who actually do have friends and family and still like to go to a pub anyway—who appreciate a place to go. As one who has traditionally worked on Christmas Eve, I know I like to have a pint after work. And there are usually enough bar staff who—gypsies themselves—are just as happy to work. Still, just in case, it's worth tipping a bit extra, okay?

Then there are the Dukes: York, Gloucester, Kent, Westminster, and Richmond. Sounds like one of those history plays from Shakespeare. What word of York, good brother Gloucester? Ah, good Lord of Kent, he is gone—i'faith!—with Westminster to do battle with the knave Richmond. It seems a loose federation of pubs. Westminster caters to the TSE 300, Richmond to downtown shoppers, Gloucester to the raffish Yonge Street set, Kent to a crew of uptown regulars, and York to the midtown mix of practically everything but particularly the university. The Duke of York recently underwent a major renovation which included adding a third floor. And the place looks great. It looks like a million bucks, which the rumour mill suggests would about cover the bill, but regulars guess that most of it was made up pretty quickly by attracting large groups.

That's where the money is these days, getting in a gang of sixty lawyers or a hundred teaching assistants, or what-have-you. It's good for the bottom line, but it's tough for the regulars, who sometimes can't get in the door without a reservation. Still, at some point it kind of stops being a pub. To my old mind, a proper pub does not need a crew of greeters at the main entrance helping people find a table or redirecting a team of regulars to this week's destination because their regular table is overrun by yet another group booking. A proper pub does not have a "Please Wait to be Seated" sign at the front door.

No one ever said the pub life was a democratic one. Drinking men and women are ever at the mercy of their publican, the despot who can discontinue your favourite ale, take sausage rolls off the menu, or inflict Led Zeppelin upon you with impunity. The drinker is, of course, free to vote with his or her feet. We can take our business elsewhere, which is not always an easy option.

Sometimes we have no choice but to take our business elsewhere. The bar in which I courted the Evergreen Bride is, as I write, a pile of rubble on a building site, soon to become yet another block of condominiums, or is that condominia? The bar in which I drank my first public beer is now an up-market menswear emporium. And on and on.

In late 2000 (early 2001 for North American viewers) *Coronation Street* ran a storyline in which the Rover's Return—the quintessential cozy back-street pub—was on the brink of being sold to a pubco with plans to tart the place up and re-name it the Boozy Newt. This was more than the traditionalists could stand, and the perennially earnest Ken Barlow uttered a speech that brought tears to this pubgoer's eyes:

"The world is full of nasty theme pubs with flashy décor and thumping sound systems, without this place being taken over as well. It's history and tradition within these walls, and it can't be replaced once it's lost."

In the next episode, Fred Elliott, the doughy butcher, reminded us, "It's the punters who decide what they want from a pub, not these so-called experts, these market researchers with their ruddy clipboards."

It is not fine speeches, however, that save pubs. Sometimes it takes cash, and in this case it took three of the regulars to put in a bid to buy the pub themselves, offering what Fred called "the last stand against the evil tide of fancy food and foreign beer." A grateful nation rose to its feet in applause.

The idea of a drinkers' cooperative is not confined to soap operas. There's a pub called the King's Arms (though it appears mysteriously in the phone book as the Brave Hearts Medieval Pub) in Toronto's trendy Yorkville area that was endangered when its owner decided to sell up and return to England. What to do? A quintet of regulars raised the money and bought the place. One day you're a familiar face at the bar, next day you're the guv'nor. Who owns your pub? Maybe you do.

It's Supposed to Have Flavour: Tasting Beer

According to something called Impact Databank, the two biggest selling beers on planet Earth are Bud and Bud Light. Between them these two anemic beverages account for slightly more than six per cent of all the beer consumed by homo otherwise sapiens in 1999. Given that many of us drank absolutely no Bud or Bud Light in 1999, and given that it isn't even available in the Czech Republic where they drink a lot of beer, you have to assume that somebody somewhere is drinking an awful lot of the stuff. As has been said, people who drink Bud Light don't like the taste of beer; they just enjoy peeing a lot.

All the beers on the global top ten list are predictably bland, brewed for people who don't want to be surprised by a sudden burst of flavour. Anheuser-Busch didn't get where it is today by overestimating the public's palate. Yet there are people out there who really do like the taste of beer, people who like to be surprised, people who like a bit of variety. Some of these people even attend beer tastings. A few years ago, the idea of beer tastings would have been laughed at. It's beer, for Pete's sake. It tastes like beer—what did you expect? If pressed to describe one's beer, the words "suds" and "foam" sprang to mind.

Nowadays the beer experts can be as over-the-top as the wine guys. The *Good Beer Guide*, published by the Campaign for Real Ale, describes beers in terms like: "A refreshing, copper-amber session bitter with a well-defined citrus hop aroma and taste, and a nutty, malty background ending dry"; or "A strong golden beer reminiscent of hot cross buns. Fruity, malty and sweet with butterscotch notes"; or "The intense roast flavour is backed by coffee, chocolate and liquorice, and hints of spice and smoke". Other beers are redolent of "cooked vegetables", "a glorious blackberry bouquet", and "a hint of sulphur leading to a pleasant crisp apple finish". If I'd talked about beer like that in the taprooms of my youth, I'd have been out on the street by the time I got to the butterscotch.

Very few of us—this humble reporter included—have palates as finely tuned as the authors of the above descriptions, but there's nothing to stop us getting better at identifying beer flavours. The beer experts—the likes of Michael Jackson, Roger Protz, and Canada's own Stephen Beaumont—aren't feeding us a lot of bull about tasting beer. If they say they're tasting hot cross buns, they're tasting hot cross buns. The point is that there are many interesting whiffs and flavours attached to a good beer, and it's part of the fun to spot at least some of them. Drinkers brought up on the Buds of this world haven't even come to grips with the smell and taste of hops, let alone liquorice and blackberries.

Beer is just as worthy of flowery talk as wine. Beer came first, after all, and brewing is a more sophisticated process, not to mention that beer doesn't need a bunch of peasants trampling the barley in their bare feet. Best of all, no one at beer tastings expects you to spit it out after you've tasted it, which makes beer tastings a lot jollier than wine tastings.

I like wine too, but you have to admit some of those people are a bit serious about it. I am reminded of the wine bore who was holding forth at a restaurant one evening, sipping wines and declaring at high volume what the grape was, which end of the vineyard it had come from, and what vintage it was. A man at a nearby table could endure it no longer, and finally passed a wine glass to his neighbour. The wine bore held it up to the light and declared it a Chardonnay, probably New World. In due course he sipped from the glass. Quickly he spat it out, crying, "This is piss!"

"I know what it is," said the man at the nearby table, "but how old am I?"

South African novelist André Brink tells the story of an attempt to produce wine in Zimbabwe, a country generally perceived as too hot for wine. Somewhere near Victoria Falls a vineyard was planted. In time the grapes were ready for harvesting, and they were duly turned into wine. When the process was complete, the wine bottled, aged, and labelled, a French expert was invited to come and give it his blessing. He came, he went through the tasting ritual, and he raised a glass to his lips. The locals held their breath as he swished the wine around his taste buds. When at last he spoke, he asked where the wine had been made.

"Right here, Monsieur," the winemaker said, gesturing. "Just across the road."

The expert frowned and thought for a moment. "Eet does not travel well."

Apart from the spitting business, beer tasting is much like its wine equivalent. Pour your beer into a nice clean glass. It's worth noting that detergent residue can kill the head on a beer, so wash your beer glasses separately from the rest of your dishes. (Oh sure, beer tasting is supposed to be so relaxed and suddenly I'm coming on with all sorts of rules. I'm just trying to make it nice for you.) Now take a look at your beer. Hold it up. Like the colour? Are there things floating in it? Occasionally there are supposed to be things floating in it, but it's worth asking at this point. Now take a good sniff. If you can't smell anything, you're not likely to taste much either. Can you smell the hops? No? Maybe the next one will be better.

Now taste the beer. Let it hit the taste buds right up front and then further along. Are you getting one taste at the start, followed by something different as it passes through? Excellent! That's just what good beer should do. Now, this is important—don't spit it out. Swallow it. Unless it's really awful. If you have reason to believe that you've just allowed some mass-produced abomination into your mouth—your body is a temple, remember—then feel free to spit it out, perhaps in the direction of the person who has played this sinister trick on you.

A lot of drinkers pick a beer they like at the age of about twenty, and stick with it for life, which is like eating the same dinner every night or listening to the same band every day. (As I write these words I've been married to the same woman for twenty-three years, so I'm definitely not taking this analogy any further. I may be daft, but I'm not stupid.)

Beer comes in many colours and many flavours, and limiting yourself to one kind of beer seems an act of masochism. You won't always like the beers you taste, but try to see what the brewer was getting at. Sometimes a beer will strike you as funny, just as music can be funny. Brewers often have a sense of humour, and they'll brew a beer with chili peppers or ginseng, just to see what happens. It's okay to laugh at your beer. Hell, drinking beer's supposed to be fun, so lighten up. There is no set taste of beer. Predictability is boring. And even if you haven't developed the keen palate of the experts, there's no reason you can't have a darn good time. Elsewhere I note that sex and golf are two activities you can enjoy without displaying great skill; tasting beer is another. Mind you, the better you get...

There's no reason you couldn't substitute good beer for wine at mealtimes. The general rule of thumb is to substitute a lager where you would otherwise serve a white wine, and offer an ale of substance instead of a red. There are fruit beers that complement a dessert, and a Sam Adams Trippelbock—if you can get one—is just as good (and just as strong) as a glass of port afterwards.

Beer tasting on a large scale is called a beer festival, and I recommend it highly. Early every August beer lovers descend on London for the Great British Beer Festival and the chance to taste some 300 British draught beers and a growing number of imports as well. Friends, you've never seen so many casks of beer in one place. If you have to wonder if this is a wonderful sight, you're reading the wrong book. The Great American Beer Festival in Denver is even bigger.

Beer festivals are to be found in many parts of the world, even Toronto. August brings Toronto's Festival of Beer to old Fort York and, though it's not the Great British Beer Festival, it ain't bad. And in my experience it doesn't even rain (jinx alert!). At the 2000 festival I saw a man whose party piece was drinking beer while standing on his head. Imagine how drunk you'd have to be to think that was a good idea. So go along, try a few new beers, and remember to comment on the cooked vegetable quality of the beer. The others will be impressed. If they're not, try standing on your head.

To Your Health: Relax—It's Good for You

The temperance movement that arose in the latter half of the nineteenth century succeeded in persuading a good many people that alcohol was a kind of poison, and we've lived with that slur ever since. If it brings you pleasure, it must be bad for you. Only in the last few years have we heard any encouraging words from the scientific community, but some of them have been mighty encouraging indeed.

There's alcohol, of course, and then there's alcohol. Red wine has had plenty of good press in the last few years, after people started to ask why, if red meat, alcohol, tobacco, cream sauces, and the like were so unhealthy, French people didn't die at thirty. This was a very good question. By all rational reckoning, the French should have become extinct long ago, yet here they were indulging in everything that could be considered toxic and living long, apparently healthy lives, engaging in physical activity no more strenuous than watching the Tour de France whiz by once a year. And don't tell me that boules is the perfect aerobic exercise.

The fellows and gals in the white coats went away to study the phenomenon of French longevity and came back giving credit to red wine, which sent burgundy sales soaring through the roof, where they have remained ever since. En masse, women—traditional drinkers of white wine but more health-conscious than men—switched to red. Party-givers found themselves completely out of red wine within half an hour, with cases of white untouched. Subsequent studies have suggested that, in general, the health benefits of red wine stem simply from the alcohol, not from some magical quality of red wine, though red wine is richer in antioxidants than white. In other words, alcohol is good for you.

(The red wine boom was similar to the yogurt boom of the sixties, when it was discovered that yogurt-chugging residents of the Caucasus routinely lived to the age of 106. Typically, of course, very few of these ancient people actually had birth certificates, and it was later suggested that it only felt like 106 years. Living in the Caucasus on a diet of yogurt will do that to you.)

The original healthy beverage was beer. Made of the same ingredients as bread, beer was considered an exemplary, almost medicinal drink until the temperance zealots came along. When William of Orange left the Lowlands to take the British throne in 1688, he brought gin with him. William taxed beer to support his military activities in Ireland, driving up the price of beer and making gin more popular with the masses. By 1740 there were 9,000 gin shops in London (compared with the present 7,000 pubs in that now much larger metropolis). Hogarth's engravings of Gin Lane and Beer Street demonstrate the social perils of gin and the life-enhancing qualities of beer. Gin came by the moniker "mother's ruin" honestly.

Beer (and later wine) put us on the map as a species. If you didn't drink beer you had to drink water, and water was a hazard. The brewing of beer called for the boiling of water, a measure that saved lives. There are not many references in the scriptures, for instance, of people drinking water. Remember St. Paul, the life of no recorded parties, said, "Drink no longer water, but use a little wine for thy stomach's sake." Water was the ticket to cholera and other unpleasant diseases. The life expectancy of the early teetotaller was dismally low. Early man (see page 21) was not clever enough to keep his water supply pure, so he needed beer. Columbus crossed the Atlantic with wine, not water, and he had the capital of Ohio named after him.

There is a school of thought that says that Europeans learned to make beer and wine to avoid raw water, while the Asians learned to make tea. This kept both groups healthy but gave Europeans a genetic disposition toward alcohol that Asians do not share. (It is also possible, of course, that the Asians—not genetically disposed to alcohol—gravitated to tea because it suited them better. Apparently more than forty per cent of Asians lack the gene that turns alcohol first into acetaldehyde, then into acetic acid, while virtually all people of European origin can turn this little trick without thinking twice about it. Whether they preferred tea because they lack the gene or they lack the gene because they didn't develop it through centuries of drinking beer and wine is unknown.)

According to this theory, European society from the Iron Age lived in a state of at least a mild buzz until the Victorian era, when modern engineering brought clean water to the public at large. Coincidentally—or not—the temperance movement arose at the same time. For the first time it was possible for westerners to live an alcohol-free life and not perish. Alcohol became an indulgence rather than a fact of life. Ironically, we seem to be moving backwards again. A diet of beer rather than E-coli-infested water could have saved lives in Walkerton, Ontario, in the late 1990s. Now that our water is not quite so safe again, we need ways of treating it to render it harmless. Turning it into alcohol seems to work.

For years we read of studies proving that alcohol was bad for us. A pregnant woman today who takes as much as a sip of wine will be shunned and scolded, yet there can be few members of my generation whose mothers did not drink throughout their pregnancies.

Fortunately, in the last few years the people who do studies of this sort have been coming out on the side of the drinking person. It's amazing the sort of thing these people will study, and wouldn't you love to see their funding proposals? In the late 1990s researchers at the University of Western Ontario established that a stirred martini was healthier than a shaken one. "Let me get this straight, Smithers. You need a research grant for a case of gin, a bottle of vermouth, and a couple of jars of olives?" "Any chance we could have some swizzle sticks as well?"

A Japanese study revealed that drinking can be good for the brain cells. The National Institute for Longevity Sciences did IQ tests on 2,000 people between the ages of 40 and 79. Men who drank moderately scored 3.3 points higher than those who didn't drink, while female drinkers scored 2.5 points higher than their abstaining counterparts. It didn't matter what sort of alcohol they drank. Researchers acknowledged that the results did not take into account the possibility that people who drink are just naturally more intelligent than those who don't, and I couldn't possibly comment.

Around the same time the 2000 International Chemical Congress of Pacific Basin Societies—and, given what conventions are like, who's to say they weren't hitting the sauce a mite themselves?—took aboard a study done by Canadian and American researchers that showed that the antioxidants in beer can reduce the risk of cataracts and heart disease. Ale lovers will be pleased to learn that dark ales and stouts have more antioxidants than lighter beers, so are particularly healthy, especially for diabetics. The study involved giving hamsters the equivalent of two beers a day, and the results were very good indeed. Especially if you're a diabetic hamster. The Canadian input into this study seems to have been the same guys who were involved in the martini study mentioned above, which tells you practically everything you need to know about the University of Western Ontario. Let's just say there's no difficulty getting volunteers for scientific studies at Western.

The more of these studies you read, the more you think doctors should be prescribing beer. In fact my mother, in girlhood, was diagnosed as anemic and was made to drink Guinness. It was only at 89, when her Guinness input had declined, that her health degenerated. Until recently it was common for new mothers to be prescribed stout—rich in iron—as an aid to nursing. You tell me that an infant breastfed from a stout-sipping mother is not going to be a happy baby.

Beer contains the B vitamins—niacin, riboflavin, pyridoxine, and folate, to name but four impressive-sounding ingredients—which provide protection against cardiovascular disease and some cancers. The hop—a little pharmacy all in itself—contains antioxidants that fight cancers of the gastrointestinal tract, breast cancer, and thyroid cancer. Hops also reduce the risk of kidney stones and osteoporosis.

Beer is rich in potassium, magnesium, zinc, and copper, but low in sodium. Its low alcohol content makes it a wholesome, excellent source of these nutrients. Beer lowers cholesterol levels and is a good source of fibre. It's a wonder we don't drink it for breakfast, as in fact many Germans do.

Another recent study even reveals that there's no such thing as a beer belly. There's nothing in beer that inherently makes you fat (beer contains fewer calories than milk or fruit juice). If beer drinkers get fat it's because beer is an excellent appetite stimulant. Beer drinkers—like wine drinkers—are likely to eat three meals a day. And, as we know, beer helps out with the regularity, if you get my drift.

And here's one for the womenfolk. Sadly, women's stomachs produce half as much dehydrogenase—an enzyme that helps metabolize alcohol—as men. This, along with other unfair factors, makes women less able to tolerate alcohol than men. At least until menopause. As men grow older they become less tolerant of brother booze, whereas women become more so. Eventually we all become more or less equal in the eyes of Bacchus, which is as it should be.

All of this good news comes to us a bit grudgingly. The authorities don't want to unleash an orgy of pie-eyed health seekers on a binge, and they're not about to let Guinness go back to using its old slogan: Guinness is good for you. They're scared to death that some dope, desperate for riboflavin, is going to overindulge, wreck his car, and sue them. The threat of litigation makes cowards of us all.

Then there's our traditional notion that medicine by its very nature tastes bad. If it tastes good, it can't be doing us any good. Honestly, we are

so auto-repressive. Just look at the fuss over the recent studies that point out the healthy qualities of cannabis. The authorities, unable to deny the usefulness of the reefer, are now attempting to create a medicinal form of cannabis that will not have any psychoactive effect on the user. Let's not let those terminal cancer patients get a little high along with their painkillers. After all, someone might invent a cure next week and we'll end up with a bunch of healthy people with a taste for a spliff at lunchtime.

And I hate to say it, but all these studies pack the word "moderation" into their accounts as many times as they can. We find that moderate drinkers live longer than heavy drinkers, but also longer than abstainers. Predictably, no one can agree on what constitutes moderation. The American definition is lower than the German definition. The British definition changed in 1995, allowing drinkers more of what they fancy. Drinkers in the UK get to have four more bottles of beer a week than Americans, and it's better beer as well. The Canadian figures are, alas, the same as the American: fourteen "standard" drinks a week for men, nine for women. If you're going to be moderate—and it would be irresponsible of me to suggest otherwise—there's a good argument for improving the quality of what you drink. As the Unibroue folk of Quebec say, *Boire Moins, Boire Mieux:* Drink Less, Drink Better. (Given that their beers tend toward the head-crashingly strong, this is good advice anyway.)

To your very good health.

Life's a Drag: Drinking and Smoking

Some people can practice a variety of vices at the same time: drinking, smoking, caffeine, adultery, gambling, butterscotch sundaes, you name it. I admire people who can do this, but I'm not one of them. When it comes to vice, some people are generalists. I'm a specialist. Besides, butterscotch sundaes don't go with beer.

I tried smoking for a while once, but it didn't take. Smoking's like the piano: if you don't take it up when you're a kid you'll never be really good at it. But I was in a play once in which I had to smoke a cigar, and I practised on cigarettes so I'd look natural. (What I didn't realize until the big cigar craze of the 1990s is that hardly anybody looks natural smoking a cigar. Studies show that a full 99 per cent of human beings look like utter weenies with cigars in their mouths.) We were doing this play at a tiny theatre where even sitting in the back row was no guarantee of avoiding actors' spittle. I've had romantic relationships with people that were less intimate than this theatre.

Everything was going fine on opening night until we hit the cigar scene. Another actor and I were seated downstage, inches away from the audience, puffing on our stogies. Slowly we realized we could no longer see the back row. A minute or so later we couldn't see the front row, and we were practically in the front row. The only evidence of an audience was a few strangled coughs in the murky haze. It looked like old movies of London. Not only did the audience miss most of the cigar scene, they missed several scenes immediately afterwards as the fog slowly lifted. It was a confusing enough play even when you could see it, so we scrapped the cigars and I stopped practising smoking. It didn't seem to make me seem louche or dashing or bohemian or any of those attractive traits that used to be associated with smoking. I wasn't getting lucky without cigarettes, but I wasn't getting any luckier with them so I stopped.

And it's just as well, really, because smokers today are a much put-upon class of people. This has happened in a short time. Remember smoking on airplanes? There's a theory that since most airlines banned smoking they no longer circulate the air as often as they formerly had to, so we're still no better off in terms of air quality. At least the crappy air in airplanes doesn't smell like cigarettes any more. Remember smoking at work? Young folks today don't believe that not long ago people routinely smoked at their desks. How much productivity has been lost to cigarette breaks? Mind you, as comic Dave Broadfoot has noted, there's no healthier group of people today than smokers: look at all the fresh air they get. A visiting Russian dignitary, being driven through the streets of Ottawa a few years ago, commented on the liberal Canadian practice of allowing prostitutes to gather outside government buildings. Actually, he was told, these were not prostitutes but government office workers on their smoke breaks.

People used to smoke anywhere they liked. They smoked at the movies, they smoked at hockey games, they smoked through their dinners at fancy restaurants. Bit by bit the total freedom of smokers has been curtailed. If California is still the benchmark of how the rest of us will be living in a few years, smokers are in big trouble. There's even a part of Los Angeles that's threatening to ban people from smoking in their own homes. I don't know if the firefighters' union is lobbying against this measure. Their jobs are in jeopardy.

California has introduced no end of wacky trends the rest of us gradually catch up on—Chardonnay, artichokes, voodoo economics, tofu, liposuction, to name a few—so we shouldn't be too quick to mock California's anti-tobacco stance. It was California that banned smoking in bars. This measure has met with only partial compliance, possibly depending on the habits of the local police chief, but you can see which way things are going.

Emboldened by California's position, many other jurisdictions are attempting similar approaches. Vancouver, sharing not only a coastline but a fault line with California, has banned smoking practically everywhere. The city of Toronto tried it in the late nineties but didn't really carry it off. Being essentially decent people, we don't like to come across as too heavy-handed here in Toronto. I recall a debate that went on in the early eighties about how far strippers should be permitted to go. At that time they were going about as far as they could go, as Oscar Hammerstein II wrote in *Oklahoma*, and a few city burghers felt this was a trifle too far. This was Toronto, for Pete's sake. So legislation was passed that ruled that strippers should keep one item of clothing on at all times. We all knew which item that was and what it was meant to conceal, but nobody liked to spell it out too concretely in official legal documents that schoolchildren could stumble upon.

Strippers are a cagey bunch, and they quickly saw a loophole. According to the newspapers, they obeyed the law to the letter, usually choosing a headband as their one item of clothing. The city fathers and mothers sputtered in rage. "That's not what we meant and you know it!" they cried, quickly putting together another law that made it very clear indeed what they meant, though they blushed as they picked the words. (In the end, a higher court threw the legislation out altogether, turning Toronto into the sin capital it is today.)

So they hoped that Torontonians, being civilized people, would see the sense of curtailing smoking in pubs and bars. Just in case, however, they passed a law decreeing that a certain percentage of a bar or restaurant had to be designated non-smoking, and that the area in question should have its own source of ventilation. For the first few days, we were treated to the sight of local publicans skating around the issue. Bartenders developed a mantra whereby they explained to their customers that they were no longer permitted to smoke and that they could be fined large sums of money for doing so, but as long as they knew that and were determined to take that risk they might as well have an ashtray rather than wreck the furniture.

It was all the pub community talked about. Smokers insisted they'd never give up. Publicans predicted doom if they were forced by anti-smoking totalitarians to send their customers out into the cold. Dozens of pubs would be shut by Christmas if this law was enforced. Even Smokeless Joe—the publican who never had permitted smoking in his establishment—probably worried that his unique status was in jeopardy.

As days passed, it became gradually clear that the city was not actually going to do anything about the situation. Defiant smokers were not being tossed into the hoosegow. Publicans nervously kept changing their non-smoking areas. One day the bar area was non-smoking, next day it was the back part of the room, the day after it was somewhere else. But nothing seemed to happen.

The only publicans who could afford to provide separate ventilation for non-smoking areas already had pubs so large that they could easily designate entire floors non-smoking. They were all right. The city backed off, for the time being. But, they cautioned darkly, they would be back.

And the debate goes on. By the time this book appears, the city of Toronto will have introduced legislation that, as far as I can tell, will distinguish between bars and restaurants. The distinction will hinge on whether the establishment in question permits children on the premises.

Children-friendly places will be deemed restaurants, and smoking will be banned. Kid-hostile spots, on the other hand, will be declared bars, and smoking will be permitted. To the best of my knowledge the new law sets no standards for the quality of food, but then quality control doesn't figure greatly in any legislation I'm familiar with. I suspect we won't see a lot of kids in the places I go to.

I know people who swear they don't go to pubs because of the smoke, even though these days you can in fact find smoke-free drinking environments. Are these people flooding back to pubs? They are not, and I suspect that completely smoke-free pubs will not attract them either. They are—and I hate to say this of anyone—just not pub people. They had their chance to show the flag at a time when the hospitality industry was protesting that they'd all go out of business without smokers, but they didn't do it.

Now, I like a smoke-free pub myself. I don't like coming home and watching my wife wrinkle her lovely nose and say, "I can tell where you've been" before she takes my clothes out back and burns them. She herself loathes tobacco smoke—she's never had as much as a puff herself—but she recognizes that it's part of pub life. Interestingly, she doesn't mind the second-hand smoke of people she likes as much as that of strangers. The people we both hold in contempt are the people—and they're usually women, I have to say—who hold their cigarettes as far away from their own precious noses and those of their companions as they can, inevitably sticking them in someone else's face. I always regret not carrying a small plant sprayer—the sort of things that are almost exclusively used for disciplining cats—to be able to douse their smouldering tobacco.

My concern about the anti-smoking lobby is the element of pious social control that attaches itself to it. Once these people have rid the world of the curse of tobacco, they'll be after us drinkers next, just you watch. In my perfect world—coming soon to a universe near you—smokers will see the error of their ways, realize that they're poisoning themselves and making the world a much smellier place, and will stop of their own accord. God knows where American politicians will get their funding from, but that's not my lookout. Meanwhile, of course, the tobacco companies continue to target each new generation that comes along, guaranteeing themselves millions of new users for decades to come.

In the last couple of years we have looked on as cultural life in Canada threatens to shut down completely because the federal government will no longer permit cigarette companies to sponsor jazz festivals, golf tournaments, and the like. Our streets will fall silent, famous golfers and tennis players will shun us, because the tobacco pushers have been shown the door. Cultural czars plead with the feds to let music and theatre thrive again. The government winds up looking like the villain and the tobacco people get to look like saints. Heck, I've been to events sponsored by cigarette companies and nothing bad has happened to me. I haven't suddenly developed some lethal habit. Maybe these companies should be allowed back in.

But let's think for a moment. Why do tobacco companies sponsor jazz festivals? Is it because they love jazz and want us to be happy? Is it because they feel guilty about the huge profits they make from giving people cancer and emphysema? No. It's because they're banned from advertising on television and radio and in magazines. Surely the solution to this problem is not to let the tobacco people back in, but to ban other corporations from advertising on television and radio and in magazines. We could all think of products we'd prefer not to see advertised on television. And what about the quality of the advertising? I've never eaten McCain's Pizza Pockets and I'm not about to start. It's not that they taste bad—they may taste terrific, but I'll never know—but that their commercials are obnoxious and have been for years.

Would I feel better about McCain's if I attended the McCain's Pizza Pocket Theatre Festival? You bet I would. And how about the Norwich Union Tennis Championship? Count me in! Just get them off the air. I'm sure you have plenty of commercials you hate, commercials that would justify, say, a five-year ban from the airwaves. Corporations would be lining up to sponsor jazz festivals. Better they should be spending their money in a useful way rather than becoming enablers for yet another tacky reality television show.

What's the worst thing that could happen? Owing to a shortage of advertising revenues, we might end up with a little less television. The thing is, most of us would never know because we'd be out at a play or a concert or a golf tournament. There you are: with one only very slightly draconian measure the world is made a better place. Glad I could help.

The Very Fat Men That Water The Workers' Beer

Just because beer is the beverage of the toiling classes we should not assume that brewery moguls are champions of the working stiffs who make them rich. They are business people, after all, and they like to hang out with their own sort. Adolphus Busch, the man who invented Budweiser—or at least the American Budweiser, not its vastly superior Czech counterpart—didn't even like beer. This will not surprise anyone who has tasted his beer. He referred to it as "that slop", which is about right. He was the first man to pasteurize beer, which is not a nice thing to do to beer. Unless it's Budweiser, in which case who cares? They call it the king of beers, but it's a pretty minor monarchy, if you ask me, something of the order of, say, Albania's ex-king Zog.

Our own E.P. Taylor, a card-carrying magnate if ever there was one, became one of the villains of British brewing history. The owner of Northern Dancer, Taylor was a better judge of horseflesh than beer. He felt that everyone in the world should be drinking Carling Black Label, perhaps because he owned the brewery. Once he had convinced many Canadians to drink the stuff, he began to think more globally. England, for instance. They drank a lot of beer in England, Taylor noticed, but they weren't drinking Black Label. This might have been related to the difficulty of finding it in English pubs, Taylor was told, the great majority of English pubs at the time being owned by breweries. A pub that was owned by, say, the Shepherd Neame brewery would stock the beers produced by that company.

The other problem, of course, was that the English still hadn't had their brains sucked out, and they continued to prefer their traditional ale over bland, fizzy, Canadian lager. Never mind about that, thought Taylor, these people haven't seen big-time North American advertising. They'll drink lager by the time I'm through, he said, twirling his imaginary moustache and picturing the poor beer drinker tied helplessly to the railway tracks.

The key was getting the pubs, and the solution was to buy the breweries that owned them. From 1960 to 1967, Taylor and the companies he controlled bought up some 273 British breweries, closing down almost all of them and keeping the pubs. By the end, Bass Charrington controlled a fifth of British brewing and 11,000 pubs. The destruction of the rich British brewing heritage was underway, and it was a Canadian who put the boot in. And why? Carling bloody Black Label.

Taylor, of course, had learned his vile techniques on his home turf. He started with the Brading's Brewery, but a small Ontario brewery was not enough for a man of Taylor's ambitions. In 1930 he bought up nine breweries, including the Carling Brewery, and by 1952 he had scooped up nearly thirty breweries, most in Ontario and Quebec. Most of these breweries were simply shut down. Taylor was less interested in diversifying his portfolio than in shutting down the competition. Thus was consumer choice limited to an ever-shrinking selection of beers that started to taste more and more alike.

An English music hall performer of the thirties named Paddy Ryan wrote a song about beer moguls which contained the proud boast, "I'm the man, the very fat man, that waters the workers' beer." Now, I'm sure that the majority of brewery owners are decent folk—and in some cases not even terribly fat—who want only to make good beer and make an honest living doing so. There are, however, exceptions.

One of the great brewing families—all right, let's say one of the most interesting brewing families—is the Coors family of Golden, Colorado. I recall living in Brooklyn in 1971 with a woman I had met at the Löwenbräu brewery in Munich. The times being what they were, we were heading out for the coast in a driveaway car—do they still have driveaway cars?—making stops in Colorado and Arizona. A friend said he envied me going to Colorado, the home of Coors beer. In those days Coors was available only in the western states and had a cult following elsewhere, presumably for the reason that we miss what we can't have. As a beer lover, he told me, I was going to love Coors.

Over the years I have learned to be suspicious of beers that are advertised on the basis of the pure mountain water with which they are brewed. I still remember my first Kokanee Glacier Pilsner. I mean, I like pure mountain water as much as anyone, but I'm old-fashioned enough to think they should put some malt and hops in with it if they're going to call it beer. I don't recall encountering much of either in my first, disappointing taste of Coors.

In those politically intense days I don't think I knew anything about the wacky Coors family. Like the beer, the news about their interesting positions on race, unions, homosexuality, women's equality, and so much more had not filtered back to New York in 1971. I recommend to you Dan Baum's book, *Citizen Coors: An American Dynasty*.

The original Adolph Coors fled Bismarck's Prussia in 1869 and stowed away on a ship bound for Baltimore, an uncharacteristic act of freeloading that haunted him all his life. In 1873 he started his own brewery in Colorado and was a millionaire by 1890. Always a self-reliant breed that refused to borrow money or be beholden to anyone, the Coors family survived Prohibition, ever more suspicious of government. Well, when I say the family survived, I don't actually mean old Adolph, who threw himself off a ledge on the sixth floor of the Cavalier Hotel in Virginia Beach, Virginia, in 1929, seeing no end in sight to Prohibition.

Old Adolph was probably the sanest of the Coorses, a man who wanted to make good, unpasteurized beer for local sale without outside interference. His son, Adolph II, played around with the notion of making an extra-strong beer, opting instead to make his father's beer even lighter than it had been. Watering the workers' beer, as it were. The family invented the aluminum beer can, but loathed advertising almost as much as it hated unions. The Coorses hated anyone telling them how to run their business, and they became early adopters of a Hollywood actor by the name of Reagan. They wound up being boycotted by labour, women, gays, blacks, Hispanics, and environmentalists, and pretended they didn't care. Many of them were born-again Christians, although only one of them seems to have had any problem with the dichotomy of making beer and Christian fundamentalism. Adolph's was not the last family suicide, and his grandson was brutally murdered in a botched kidnapping. Another scion was blackballed from the family for marrying without his father's permission. It's a saga. The beer might be watered down, but the story is full-blooded.

Nowadays, Coors is just another big beer company, the family on the sidelines. It's a more efficient, more profitable company now, with a big advertising budget, and there are still a lot of Americans who refuse to touch it. And not just because they don't think it's good.

And what about Molson, those fine nationalistic brewers? For a time, both of the big two breweries were foreign-owned, but Molson bought itself back. (Labatt is owned by Belgian Interbrew.) To demonstrate its proud patriotic fervour, Molson in 2000 launched a hugely successful television commercial in which a plaid-shirted regular guy loudly pointed

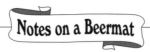

out the differences between himself and the Americans, ending with a shouted "My name is Joe and I am Canadian!" Which, coincidentally, was also the name of the beer he was promoting. Within a few months of this ad appearing, the actor who played Joe was in Los Angeles looking for work, and Molson had sold the fabled Montreal Canadiens to a businessman from Colorado. My name is Joe and I am vaguely Canadian, when it suits me.

Even Guinness is not above beastliness. The company that built up such goodwill with its long-standing Guinness is Good for You campaign (eventually quashed by the anti-beer lobby) and the imaginative use of toucans in its marketing turns out to be no better than the rest. In 2001 it called in the lawyers on Hart Robinson, a small Ontario brewery and issued a cease-and-desist order. The brewery's crime lay in naming one of its beers Dragon's Breath, in direct contravention of the Because We Say So act. Why is it wrong to name a beer Dragon's Breath? Because Guinness says so. Because Guinness brews something called Dragon Stout in Jamaica. Anyone who confuses Canada with Jamaica needs the help of more than lawyers. I've had Dragon's Breath and Dragon Stout, and I think I could tell the difference in a blindfold test.

Dragon's Breath, originally brewed for the Kingston, Ontario Brewery, has been available in Ontario since at least 1992, without—as far as anyone can tell—damaging the domestic Jamaican market. Yet, unable to afford a suitful of legal help to combat the Irish-Jamaican juggernaut, Hart Robinson seems likely to take a pleasing, hoppy pale ale off the market. My 2001 *Good Beer Guide* lists no fewer than thirteen British beers with the name "dragon" in their name, from Dragon Fire to Dragonslayer. There's even a Welsh brewery that makes a strong (but not hoppy) bitter called Dragon's Breath, which rings a bell. I trust the suits of Guinness are in full cry there as well, unless they've decided that northern Wales is even less like Jamaica than Canada.

Accustomed to near-monopoly in its native Ireland, Guinness seems to think it a natural state. They're teetering on the edge of not being good for us.

I'm Just a Barmaid Connoisseur: Bar Staff

I once worked in a pub with a woman named Mary. Mary was a terrific barmaid—bright, pretty, friendly, and omnicompetent. This was in England before decimalization, so you had to be quick with figures: what's 1/10 plus 2/4 plus 11d plus 2/6? Mary's customers loved her, so we were all surprised when the manager fired her. Apparently Mary was too friendly and down-market. The manager—a very stupid man—wanted to make the place a little tonier, less chummy, and he replaced Mary with a hapless young woman from Leicester who couldn't add.

I think about Mary sometimes when I see bar staff at work. Like taxi drivers, booksellers, and major league shortstops, some are better than others. If you ever take cabs, you know that sometimes you know as soon as you get in that you're going to have to work hard for this ride home: "You need to turn left here... no, left... no, here!... oh for God's sake, if you'd put down the cellphone for a... please turn left... please..." Other times you get in and relax and enjoy the ride.

It's the same with bar staff. A good bartender or server can add immeasurably to your drinking experience, and should be remembered in your tipping thoughts. Different bars, of course, call for different kinds of people. There's a man named Harold who has for countless decades graced the rooftop bar at what used to be the Park Plaza Hotel in Toronto. I say "graced" very deliberately, because Harold has the style and class you want in a pricey hotel bar along with an unhurried friendliness. It's easy for people in Harold's shoes to become supercilious and pompous, two words you would never use of Harold, a local legend who has been immortalized in novels.

Harold's elegance might be misplaced at, say, the rather more earthy Grossman's Tavern, which is why one values the brash, wise-cracking Dawn. One afternoon as a group of us were leaving Grossman's, Dawn called out to us, "Sure, go somewhere else and get ripped off for your beer. You'll be back!" If she did that at an upscale hotel bar, her career would be a short one, but she's universally admired at Grossman's. I've written elsewhere in this book about John, the philosopher-waiter at the old Embassy Tavern. The Embassy had a couple of other waiters who ruled through fear. You'd have to have been really drunk to mess with these guys. John ruled through some strong, quiet moral force. There was a waiter called Tommy at the Morrissey Tavern who had a similar quality. I saw Tommy use physical force a couple of times, but it was definitely his approach of last resort.

Today's drinking scene seems to call for less physical strength, or perhaps I'm just drinking in classier places. It's also possible that I don't stay up as late as I used to, so I've left before the violence kicks in. I once saw a waiter at the late, not terribly lamented Young Station deal with a difficult customer by taking about a seventy-foot run and blindsiding the guy with a blow that levelled him, with not much chance for a replay any time soon. You hang out in bars, you see just about everything.

The Duke of York used to have a server called Olga, a slender Irish woman from County Antrim who made her customers feel the world was a better place. Well, that and the beer. I never saw Olga punch anybody, and I'm not sure if I'm glad about that or not. She eventually went back to Ireland and took a suitcase full of hearts with her. More recently the Duke has been home to a fellow from Timmins, Ontario, who does a bit of wrestling on the side. Dale doesn't look particularly menacing—in fact he seems a damn nice guy, and I suspect he probably is beneath that damn nice exterior—but he's clearly capable of dropping a troublesome drunk. I'm a peace-loving guy, me, but part of me wouldn't mind seeing Dale twist a troublemaker into a knot. I can even think of one or two candidates.

Sometimes you get to know people outside their working hours. I once played golf with a guy called Ed who slung beer at the old Red Lion (as opposed to the new Red Lion). Ed was an interesting man from the far north somewhere, who got up early and played golf five days a week, then downed numerous beers before going into work, where he hauled pitchers of the stuff to the softball teams that gathered at the Lion. In the off-season he travelled to places like India or South America. Interesting guy.

The guys who run the Graduate Students' Union Pub on the University of Toronto campus are an odd duo. Harry is gay and acerbic with a taste for art and tattoos. When he's behind the bar you're likely to be bombarded with high-volume music of what might be the techno variety, as if I'd know. Ed, on the other hand, is straight and married, taciturn and middle of the road, with a taste for easy listening music. Like his namesake from the old Red Lion, Ed would rather be golfing. Ed listens patiently when Harry comes up with a new design concept. Between them, they make the place work.

Bar staff, of course, do more than smile and serve you beer. Not long ago I ventured into Paupers Pub on my way home, as I occasionally do. There's a spot at one end of the bar I particularly like, with its own little lamp so guys like me can read even after they turn the lights down to make it atmospheric. Walking in, I saw the seat was free. It was my lucky day. As I took off my coat, Patrick—the server whose Subway Game is recounted in these pages—called me down to the other end of the bar. There was something he needed to talk to me about. Reluctantly I abandoned my favourite spot and went over to where Patrick waited. "It's all right," he said quietly, "there's nothing I need to talk about. I just don't think you want to get too close to the guy you were about to sit beside." Patrick was right. Next to the ideal seat with the little lamp sat the most tiresome human on the planet, a loudmouth and a bore, and I was saved from a fate almost indistinguishable from death.

I'm sure I'm not the only man on the planet who has been accused of falling in love with any woman who brings him beer. Not that it's true, of course. There have been a couple of women who brought me beer without invoking Cupid's arrow, but why dwell on the negatives? There used to be a server—we called them waitresses in those days without a second thought—at the old Sticky Wicket who had it all: talent, looks, people skills, you name it. The Sticky Wicket was a hard bar to leave when she was in charge. Back in the golden age when people occasionally had long lunches and the world was a better place altogether, a small group of us gathered for a pint and a bite to eat. Lunch concluded, we settled up and prepared to leave, whereupon one of us suggested one more pint. We had that and settled up again, and yet once more another pint was proposed, motion carried. One of our number dredged through his pockets and located exactly the price of pint, tax included. He sadly reported to our near-divine waitress that he lacked the funds for a tip. She looked at him kindly and said, "That's all right. You always tip too much anyway." I vaguely recall that we all proposed to her on the spot.

I used to fall in love with the aforementioned Olga every Friday night at the Duke of York. I have a soft spot for Kathy at the Madison, and I was sad when Claire left Paupers to reinvent herself as a civil servant. Down at the Graduate Students' Union Pub, Ed's wife Michelle, a lively anthropologist, used to tend the bar on Fridays, and beer sales soared. She certainly sold a fair bit of it to me.

The late David Parry used to sing a song by English songwriter Keith Marsden called *Greasy Mack*. The narrator of this fine song is aware of his reputation. People see him "flit from pub to pub" and they assume that he's a sot. He is accused of every perversion going, but without cause. He lacks the "knack" for the standard male hobbies of stamp collecting, vintage wines, or growing potted plants. No, he's "just a barmaid connoisseur". It's not such a bad thing to be.

I'll Need to See Some I.D.: Drinking and the Law

Some chapters ago we discussed the origins of beer. You may recall early man (or early woman)... damn, let's just say early person. Early person tasted a bit of soggy barley that had come into contact with a bit of windborne yeast and fermented. Early person got a buzz, and saw that it was good. You can bet that within a month some other early person had introduced legislation governing the permissible strength of fermented soggy barley, the hours of the day during which fermented barley could be ingested, the minimum age of fermented barley consumers, the required signage in premises that provided fermented barley, and in what circumstances fermented barley users could legally operate fire.

Well, it's human nature, isn't it? If you don't pass a law, somebody somewhere is going to get away with something, and then how will you feel? And there's something about alcohol that brings out the legislator in people. Not the people who are enjoying it, of course, but the other people.

Growing up with Ontario's frequently odd drinking laws, I often wondered where these curious bits of legislation could possibly have come from. I mean, it was against the law to drink standing up. Who thought of that? When they were sitting around inventing laws, did someone get up and say, "Look, why don't we make it illegal to drink standing up? That'll fox them." And did the others say, "Excellent idea, George. They'll be scratching their heads over this one." Had there been a problem with standing drinkers? Had someone felt driven to cry out, "Why won't they just sit down?"

And it wasn't even drinking. You couldn't stand up with a drink in your hand, whether you drank from it or not. I suppose we should have been grateful that they hadn't thought to regulate which hand we drank with. "I'm sorry, pal, but you've been drinking left-handed again. I'm gonna have to ask you to leave."

The first clue I got to the origins of drinking in Ontario came when I went to Scotland for the first time. It was like coming home. I'm sure there are very nice pubs in Scotland, but the first two or three I encountered reminded me of Ontario taprooms. They had the look of rooms that couldn't be wrecked, because there was nothing breakable in them. And they could be hosed down after an evening's drinking. You could fight, bleed, throw up, wet yourself, and there'd be no evidence of it the next morning.

There can't be many Ontario towns whose telephone books don't have pages of names starting with the letters "Mac". The English might have owned much of it, but it was the Scots who lived here and did the work. Canada was no colder than Scotland, after all. And Scotland—like the Ontario I started drinking in—was made up of exactly two groups of people: people who drank too much, and people who drank too little. And the people who drank too little got to write the laws that governed the people who drank too much. You could characterize these people as joyless, except that some of their laws demonstrate a wry sense of humour.

I remember at one time in Ontario you were permitted to drink outdoors on your property only as long as no one could see you doing so. Many areas—and I know the Toronto suburb of Etobicoke was one—had legislation limiting the height of fences and hedges. So you could drink outdoors on your property in Etobicoke only if you had short neighbours who lived in bungalows.

And it wasn't just Ontario, of course. There is hardly anywhere on the planet that doesn't have some wonky drinking laws. Until recently practically every pub in the UK had to close between 3 p.m. and 5:30 p.m., and hardly anyone could remember why. In Pennsylvania you can't buy a six-pack of beer. Beer can be sold only in cases of twenty-four, and don't bother asking them to explain it. The state of Georgia passed a law, at the end of Prohibition, that defined beer as having a maximum strength of six per cent alcohol by volume. Early in 2001 a group of adventurous beer drinkers sought to have this law overturned so that they could enjoy the occasional strong beer, but the state's wise, all-knowing legislators—presumably fearful that outbursts of fun might break out—left the comfort of their interns and turned out to defeat this radical measure.

The granddaddy of heavy-handed alcohol legislation—and I'm ignoring the Muslim world here—was Prohibition. Canadians didn't suffer nearly as badly as Americans from this scourge of righteousness. Between 1920 and 1933, not an American touched as much as a drop of alcohol. Ha-ha—just joking! It has been estimated that by 1922 there were more speakeasies in America than there had been bars in 1920. It was

Prohibition that succeeded in organizing crime in the USA. Before 1920 crime had been chaotic, but the Volstead Act offered an incentive to criminals who were organized. Millions of dollars were made by people we would characterize today as gangsters, although they might have seen themselves as businessmen providing a popular service. The authorities spent millions of other dollars in a futile attempt to uphold the law. The murder rate soared, and no doubt a few people succumbed to unregulated rotgut liquor. And nobody stopped drinking.

The proliferation of lawyers in the postwar era has made the drinking world a minefield. Early in 2001 an Ontario woman was awarded a large sum of money after she sued her employer for letting her drink and drive after a company Christmas party. Her boss had offered to call her husband to take her home, had offered a taxi ride. He had not, however, hog-tied the woman, delivered a fire-and-brimstone sermon, and personally made sure she got home safely, so he was on the hook when the woman—having by now gone off to a pub for a couple more drinks—crashed her car some time later. We are not sure what percentage of the damages was claimed by her lawyer.

Not that I want to sound critical of lawyers. A lawyer can be a wonderful thing. Just ask Mo Vaughn. Early in 1998, Mo Vaughn—a robust firstbaseperson for the Boston Red Sox—left a Rhode Island strip club and, on his way home, somehow drove into a car parked off the highway, and rolled his pickup truck. Investigating officers testified that Vaughn failed eight sobriety tests at the scene. On his third attempt to recite the alphabet, he managed only A-B-D-C-H-L-M, which suggests a willingness to pitch in but not much more.

All this would seem to indicate a verdict of guilty, but you'd be underestimating the skills of Vaughn's lawyer, one Kevin Reddington. This latter-day Cicero posited that his client might not have been drunk, all evidence to the contrary. His alphabet problems might have been caused by his having been (a) sleepy, (b) dazed by his recent accident (which he had caused, don't forget), or (c) unstable because he had gained weight in the off-season.

The judge—who I'm betting was a Red Sox fan—ruled in favour of the defendant, and charges were dropped. My point here is that a lawyer who can turn weight gain into a legal defence is worth remembering next time you're facing charges in Massachusetts. The name is Reddington, Kevin Reddington.

The issue of drinking and driving is a sensitive one. One of the reasons I live in the heart of a city is that I'm always a cab ride from home. I don't want to drink and drive. I'd rather have a few pints and then go through the merry fun of explaining where I live to a cabdriver who's talking on his cellphone. It's part of a good night out.

There are, as we know, people who do drink and drive. I did it on occasion when I was young and even more stupid than I am now, so I'm not going to take a pious tone about it. I have before me a brochure I picked up in an English pub called *Dying for a Drink?* That's the name of the brochure, by the way. The pub was called the Royal Oak. Published by the Department of the Environment, Transport and the Regions and dated July 2000, this brochure tells me a lot. Among other things, it tells me that it was printed on paper that is 75% post consumer waste, 5% pre consumer, and 20% TCF pulp. I'm not sure what any of that stuff is, but I'm not putting the brochure in my mouth.

The purpose of *Dying for a Drink?* is to make us think twice about drinking and driving in Britain, and it's full of common sense and interesting information, including a reference to how much alcohol can remain in your bloodstream the morning after a night on the ale. You could get busted driving to work. Lucky thing I walk.

One of the interesting facts is this: "Nearly one in seven of all deaths on the road involve drivers who are over the legal limit." Well, for starters, there's that weasel word: "involve". If the Department of the Environment, Transport and the Regions means "are caused by" why doesn't it say so? Apparently in the UK, if a sober driver with a drunk passenger is "involved" in an accident it is automatically treated as a drink-related incident. You can't be too careful with statistics.

But even if one British road fatality in seven is actually caused by drunk drivers—which is a bad thing, no question—we're left with the daunting fact that 86 per cent of British road fatalities are caused by sober people. What's being done about them?

I have another brochure on my desk. Actually, I've got a lot of stuff on my desk, including possibly a cat or two, but it's the brochure that's at the top of the pile. It comes from the Ontario government and it's called *Break The Law Pay The Price*. Personally, I'd have put a comma in there somewhere, but the Ontario government laid off the punctuation guy in a cost-cutting drive. (I gather he lasted longer than the water inspection guy.)

According to *BTLPTP*, "Drinking drivers are responsible for one-quarter of all people killed on Ontario roads." In other words, only 75 per cent of Ontario traffic fatalities are the work of sober people. Either we have more drunks in Ontario, or our sober people are better drivers than Britain's.

Now, despite the damning evidence in these brochures that sober people are causing carnage on our roads, the people who know what's good for us are busy trying to lower the legal blood alcohol limit. Early in 2001 the Quebec government announced that it was lowering the limit from eighty milligrams to fifty, throwing in a complete drinking ban for professional drivers—cabbies, bus drivers, and the like. This last measure was a reaction to—well, nothing at all. Were drunk ambulance drivers creating havoc on the roads of Quebec? No. But it gave the government of Quebec the appearance of having taken a strong stand on something. Predictably, the Ontario government immediately made noises about following suit.

The lowering of the blood alcohol limit is a canard, or—as we say in English-speaking Canada—a duck. Is there any evidence that drivers with sixty or seventy milligrams of alcohol in their bloodstream are doing untold damage on our roads? Nope. The police don't seem to think so, and they're out there more than I am. *Break The Law Pay The Price* notes, "Most drinking drivers killed in crashes had blood alcohol levels almost double the legal limit."

Exactly. The problem drunk drivers have more than fifty milligrams before they set out in the evening. They have fifty milligrams with their breakfast. They're guys like Richard Sawyer McLeod of Alberta, who in 2001 rang up his seventeenth drunk driving conviction to go along with eighteen raps of driving while disqualified. Mr. McLeod has not had a valid driver's licence since 1967, but he keeps on driving anyway, except when he's in jail. Guys like Richard Sawyer McLeod drive home from court. Lowering the limit thirty points will not make a difference to McLeod and his ilk. All it will do is get law-abiding people into trouble. Tougher enforcement in England has led to countless idyllic country pubs going under because their respectable customers are afraid to go out at night for fear of being a few milligrams over the line. These are members of the non-criminal classes who just don't want to be arrested.

The anti-booze crusaders are indifferent to their plight. When they get the limit lowered to fifty milligrams, they will begin their campaign for twenty milligrams, then no milligrams at all. The issue is not driving, it is drinking, and their goal is zero tolerance. I don't know—I was brought up to believe that tolerance was a good thing. These people succeed because they have so much time to attend meetings. While the rest of us are sitting in pubs, they're holding meetings.

And where does it end? In 1999 a California man—and why is it so often California?—was pulled over by the police for driving too slowly. He failed a sobriety test and was charged with Driving Under the Influence, although a subsequent urine test showed that he had no alcohol or drugs in his system. Taufui Piutau—for that is the man's mellifluous name—acknowledged that he had been drinking kava tea, and possibly eight to ten cups of it, with his church friends. Although California law is vague on how many milligrams of kava kava you're allowed in your bloodstream, the DA's office carried on with the prosecution of Mr. Piutau, which cost the father of four his job with Federal Express.

Nearly fifteen months later, the case ground to a halt with a mistrial, a hung jury unable to reach unanimity, though ten of the twelve jurors favoured acquittal. A grumpy District Attorney grudgingly acknowledged that the state would probably not pursue the matter further. Mr. Piutau's lawyer, one Scott B. Ennis—a name to remember if you get into trouble in San Mateo—argued in court that what the officers saw as impairment was probably a combination of gout and cultural misunderstanding, though it was not immediately clear exactly whose gout was at issue. At last word, Ennis was carrying on with a twenty-million-dollar wrongful dismissal suit against Fed Ex.

Kava kava is known for its relaxing qualities, which is part of the problem. The authorities can't abide the relaxants. It's fine for caffeine-crazed javaheads to drive around like maniacs, but relax for a moment and you're headed for the big house. If driving under the influence of herbal tea becomes illegal in California, they won't be able to build new prisons fast enough to hold the perpetrators. Marin County will become a ghost town.

It's that pleasure thing again. What the Republicans really hated about Bill Clinton—apart from his being a Democrat in public office—was not that he received sexual favours from a consenting adult in the Oval Office but that he visibly had fun. A lawyer friend of mine likes to point out that there is no reference to fun in any Act of Parliament, and I suspect the American constitution is just as bad. It permits the pursuit of happiness, as I recall, but it stops short of fun.

When the Republicans succeeded—by hook or by crook, but mostly by crook—in retaking the White House, we were treated to the spectacle of John Ashcroft becoming attorney-general. Ashcroft was available for the job because the voters of Missouri had tossed him out of office, voting for a dead guy instead. To be fair to the Missouri electorate, it wasn't easy to tell the difference. John Ashcroft doesn't hold with dancing. It's not that he

doesn't like dancing, or isn't good at dancing, like George W. Bush. He thinks dancing is a sin. He won't dance, don't ask him. Ashcroft is straight out of the world's oldest religious joke: Why do Baptists disapprove of having sex standing up? Because it might lead to dancing.

An attorney-general who thinks dancing is wrong is unlikely to look kindly on America's drinking classes, even though his president is from Texas, the state where drinking while driving is practically an institution. Not that the president does that. Not any more. Indeed the born-again president quickly barred the White House kitchen from even cooking with alcohol.

But I digress. Like you, I'd welcome safer roads and highways, but the new Puritans will do little to achieve that end. The figures show that the overwhelming majority of accidents are caused by bad drivers, a handful of whom have been drinking as well. Let's get bad drivers off the road, but let's keep the "sinner repent" morality out of it.

Rex Gladstone, or: The Meaning of Pub Names

I refer elsewhere in these pages to a Toronto pub called the Rose and Crown. There are many English pubs that bear this name, which commemorates the victory of Henry VII over Richard III in 1485. The rose is that of Lancaster, and the crown is the crown of England, won by Henry. You won't find a lot of Rose and Crowns—or should that be Roses and Crown?—in Yorkshire, which was the losing side.

Pubs called the Royal Oak take their name from the tree in which the future Charles II hid after getting whupped by Oliver Cromwell in 1651. The King's Head can refer to any masculine monarch, but it is most appropriate in the case of the head of Charles I, which became involuntarily separated from the rest of the king one January morning in 1649. Publicans have traditionally been more inclined to support the fun-loving Stuarts over the gloomier Roundheads, and there are still pubs called the Blackboys, which is not in fact the racial slur it appears but an affectionate reference to Charles I. There are many pubs that pay tribute to royalty with names like the Queen's Arms, the Crown, and the Feathers (a reference to the coat of arms of the Prince of Wales). Older pubs recall the Crusades: the Turk's Head, the Saracen's Head, and the Trip to Jerusalem. And of course there are countless tributes to any number of dukes, earls, and counts. You can learn a lot of English history by hanging out in pubs.

Wouldn't it be nice if we honoured Canadian history in our pub names? If nothing else, it might lend an air of gravitas to our filthy habits if we could say, as we lurch through the front door, "Sorry I'm late—I stopped in for a quick one at the Rowell-Sirois Commission." Or if we could agree to meet later at the Lord Durham's Report. Or at the Avro Arrow Cancellation, or the Discovery of Insulin, or the Anne Murray's First Grammy (popular with feminists), or Ye Olde Nothwithstanding Clause. I'd even settle for Mike Harris's Head. And who wouldn't like to call home and report, "I may be a while. I'm in Kim Campbell's Arms"?

There's something powerful about names. You may be familiar with the comic gambit of finding your soap opera name. It's simple: you take your middle name and combine it with the name of the street you grew up on. I know someone whose soap opera name is Kimball Bessborough, which is a really fabulous name. It's hard to do better than that. It's especially difficult for me as I don't have a middle name. Call me Zero Welbeck. Apparently there's another version that creates your name as a stripper. It involves the name of your first household pet, and I don't remember the rest of it. It helps if you grew up with a cat called Fluffy.

Any writer of fiction will tell you that finding names for characters is one of the toughest parts of writing. Get the name right, they say, and the character will follow. Call me Ishmael: brilliant. Call me Nigel: not so good. Leopold Bloom, Holden Caulfield, Miss Havisham, Gussie Fink-Nottle, Sir Toby Belch, Heathcliff—the characters are half-written as soon as you read their names.

It struck me one day, many years ago, that one could write a novel— or at least a fairly serious novella—using altogether plausible characters whose names could be drawn from the names of Toronto drinking spots. This had to be many years ago, of course, before we traded in our venerable old watering holes for places with winsome names like the Toad in the Hole or the Friar and Firkin. Even P.G. Wodehouse, who had a gift for hyphenated names, would have drawn the line at someone called Toad-in-the-Hole. "I say, Friar-and-Firkin" just doesn't work.

No, it has to be the old names. A lot of them are gone now: the Morrissey, the Sheldon, the Drake. Others remain: the Rex, the Selby, the Gladstone. Now, I still haven't actually written that novel, but I've got the characters so I'm well on the way. I see a man called Rex Gladstone, and maybe you can see him too. He's a good-looking fellow with a powerful jaw, and a biggish chap too. In later years people will see Rex as a bit on the heavy side, but for the moment he cuts quite an impressive figure. He has a pretty serious job, I imagine—something in banking, perhaps—but he's not averse to a bit of fun. He's a loyal friend and an imposing adversary. He looks good in a well-tailored suit, but he can raise a young woman's heartbeat in his tennis whites too.

Rex is engaged to—or has possibly just been romantically linked with—the lovely Selby Linsmore. Of that Fine Old Ontario Family, the Linsmores. Selby is always immaculately turned out, and needless to say she knows absolutely everyone who needs to be known. She might be ever so slightly on the cool side, however, and even the sight of a glistening Rex

Gladstone attacking the net at the tennis club in the mixed doubles semi-final fails to bring a flush to her exquisite features.

Rex understands that marriage to Selby will be the making of him, but he's accustomed to a bit more ardour from women. Like pretty young Beverley Paddock, for instance. Beverley has no family at all to speak of, and in fact she speaks of them as little as possible. She doesn't come from money, like Selby, but there's a certain spunk to the girl, and she knows how to please a fellow. She's just not the sort of girl you'd marry. Let alone take to the tennis club.

Enter Clinton Morrissey. Of mixed blood, Clinton came to Toronto from his native Caribbean, touring as a fast bowler with a better than average cricket side. He has always preferred tennis, however, and has just become the assistant teaching pro at the tennis club to which both Rex and Selby belong. Not surprisingly, Clinton is a handsome man, and even the ice-cool Selby melts a little when he makes a curiously effective adjustment to her grip.

Rex—who is, quite honestly, no smarter than he strictly speaking needs to be—sees the change in Selby. He confides his concerns to his friend Cameron Brunswick. I still don't quite have a fully-formed Cameron Brunswick in my mind just yet, but I certainly like his name. Cameron suggests that Rex surprise Selby in some way, take her somewhere she'd never normally go. Like where, asks Rex. How about the circus, proposes Cameron, who is slowly turning into a character I like.

The circus—luckily for the plot—just happens to be in town and Rex books the two best seats in the house, hoping that the danger of aerial daredevils and the sweat of horses will rouse Selby in a way he's never managed. They sit through several acts, including a comic piece involving a troupe of First Nations performers, in which a man called Black Bull quarrels with another man called Red Lion over the affections of a woman they both fancy—pretty little Wheat Sheaf.

And then Rex and Selby are snapped to attention by the loud crack of a whip. A full-grown Siberian tiger snarls and crouches, as if about to attack a woman in an abbreviated leather costume. She cracks the whip again, high in the air above Rex and Selby's heads. Rex is transfixed. The woman is beautiful—dark and lean. Her strong, olive-hued arm ripples as she handles the whip. The tiger, feeling her power, slowly yields to her, finally rolling over and allowing her to rub his furry chest. That done, the woman—now standing feet away from Rex and Selby—acknowledges the wild applause of the audience, bowing deeply, her full breasts threatening to tumble free from her skimpy leather top. (Whew—I'm enjoying this.) The circus announcer cries out over the popular roar, "Ladies and gentlemen—direct from Venezuela, the incomparable Isabella El Mocambo!"

Rex, his lip trembling, cannot take his eyes from this wild creature, so he is unaware that next to him Selby is similarly bewitched. "Brava!" he calls out to the circus performer. Isabella smiles and turns her huge dark eyes to—no, not Rex, but Selby! Then, with one last triumphant crack of the whip, she turns on her stiletto heel and exits, the crowd's cheers still ringing in the air.

A crew of clowns rushes in, but Selby suddenly gets up. "I need some air," she says breathlessly, and she walks out. Rex, uncertain if his legs would even carry his weight, such is his state of excitement, remains in his seat. Should he follow Selby, even if he could? If Cameron Brunswick were there he'd have advice for Rex, but Cameron—unknown to Rex, whose experience of the world is limited—is, as we speak, in a Church Street leather bar, trussed like a Christmas turkey, while... well, I don't know while what. Let's face it, I've never been in a leather bar in my life.

Okay, so I haven't figured out the rest of the story yet, but I really think I'm on to something here. Cameron Brunswick, for starters, certainly came as a surprise to me. I suspect before the story ends someone will need the services of patrician attorney Waverley Drake. The plot is almost certainly going to hinge around something that is said or done by a visiting aristocrat: Sheldon, Duke of Connaught. I think this story has legs. They're not as good as Isabella El Mocambo's legs, but they're legs nonetheless.

Part II: Drinking in Particular

Two Practically Perfect Pubs

Having determined that pub perfection is unattainable, let's cast our little red eyes on a couple of pubs that come pretty darn close. These are both English pubs in slightly out-of-the-way places. They are not tourist meccas, they don't have Web sites, and they are generally unknown to people who live more than ten miles away. There are lots of other pubs like them, I'm sure, but these are two that I know.

Lewes is an old town in East Sussex, a few miles northeast of Brighton. It has a ruined castle, a house that once belonged to Anne of Cleves (the locals soft-pedal the regrettable fact that there is no evidence she ever set foot in it), an old priory, several antiquarian bookshops, and an excellent brewery. In the nineteenth century it had seven breweries, but there's no point regretting what we've missed. It has a vibrant high street, which is not so common in England these days, and a few good pubs. The best of these pubs is the Lewes Arms, an early nineteenth-century inn that has attached itself to the old castle wall like a benign barnacle.

The Lewes Arms has several of my Perfect Pub criteria—no piped-in music, no television, good beer, genial staff, a dog-friendly environment—but it also has those intangible factors that distinguish a great pub from a good one. It isn't a beautiful pub inside, but the moment you step inside you feel you've come to something not unlike home. There is a tiny front room and a slightly larger room on the far side of the bar, plus a third room off the corridor you enter from the front door, with access to the bar via a hatch. There's another room upstairs that is used by the folk music club among others.

The pub-minded know a good pub when they see it, and the Lewes Arms is seldom empty. You know you're in the best pub in town when all the interesting people are there, and they're certainly at the Lewes Arms.

The young mingle with the old, but the young are outnumbered by the old—or at least the middle-aged—so they don't get it all their own way.

The best pubs have a customer base of all ages. Any pub that is dominated by the young will almost certainly drive away the older drinker. Some towns are full of young people's pubs. Anne and I spent Christmas in Saffron Walden in Essex some years ago, and all the pubs appeared to be young people's pubs—all loud music and hostile looks when a wrinkly face peered in at the door. We finally found the pub the older people went to but it was so crowded we couldn't get in.

The landlady of the Lewes Arms is one Claire Murray, as far as I can tell an altogether sweet-natured woman who wants the best for her pub and her customers. One night we watched a man who had—apparently uncharacteristically—taken aboard more than the daily maximum recommended by the health authorities. He did a round of maudlin farewells through the place and finally lurched out into the night. Claire watched him go then put on her coat and followed him to see he came to no harm on his way home. (It turned out that he spotted her when he was most of the way home, then tried to insist on walking her back to the pub.) When I'm in Lewes you'll find me at the Lewes Arms. It is a true community centre, and I love it.

The town of Dursley in Gloucestershire is celebrated for not much, quite honestly. It is one of the few unattractive spots in the Cotswolds, although its setting is wonderful. Dursley is on the route of the Cotswold Way, so hikers pass through town, walking right past—if they're completely daft—a pub called the Old Spot. (Dursley is also the source of the name J.K. Rowling gave to a pack of villains in her Harry Potter books, and the town is not grateful to her for its newfound celebrity. She just liked the name, that's all.)

I have family in the greater Dursley area, so I've spent a bit of time there over the years. My favourite pub for the longest time was the New Inn at Waterley Bottom, just up and over the hill from Dursley. When I first knew the New Inn, it was run by a couple named Ruby and Ric Sainty, and it was heaven on earth. Ric—if the local gossip was to be believed—ran off with a barmaid some time in the eighties and took over a pub in Bristol, but he came back in 1993 and took over a dowdy Dursley pub called the Fox and Hounds, changing its name to the Old Spot. (Old Spot is a local beer named for a breed of pig raised in the area, so don't complain that you don't learn anything from me.)

Ric now has a different wife—neither the earlier wife nor the barmaid—and together they have transformed the Old Spot into a pub that was named runner-up for the Campaign for Real Ale Pub of the Year a couple of years back. It's an attractive pub with an ongoing pig motif, though it's not your classic picture postcard English pub. It's quiet, even when the local folk music people take over one end and fill it with the unamplified sound of guitars, a fiddle, a dobro, a mandolin, a concertina, a button accordion, a banjo, a double bass, a bodhran, and human voices.

Ric and Ellie have recently retired, leaving the place in the hands of a pair of managers, one of whom is the alleged barmaid from the earlier story. Ric has a house up the hill and will doubtless still be seen at the Old Spot on a regular basis, if only to ensure that his glorious vision is not mucked about. If I lived in Dursley, I'd be at the Old Spot every day. It offers excellent beer (including Old Ric, brewed by the local Uley Brewery) and just about everything you want in a pub. Again it's the intangibles, it's the regulars, it's the proprietor's dogs… it's the practically perfect pub.

Drinking Globally: The Wide World O' Booze

Travel, as we know, can be a broadening experience. I think we all do things on holiday that we don't much do at home. We go to museums, we visit historic sights, and we go on tours. But there's no point being silly about it. For the drinking person, travel offers a rare opportunity to see how people drink in other cultures. Some people actually get grants to do this, and they call it anthropology. You and I do this on our own dime. Mind you, we don't have to write an impenetrable report about it afterwards, so all in all it's worth it.

I've already written about drinking in England, but they drink in other countries as well. I find the most difficult part of drinking in France is getting anyone to understand me when I try to order a Pelforth. There is a French beer, brewed in Lille, called Pelforth, which is obviously a very un-French name. How to pronounce it? Possibly my favourite sentence by P.G. Wodehouse is the opening line of a novel called *The Luck of the Bodkins*: "Into the face of the young man who sat on the terrace of the Hotel Magnifique at Cannes there had crept a look of furtive shame, the shifty, hangdog look which announces that an Englishman is about to talk French."

Well, that's how I feel when I try to order a Pelforth. It's not even that Pelforth is the best beer in the world or anything, but I kind of like it. It has more character than most French beers, but how do you say it? Do you Frenchify it and leave off the 'th' at the end? Pelforrrr? Do you pronounce the 'th' as a Gallic clipped 't'? Pelfort? Or do you recognize that it's one of those odd French things and say it in a vaguely English way, as it's spelled?

Dear reader, I have no idea. I've tried all three approaches on various occasions and have been rebuffed each time. I think we've all suspected from time to time that the French are having us on, that they understand exactly what we're trying to say but they're damned if they're going to give us the satisfaction of thinking that we speak intelligible French. My friend John Jackson and I once went into a patisserie in Paris and ordered several delicacies. The patronne would not sell us these items until we could pronounce them to her satisfaction. Still, they were very good when we left the store a couple of hours later.

Anne and I were in Marseilles once and stopped for lunch at a café. We ordered food for both of us, a glass of wine for Anne, and a Pelforth for me. The waiter looked at me quizzically, but you expect that, don't you? At least he didn't deny that any such thing existed, which is what I usually get. A little while later he reappeared with Anne's wine and a large plate with a sausage-shaped thing on it. *"Et c'est quoi, exactement?"* I said, or something like it. *"Votre francfort, monsieur,"* he replied, with the warm glow that comes from having completely foxed a tourist. There is, apparently, an odd quirk of the Marseilles dialect that makes no distinction between a dark beer from northern France and a frankfurter. My French is Wodehousian, but it's not that bad. Pelforth, francfort—even I can tell the difference. It still beats trying to pronounce '33', the name of a very popular French lager. *Trente-trois* is a combination of sounds designed to confound the non-Francophone palate. Small wonder the locals all drink wine.

There's another French beer I like and I discovered it not all that far from Marseilles. We had rented a car—this was 1986 and I think we're still paying it off—and had stopped for the night in a small town called Brignoles. We found accommodation, settled in, and went out to see the sights. There weren't a lot of them. We visited one café, stayed for a bit, then crossed the street and visited the other café. The second café was more lively than the first, and our hostess, having established that I was in search of interesting beer (or a hot dog), smiled and said, "Adele Scott?"

I smiled back, as you do, but stopped short of answering in the affirmative. The nature of the question was unclear. Should I know Adele Scott? Was I being offered Adele Scott and would it be deemed impolite to turn her down? Driving in the English countryside once I saw a hand-lettered sign advertising Local Honey For Sale. I didn't stop. I mean, you don't know what she's going to be like, do you? Same thing with this Adele person.

After a bit of this back-and-forth smiling and non-communicating, she held up a beer bottle and said once again, "Adelscott!" I didn't know at the time that Adelscott was a French beer made by the Adelshoffen brewery in a sort of Scottish style using whisky malt. It has a smoky flavour and it's really rather nice. It's also rather strong, which I also didn't know at the time.

There was another woman at the bar, and she might have been there a long time. Certainly hours rather than minutes. Possibly days rather than hours. She might have been a few Adelscotts to the wind, and why not? She wanted to meet these exotic tourists who had breezed into town and wanted—perhaps to keep us from speaking French—to address us in our native tongue. Unfortunately her knowledge of English made us sound like Charles Aznavour by comparison. She thought a moment, made a facial expression that signified great concentration, and finally uttered a word we slowly recognized as "friend". "Ah," we cried, in international good cheer, *"ami!"*

Another round of drinks seemed called for to help us celebrate this outburst of friendliness. Really, it was all going very well. Emboldened by her success, our new ally recalled that she knew another English expression. Dredging it up was clearly going to take a moment or two, and her brow furrowed at the effort. Finally she had it. She leaned forward toward us, and we leaned forward toward her. The entire bar fell silent. No one wanted to miss this moment. Slowly she formed the words: "You... fucking... dog."

God knows what she thought she was saying, but she seemed a bit surprised when we broke into laughter. A grim-faced young woman hurried to her side and—clearly bilingual—whispered to our friend what she had said to us. The healthy glow disappeared from her face. She was mortified, both by the international incident she might have triggered and by the knowledge that someone had taught her these words at some point in her life, possibly under false pretences. We tried to assure her that we took no offence and that we still regarded her as our friend, but she was disconsolate. It certainly seemed to sober her up in a hurry.

Now, if we'd been at a museum or some damn thing, we'd have missed all of that. Trust me, if you want to know what's going on in a place, head for the bar.

The Germans get a bit of a bad rap, fun-wise. They are, in fact, capable of feeling and expressing pleasure, and it helps if they've been drinking. They're a bit like Canadians that way. I've enjoyed myself in German watering holes ranging from huge Bavarian beerhalls to little hole-in-the-wall sorts of places. As I mention somewhere else in this book, the German language becomes a whole lot easier after a few beers. You start making up nouns the way Germans do, just piling up words on top of one another, and German people seem to understand. The French would just give you one of those withering French looks, but the Germans are just as likely to buy you another beer.

One rule of drinking the Germans seem to understand instinctively is that, if you're going to bore the pants off someone in a bar, it's up to you to buy the beer. For the young, impecunious drinker, this is not the worst of all possible arrangements. (This rule is not recognized in many other places. I have met barroom bores who actually expected me to subsidize their drinking. Well, really.) I was in a bar in Bremen one afternoon in the late sixties. I quickly discovered it was obviously close to some sort of military thing, as there were soldiers about. An older man befriended me. I don't know if he hung out in this bar because he liked to be around young soldiers or because it brought back memories of his own military past. I belong to the don't-mention-the-war school when it comes to Germans, so I didn't ask.

He bought me a beer and started talking calmly and in English about, as I recall, Winston Churchill. If he didn't start out on Churchill, he very soon got there. His view of Churchill was not enthusiastic. Well, it was enthusiastic all right, but not pro-Churchill. I recall the expression "the greatest war criminal of all". As he warmed to his subject he raised the volume a bit and began to lapse back into German. Eventually he was ranting—there's no other word for it—entirely in German at great volume.

Then he stopped. He bought us both more beer, and began again. Calmly and in English. The same thing happened again. Again he stopped, bought more beer, and resumed as he had before. After about four beers I decided I had heard enough and made my apologies. It was practically the first time I had got a chance to speak. Don't let them tell you there's nothing funny about the Germans.

Be careful in Switzerland. Don't get me wrong. It's a damned nice country, with mountains and lakes and chocolate and all the things you expect. But twice in Switzerland I got fooled. They have bars in Switzerland that don't sell alcohol. I went into a bar in Neuchatel that looked like one groovy place. The Rolling Stones were playing through the speakers (this was still the late sixties, so I was happy to hear them), and everyone in the place looked just as they should.

I sat at the bar and ordered a beer. The bartender looked at me a bit funny, but I'm used to that, and he brought me a bottle and a glass. You tend to do a lot of reading in Switzerland, there being several dozen official languages. I once saw *Rebel Without a Cause* in Switzerland but I could hardly see anything for all the subtitles. I learned a lot of French, German, and Italian that day. Well, it was the same thing with this bottle of beer. I've never had so much to read on a beer label, but I'm enough of a linguist to recognize that I'm being warned that there's no alcohol in my beer in several languages.

Only then did I take a proper look at my surroundings. All the hip young folk around me were actually drinking Pepsi or some damn thing. The bottles behind the bar were bottles, all right, but not the sort of bottles you expect behind a bar. The place was a fake bar, and I hadn't spotted it. My non-beer was exactly that: non-beer.

And I'll be damned if the same thing didn't happen several days later, somewhere else in Switzerland. Fool me once, shame on you; fool me twice, shame on me. I came of drinking age in Toronto, at a time when the authorities did all they could to prevent people from drinking, but even they never tried a stunt like this. Why do the Swiss tolerate this sort of thing? Perhaps it's changed, but I've never gone back to find out.

The Americans would never pull off a trick like that, although Prohibition came pretty close. Actually Prohibition mostly seems to have meant that Americans got their booze from a different bunch of crooks than they were used to. For that matter, a lot of Americans continued to get their booze from exactly the same places they always had.

I'm not sure any New York bars ever bothered closing down during that misguided dark age. McSorley's Old Ale House was popular with politicians and never seems to have had any problems with the authorities. I chatted once with the proprietor of the Old Town Bar on East 18th Street, who said that they had removed their sign outside during Prohibition but that otherwise life had gone on as usual.

There's a bar called Chumley's in the Village that still has no sign outside. It opened in 1927, at the height of Prohibition, and has carried on successfully ever since. But you won't stumble upon it, unless you're a charmed stumbler. Even as you stand at the front door, at 86 Bedford Street, you'll have no hint that you're standing outside a bar with many beer taps unless one of the inmates comes lurching out. It's a quiet street, Bedford Street, and you can impress the bejeezus out of people who don't know about Chumley's if you walk along and calmly push open the door and step into a bustling New York bar. Just don't try it until after about four o'clock in the afternoon or the door will be locked and you won't impress anybody at all.

Chumley's has been tarted up slightly in recent years, but the bar area retains its sawdust on the floor and the three large Labs that lie about looking somehow baleful and winsome at the same time. There are two main themes to the decor: dust jackets and photographs of the many authors who have swilled on the premises and photographs of firefighters. Chumley's also has one of the quirkiest jukeboxes I've encountered. I mean, I've seen retro jukeboxes before, but none that offer a full CD of Joni James. You have to be pretty retro yourself to remember Joni James. You can also hear Handel's *Messiah*, if you need a change of pace.

Until recent years New York was a lousy town for beer drinkers. It used to take me a day to remember that I drank gin in New York. Gin was better value, given the generous servings you tend to get south of the Canadian border. The beer usually went by the name of Bud or his scrawny kid brother, Bud Light, and the purveyors of this stuff charged hefty prices for a thick mug that held paltry amounts. Just as well, really. The only time I was happy to see Bud was July 4, 1983. We were visiting our friend Syd Holden in Brooklyn Heights, and we went up to Yankee Stadium to catch the Yankees against the Red Sox. Syd's from Boston, so we were all cheering for the away team. There's something unhealthy about people who support the Yankees, I've always felt. It's too damn easy.

It was a very hot day, and we were sitting in the bleachers. I was keeping score on an envelope that I had with me for some reason. Dave Righetti was pitching for the home side, and pitching well. Given that we were all cheering for the Red Sox, I didn't feel it was jinxing anybody to point out after several innings that we were watching a no-hitter. It was still a close score and Syd was sure that the forces of good could still prevail. With two out in the ninth, Righetti got Wade Boggs swinging on strike three, and we all went crazy. Well, the three of us went less crazy, having hoped to the end that the Red Sox could come back, but it's still the only no-hitter I've ever watched live.

Did I mention that it was hot that day? It was very hot, somewhere in the mid-nineties on the American scale, and we were ready for a cold one. There are a couple of industrial, pour-beer-down-the-throats-of-many-thousands-of-Yankee-fans kind of bars right outside Yankee Stadium, but they were predictably packed and we walked a block or two looking for something more congenial while the area cleared out. We found a backstreet bar not far away, an actual neighbourhood corner bar. We didn't expect anything more exotic than Bud, and we weren't disappointed. Still, it was the fourth of July, the Yankees had just won a no-hitter, it had maybe cooled down to about ninety degrees, we were in a part of the Bronx we would probably have been warned against, and we pounded back a few ice-cold Buds, the bottles soaked with condensation. They were too cold to taste, which is the only way to drink Bud. We were happy, and I haven't had a Bud since.

Even today you can't be sure of getting a decent beer in New York. The Bud brothers are everywhere, unless you know where to look. The lover of good beer (or tequilas mezcals, or single malts, for that matter) heads for a place called d.b.a., down near the foot of 1st Avenue. The frills at d.b.a. are all behind the bar, and I'm not referring to—or at least not just referring to—the bar staff. They don't do food at d.b.a., though they're happy to direct you to local takeout places if you want to eat while you drink. (On my most recent visit I saw a couple of guys at a table enjoying a picnic of several cheeses and a fresh baguette; they looked as happy as clams.) They don't have live bands—though they do make you listen to music—and they don't have banks of television screens. You're there to drink, and to drink well. And the neighbourhood's improved enough in the years since d.b.a. opened (1994) that you're less likely to be murdered when you leave.

There are places in New York with bigger draught beer selections, but d.b.a. always offers an intelligent choice of beers, with always at least a couple of real ale opportunities. And it's not every bar that tells you, on a blackboard above the bar, when each of the casks was tapped, so you know how fresh everything is. They love their beer at d.b.a. and they're happy to talk about it, happy to give you a taste of something you're not sure of. Dropping in one night, I found myself in the midst of a celebration of microbreweries from New Jersey. Who knew? The name, by the way, probably stands for Doing Business As, but if you inquire you'll probably be told Don't Bother Asking.

I've spoken to Canadian beer guru Stephen Beaumont about d.b.a., and he reckons it's either the best bar in America or tied for first with a place called Toronado in San Francisco. If you don't trust me, trust him.

The aforementioned McSorley's in the East Village dates back to 1854, and it hasn't changed much since John McSorley first opened the doors, except that there's probably more clutter now. Oh, and about thirty years ago the National Organization of Women brought legal action to end the bar's discriminatory practice of refusing to serve women. Eventually McSorley's yielded to the law, but some years passed before they installed a women's toilet.

That bit of oddness aside, it's a nice place to be, particularly in the afternoon. We were there one fairly busy afternoon, sitting beneath a pay phone, which turns out to be the bar phone. If you call McSorley's that's the phone that rings. The staff showed no interest in answering the damn thing—hell, the place was already busy enough—so Anne started picking it up. Most of the callers were looking for the address, though some needed directions. She didn't do terribly well with the guy calling from the Lincoln Tunnel, but she was great with the guy who claimed to be on the Upper West Side.

"Can you be more specific?" she asked. "Where exactly are you?"

"I'm near Bloomingdale's," the man replied.

"Bloomingdale's?" my wife from Toronto said. "Then you're not on the West Side, are you?"

I wanted her to add "Welcome to Noo Yawk!" and hang up, but she was too polite.

There's not a lot of choice at McSorley's. There's dark beer and light beer—formerly made locally but now made by Stroh's—and it comes in little mugs that need constant refilling. They'd need even quicker refilling if it were better beer. And a good mid-afternoon pick-me-up is offered by the cheap cheese plate: soda crackers, cheddar cheese (and not bad cheese either, for the Americans), and raw onions. A bit of strong mustard, and life is close to ideal. It was said soon after the turn of the last century that wives knew that their husbands had been in the safe, floozy-free environment of West 7th Street, because you could always tell a McSorley's onion.

The man who wrote best about McSorley's was Joseph Mitchell, who wrote the definitive study of the old saloon for *The New Yorker* in 1940. At that point McSorley's was eighty-six years old and still on only its fourth owner. He writes of the regular who, on the day of his retirement, announced, "If my savings hold out, I'll never draw another sober breath." I'm not sure I haven't seen him in there still.

Some years ago I was on a bit of a pub crawl in New York with the aforementioned Syd. We had done Pete's Tavern—an old haunt of O Henry—and one or two other spots I don't now recall, and we were headed across town to the Village when we happened upon the also aforementioned Old Town Bar on a very dark, almost moribund East 18th Street. We never did get to the Village. At that time—this would have been the early eighties—it was the bar that time had forgotten. It even held to the old New York tradition that the house bought every third drink. I enjoyed that tradition once at the late and still lamented Lion's Head in the Village, a grand old Manhattan landmark.

East 18th Street is perkier now than it was then, and the Old Town is more popular than it seemed that long ago night. It made it into the opening credits of David Letterman's show, which drew the crowds. A hipper clientele has improved the draught beer selection a bit, which it certainly needed. There is Liam Neeson memorabilia on the walls, which probably means that he's moved on by now and drinks somewhere else.

The Blind Tiger is a fairly new bar on Hudson Street on the West Side. It's not far from the famous White Horse Tavern, where Dylan Thomas infamously—and allegedly—drank the many neat whiskies that may have led to his doom. Everybody should drink at least once at the White Horse, but there's much better beer at the Blind Tiger, a bar that offers a pleasing range of microbrews. And on weekend afternoons the house offers free bagels and cream cheese.

There's a Waterfront Ale House in Brooklyn, but I don't get to Brooklyn much since Syd left town. Fortunately they opened a branch in Manhattan on Second Avenue in midtown. Fine beers and good food too.

When Anne's shopping at Lord & Taylor I wait for her at the Ginger Man on East 36th Street. With 66 taps on display, there's plenty of beer to choose from, but it's definitely the sort of place where you want to feed the jukebox rather than listen to the pap you'll have inflicted on you otherwise.

When I'm in Chicago I try to have lunch at least once at Andy's on East Hubbard. Andy's is a jazz club that offers live jazz three times a day: at lunch, after work, and in the evening. At lunch there's no cover charge, just a chance to buy Goose Island Honker's Ale from a woman who typifies a certain kind of big-town barkeep: not as gruff as she seems, but almost certainly tough if she needs to be.

The Goose Island Brewery has a bar of its own on the way to Wrigley Field, and it gives an opportunity to taste the other beers on its list other than the fairly ubiquitous Honker's. Closer still to Wrigley is a bar called Sheffield's which has a fine list of beers and a pleasant garden. I like Sheffield's because it was the first place in a quarter-century to ask me for ID. They were checking everybody, including at least one other geezer, but still it was nice to be asked. The Clark Street Alehouse has a lot of good Midwest microbrewery beer and a sound system to loosen your teeth. A lot of Chicago bars don't open until at least mid-afternoon, so call first. Late in the nineteenth century Chicago's bars were famous for never closing. Part of the ritual upon opening a new bar called for the proprietor to declare the place open, then take a walk and throw the keys into Lake Michigan.

In 2000 the Christian Booksellers Association held its annual conference in New Orleans, which seemed an odd location. A lot of people find themselves harbouring ideas in New Orleans that aren't always in keeping with a strict reading of the New Testament. It seems to me a city that does a better job fulfilling the physical pleasures than the spiritual ones. In a *Publishers Weekly* report of the conference, one Christian bookseller from Texas declared that she had enjoyed herself but added that New Orleans wouldn't have been her first choice. "There's not a lot here for Christian folk to do," she pointed out.

That may be so, but we sinners find plenty to occupy us. Writer Calvin Trillin once asked a local gourmand where he should eat in Louisiana. He was told: anywhere. The same rule applies pretty much to drinking. At first glance there appear to be no drinking laws at all in New Orleans, but I'm aware of at least two. If you're going to drink on the streets your beverage must be in a plastic or paper container, not glass or metal. And you can't drink on the streetcar that goes out to the Garden District. That seems to be it, legislation-wise. I'm sure there must be other rules, but those are the only ones that stand out.

There are many facets of life in New Orleans that remind you that you're not in Canada any more, but none more than walking around the French Quarter on a hot night with a large plastic cup of beer, listening to live music from the many clubs. Sure, it's become overrun with t-shirt stores—the first evidence of a dead culture—and it's become something of a theme park, but it's a theme park for grownups. Leave the kids behind.

Like most hot, sultry places, New Orleans is not a great beer town. The local institution is Dixie, a standard hot-weather lager of no real distinction, though it's useful when you're trying to restore fluids to the system. They also brew a Blackened Voodoo Lager, which got them in bad odour with southern Christian folk who don't hold with that voodoo stuff. There's some decent beer from the Abita brewery just out of town, and I've enjoyed Rikenjaks when I've been able to find it.

There are as many bars in New Orleans as there are Mormons in Salt Lake City, so you're never far from a drink. If you're restless, there are lots of hole-in-the-wall sorts of places that offer takeaway beer as well. The pub-minded tourist simply has to get to a couple of places: the Napoleon (no, he never drank there, but there's a story that they offered to take him in) and the venerable old Lafitte's Blacksmith Shop. The place I gravitate toward is a place called Coop's, down on Decatur Street. The last time I was there they were serving a decent Scotch Ale from Rikenjaks, but I guess I went too often because they ran out of it. Along with pretty good beer and an excellent southern bar ambience, Coop's will do you an altogether serviceable meal—the wonderful local food at good prices.

It is worth noting—well, I think it's worth noting; you can decide for yourself—that the fine fellows who own d.b.a. in New York have opened a d.b.a. in New Orleans at 618 Frenchmen Street. It wasn't there last time I was in the Crescent City, but I'm told it's there now.

You never know where you're going to find a drink on your travels. The vicissitudes of life have delivered me to Syracuse, New York, only the once, but it was long enough to discover Clark's Ale House, a bar of great character, multiple fine beers, and only one sandwich. Still, it's a very good sandwich. Just beyond the border of Cambridge, Massachusetts, just as you get into Somerville, you'll find—if you're lucky—Redbones Barbecue, the only place I've ever found Sam Adams Trippelbock on tap, served from a little barrel behind the bar. I don't speak of life-altering experiences lightly, but this was just such an experience.

A longer-than-expected delay at the Atlanta Airport led to the discovery of a bar that sold only Sam Adams beers on tap. I was almost sorry when our flight materialized. It turns out that there's no international law dictating that airports have to sell bad beer. They do it only to make your airport experience even more unpleasant. Maybe someday the touring drinker will even be able to get a decent beer on an airplane, but I'm not holding my breath.

Our friend Syd, mentioned above, moved to Florida a few years ago. When we went to visit him he took us to the Palace Saloon in Fernandina Beach, which purports to be the oldest saloon in Florida. I'm prepared to believe that claim until I see evidence to the contrary, and I've no doubt there are half a dozen bars in Florida making the same claim. I just haven't been to the others. It is worth noting that Syd has lived in a few places in the last ten or so years. We used to visit him when he lived in Brooklyn Heights. We visited him when he lived in Cambridge. We visited him in northern Florida. There was a time he went to work in Riyadh, Saudi Arabia. Riyadh is one of those chop-your-hand-off kind of places when it comes to the pub life. We didn't visit Syd in Riyadh.

This Sceptr'd Isle: Drinking in England

Like everything else, pub life in the United Kingdom is changing, usually for the worse. Pubs are being closed or they're being gutted and turned into ghastly theme pubs. Where it once cost about the same to drink at home or in a pub, it's now cheaper to drink at home. And many do, especially since central heating became more widely available. Still, I recently saw a figure pointing out that Americans drink only twenty per cent of their beer in bars and restaurants, while the English continue to drink seventy-five per cent of their beer in pubs. And rightly so, for the pub is not just a place to drink. It's the village hall. It's where people go to hear the news, find jobs, make friends, meet the people they'll spend the rest of their lives with.

The English pub is something that has evolved over the centuries. The earliest pubs existed to serve travellers, usually pilgrims. Chaucer's pilgrims set out from the Tabard, an inn in Southwark. As travel grew more sophisticated, inns proliferated along coaching routes, in much the same way that Canadian towns sprang up along railway lines. Travellers needed a bed for the night and a meal, and while they were there they might as well have a flagon or two of ale as well.

When railways began to supplant the coaches, pubs appeared to cater to the needs of train travellers. Long after the British railway system was gutted in the 1960s, you can still find pubs called the Railway or the Station Inn, far from the nearest train line. It's a little disconcerting the first time you come upon one of these stranded railway pubs.

One of the most impressive pubs in London was built by a man named Frank Crocker, who had been given a hot tip that a major railway station would be built practically across the street. Crocker built the Crown Hotel, an ornate palace of a place, and waited for the fortune that would surely follow. Alas, the train line veered away from Crocker's hotel and Marylebone Station wound up a mile away. A broke and broken Crocker jumped to his death from an upstairs window. Pub historians are quick to cast doubt on virtually the whole story, but it's a good one nonetheless. If it isn't true, it certainly should be. The pub—now called Crocker's Folly—still stands in a quiet residential street in St. John's Wood, not far from Lord's Cricket Ground.

Call me a rain-soaked anglophile, but there's not much I like better than a good English pub. People talk of a good old typical English pub, but there's really no such thing. Some of them are fancy, with acres of frosted glass, mahogany bars, and great marble urinals a fellow's almost reluctant to pee into. But they're not all like that. In 1967 my cousin took me to a Gloucestershire pub that didn't even have anyone tending the bar. The customers served themselves then reported what they'd taken to a woman who came around with a change purse. She told you what you owed and you paid her.

That pub doesn't exist any more. Nor does the Berkeley Hunt in Purton, an unadorned pub on a canal that runs parallel to the Severn River. The Berkeley Hunt, when I knew it, was run by a Mrs. Musselwhite, known to all as Ma Musselwhite, rumoured to be if not the oldest licensee in England then certainly damn close to it. The pub didn't have anything as highfalutin as a bar. You came in the front door and found yourself in a narrow corridor with a kind of serving hatch in front of you. There, if you were lucky, stood Ma herself. The beer was behind her in casks, and your beer came straight out of the barrel. By this time the casks were metal rather than wood, but you can't have everything.

Once served, you joined the throng that gathered in the doorway or, in good weather, stood outside in the garden beside the canal, or you moved into either the room on the right or that on the left. There is a general principle in English pubs that if you have two rooms one will be tonier than the other. In the Berkeley Hunt I think it was the room on the left, on the basis that the furniture was a mite softer. But I'm not sure I ever saw anyone drink there. I once spent Christmas Eve in the Berkeley Hunt, and we all gathered in the room on the right, sat in a large circle singing songs and sharing something I've never tried to define. (The Germans have a word for it—*Gemütlichkeit*—which is almost as much fun to say as it is to experience.) Shortly before midnight, Ma Musselwhite herself came around and took orders for a round of drinks on the house.

I once spoke to a younger member of the family who said they were keeping the place open only as long as Ma wanted to run it and was capable of doing so. When I came by one year and saw the place closed up I knew an era had ended. God bless you, Ma.

You never know when you're going to have a magic pub moment. In May 1980 I found myself alone in London, my wife back in Canada. It was Cup Final day, a big day on the English sporting calendar. I watched the match on television in the afternoon, a surprise win for West Ham over fellow London club Arsenal. That evening I took the tube up to Islington to see a play in a small theatre at the back of a pub called the King's Head. After the play I decided the King's Head was too crowded so I headed down the street to find something a little quieter. Islington now is very chic, but it wasn't at the time. It was also, it is worth noting, the part of town in which Arsenal—that day's losing team—played.

I don't know what the pub was called, but I went in. Similarly I don't remember what was on tap, but I know that an older fellow played a piano and the whole community was there. Over to one side stood some lads who had been to the match and were looking sombrely at their programs. There were youngsters and there were grannies at this pub, and I may have been the first tourist who ever set foot in the place. Even though I was actually living in London at the time, it wasn't that part of London and I hadn't been living there for generations; I was a tourist. A Salvation Army couple came in to solicit donations. They were made welcome, but they weren't going to get out until they sang a song. They did us a rousing hymn, accompanied by the old fellow on the piano, and we all cheered. And I swear that before the evening ended we sang *Maybe It's Because I'm a Londoner*, the great anthem of the capital. I was probably the only outsider in the room, but I joined in with gusto, wishing I had been a Londoner. For once in my life, I could actually imagine being an Arsenal supporter. The impulse didn't last, but it was powerful at the time.

Not all pubs are friendly, welcoming spots, it must be said. Some years ago Anne and I sought out a Wiltshire pub that was described in the *Good Beer Guide* as "One of a dying breed; as basic as they come." It was what had clearly been a rustic pub now being encroached upon by creeping suburbia. We drove past it once because its ancient, weathered pub sign was illegible. When we stepped in, we saw it was indeed basic. The venerable landlady gave us a look that suggested we'd come to the wrong place. In a room to our right sat the regulars. They were men to a man, all in black, with a couple of working dogs. It was hard to say where these rustics lived or worked in this new genteel area; possibly they were bused in each day.

The regulars fell silent as we came in. Not that we actually entered their room; that would have been an invitation to violence. Feeling a chill in the air, we ordered half pints as a compromise position. We weren't about to retreat altogether, you understand, but we didn't feel like lingering either. We sat alone in the only slightly more tony room, where we could see into the regulars' room through a doorway, or at least we could until one of the regulars pointedly kicked the door shut. Only then did they resume conversation, which from where we sat sounded rather like, "Orrr, arrr, orrr, errr..."

We have not been back to the Bruce Arms, but the pub guides suggest that it is now a friendly, welcoming spot under new management, still retaining its unspoilt charm. Maybe so; I just want a guarantee that the guy who kicked the door shut isn't still there.

There are plain pubs and grand pubs, but the rules are the same. There are no waiters in an English pub. You go to the bar and get your drinks. Some of my best friends are waiters, but I have to say that the English setup works wonderfully well, especially if you're just pushy enough to make your way to the bar and get the bar staff's attention. It's an efficient system. One recent New Year's Eve I watched three bar people serving a very busy Sussex pub without making anyone wait for long. Sometimes the landlady pitched in as well, but there was scant space for a fourth person behind that bar. Her presence meant one of the others could take a smoke break and go look for abandoned glasses.

I've worked in a London pub and I know that pub wages aren't bad, or they weren't in 1969, at least compared to other jobs I did in London at that time. I'm not saying anyone's getting rich behind a bar, but they're not dependent on tips. I have seen a London barman tipped by an American tourist and calling the fellow back because he'd left change on the bar. Tipping is not the accepted practice, but if you like the service you're getting from someone behind a bar you say, as you're ordering your drinks, "And will you have one yourself?" The person will then say, "Thank you, I'll have a half pint" or whatever, and will charge you accordingly. All is well, and you will be favourably regarded thereafter.

The traditional English practice of buying rounds is slipping away, for fairly sensible reasons. Traditionally, if two people drank together, one would buy the other a drink, after which the second would reciprocate. If three drinkers gathered, each would play his role, and so on up the scale. Find yourself one of a group of half a dozen, and it becomes clear that you're there for six pints, whether you want them all or not. It was chummy, all right, but not conducive to productivity. And woe be to you if you left before your round came along.

So, what are you drinking? It used to be fairly simple for the beer drinker: a pint of bitter. (Please note bitter, not bitters. Bitters is a vile herbal drink designed to do battle with a hangover.) This was in the days when pubs were owned by breweries and a pint of bitter was the normal draught ale made by that particular brewery. Nowadays, there is likely to be a choice of bitters, but there are worse things than choice. My advice is to make sure that what you're drinking comes from a handpump, the tall, slightly phallic device that signals the presence of real ale. English lager exists to separate fools from their money, and the other beers on offer will not be as fresh or as tasty as a real ale. Don't hesitate to ask the bar staff for advice, especially if they're over twenty-five.

It is worth noting that if you ask for a martini in an English pub, to this day you will probably be served a glass of vermouth. You may also be asked if you'd like lemonade with that. The standard measures for liquor have grown marginally in the shift from sixths of gills to a metric measure, but they're still smaller than Canadian measures (and a tiny fraction of what you generally get in a good American bar). Feel free to ask for a large one, which will be a double. You're on holiday, for Pete's sake.

English drinking hours continue to bewilder visitors from practically anywhere. Explain to anyone that pubs in London close at 11 p.m. and they'll laugh at you. Hell, you can drink later than that in Kenora. That may be true, but it doesn't alter the fact that at ten to eleven all across London barmen are calling out "Last orders please!" And ten minutes later you'll hear a bell and the cry, "Time, ladies and gentlemen please, let's have your glasses!"

They talk about changing the drinking hours, and some day they will. They've made it possible to drink during the afternoon, which was illegal only a few years ago, and you can drink all day on Sundays now, at least until 10:30 at night. But that's assuming the publican actually wants to open the doors, for he's under no obligation to do so. Outside the cities, most of the pubs are run by a family who live on the premises. They open at lunchtime, close for a few restful hours, and re-open for the evening. As far as they're concerned, they're working plenty of hours thank you very much, and I suppose they have a point. If they stayed open longer they'd either have to work longer hours themselves or pay someone to work those extra hours when they wouldn't have enough customers to justify it.

When I worked at the Argyll Arms, just off Oxford Circus in London, I turned up at 9:30 a.m. to get the place ready to open at 11. We were busy at lunchtime, but I got a short lunch break myself. We then closed at 3 p.m.

for the afternoon. All being well I got away at 3:20. We re-opened at 5:30 p.m., which meant I had to be back ten minutes earlier, and we then worked through till 10:30 with a dinner break in there somewhere. We were quiet during the evening, which was a blessing, so we closed half an hour earlier than the other local pubs, which meant I could get away for a couple of quick pints elsewhere after we closed. Still, it was a long day with a virtually useless two-hour break in the middle of the day. If you went home in the afternoon there wasn't enough time to do anything, and it wasn't as if you could go to a pub because they were all shut. As I recall I was making £16 a week, with Wednesday evenings and Sundays off. Still, I've been less happy in jobs.

Then there's food. There are almost no English pubs today that don't serve some sort of lunch. The ploughman's lunch, which is not a traditional meal but something that was created in the sixties as a cheese marketing initiative, is served practically everywhere. Much of southeastern England boasts a baked potato—called a jacket potato there—served with cheese, chili, tuna, or baked beans, depending on your needs. Farther north you might get Yorkshire pudding served with a choice of fillings.

Dinner, in some parts of England, is still an adventure. The Cotswolds are chock-a-block with pubs serving dinner, while other parts of the country are still incredulous that people might want a meal after dark. Once it was even worse. Anne and I almost reached the point of consulting legal persons in the late seventies and early eighties, whenever we visited the British Isles. A cheese sandwich in Mansfield once saved our marriage, as did a couple of leftover ham rolls in Gretna, up in Scotland. Travel writer Bill Bryson has written of the stunning ability of the English to take pleasure in the smallest things. The cheese sandwich in Mansfield was as glorious an experience as I can recall in England, with the possible exception of the 1983 FA Cup semi-final (Sheffield Wednesday 1, Brighton and Hove Albion 2). Fainting with hunger, we asked the landlord if there was any food at all of any sort to be had. He thought for a moment, it being later than 2 p.m., and admitted that, if pressed, he could invent a cheese sandwich or possibly two. There was never a better cheese sandwich than that cheese sandwich, and I raise a glass to the unknown publican of Mansfield. I hope that success and happiness have dogged his every step since that evening.

You should know that even the pubs that stay open all afternoon seldom serve food after about 2 p.m. This falls under the "There's no call

for it, guv" rule that says that the publican is the sole judge of what his customers want, not that he'd ever actually ask. There's a pub in Lewes that serves food from noon until 7 p.m., so you can get a nice meal at four in the afternoon but will probably be too late if you get peckish at, say, your normal dinner time.

But enough carping. The English pub continues to evolve, sometimes for the better, sometimes not. Many pubs, for any number of reasons—tough drinking and driving legislation, the increasing likelihood of people staying in to watch *East Enders* instead of going to the pub, or the growing tendency to drink at home, throwing back smuggled French lager which bears a much lower tax rate than English beer—are closing their doors forever. This is the greatest tragedy. As pub-lover Hilaire Belloc said, "When you have lost your inns, drown your empty selves, for you will have lost the last of England." Amen.

Patrick Kennedy's Subway Game, Eastbound

There are lots of games involving drinking, most of which take place inside pubs and usually require a display of physical dexterity or the total recall of arcane trivia. A hospitality industry professional friend of mine has invented a drinking game of an altogether different sort.

If you've ever visited a Toronto pub called Paupers, you have probably encountered Patrick Kennedy. Patrick's a bit of a local star. To his embarrassment (he's not an attention seeker), he finished runner-up in the 2000 *Now* magazine Best of Toronto readers' poll in the Best Restaurant Server category, but then this is the same poll that named Red Lobster the Best Seafood Restaurant in town, which gives you some idea what sort of people are voting. Democracy's a slippery notion. When not waiting on tables, Patrick is frequently to be found somewhere near the bar, chatting with his regulars long after his shift has ended. Many people assume Patrick to be the owner, such is the proprietary attitude Patrick takes toward the place. This misapprehension is helped along by his authoritative manner and aldermanic bearing, although he sports a rather un-aldermanic ponytail. Well, let's just say that I've never seen an alderman with a ponytail.

Patrick's Subway Game requires the use of a subway, so this is a game that can be played only in select cities, and then only in areas of those cities that are served by a subway. A bus or a taxi simply won't do. It is important that you can't see what you're getting into, so it's essential to arrive at your destination from beneath the ground.

The idea is this: you take a subway map and find a station you've never been to before, in a part of town you don't know. Then you board the subway and travel to the station you've selected. Emerging from the tunnel of transit, you proceed to find some kind of licensed premises. Then you have a beer. And, well, that's about it really. It's not about winners and losers and scoring points. It's about finding hidden treasures, and it's the playing that counts.

In some cities, of course, the Subway Game could keep one occupied for years. The relative ubiquity of the English pub would make the London version rewarding, if possibly a trifle too easy. Though who knows what you might find near the South Ruislip station, or Theydon Bois or even Gants Hill. What pleasure to go a-searching though. New York, as well, offers a wide variety of subway stations but I don't know what joy you might find in, say, mid-Queens. (And I still don't, as you'll discover in later chapters.)

I decided to put the Toronto version of Patrick's game into action. The Toronto subway, alas, is limited, and there are too many stations I can already identify with a pub of some sort. The East End, however, is a bit of a cipher to me, so on my first outing I settled upon the Coxwell station out on the Danforth. I may have seen the corner of Coxwell and Danforth at some time in my life, but I certainly don't remember it.

You can possibly imagine my excitement as the subway rolled to a stop and I left the train. You might then imagine my frustration as I realized I had got off a stop early, having miscalculated the number of stops after Pape. The doors closed behind me, and the train sped off to wherever it goes after Donlands, where I now found myself. Well, actually I know where it goes: it goes to Coxwell, and that's where I eventually wound up as soon as another train came along. Tip number one: in almost all cases, subway stations actually have their names emblazoned on the walls so you know where to get off. Sometimes the driver or conductor will also announce the names of approaching stations. When you hear the words, "Next stop XVBERRRGGSVMP," you'll know enough to read the signs on the station walls.

When you leave the Coxwell subway station you come out on a quiet residential street. Well, first you have to negotiate a brace of piranha-like Girl Guides selling their celebrated cookies inside the station, then you come out on a quiet residential street. Cost so far: subway token, purchased in moderate bulk, $1.77; box of Girl Guide cookies, $3.00. Well, you never know—there might be nothing to eat at Coxwell and Danforth. And you didn't meet these Girl Guides. It would have taken a braver man than I to say no to them. And, for that matter, I wouldn't be surprised if they were actually Brownies, though I'm no authority on the subject.

The only sign of urban life on Strathmore Boulevard is a cheerful, if aggressively Protestant, church called Church of Christ, but soon you're out on Coxwell Avenue. To your left you see the law office of one T. Edgar Reilly, working out of an old house across the street from Rocco the

Cobbler. A moment later you're on the Danforth, standing in front of a bar called TKO's: The Sports Pub. I had expected the Subway Game to be more difficult than this.

Uncharacteristically reluctant to seize the first pint offered to me, I walked along a few blocks eastward. After all, there seemed little purpose in travelling all this way only to have a quick pint then head back to the subway, never knowing what pleasures have been laid on for the proud denizens of the Coxwell-Danforth area. Surely people don't live there just because the houses are cheap or because they like to live as close as possible to Rocco the Cobbler, as fine as I'm sure his work is. Though I didn't see his name in the Now magazine readers' poll.

As I passed a storefront operation called Open Heaven Ministries Inc. I began to wonder if this was perhaps not a big drinking part of town. My limited experience with enthusiastic Protestantism tells me that the people who frequent places with names like Open Heaven Ministries Inc. do not pop into TKO's for a bracing snifter afterwards. Yet I pushed on. I was excited to find a place called the Prince of Wales, which proved to be a supermarket. I passed on Europe Planet Bar-Grill-Pub, although I liked the name, and I may regret my decision for many years to come.

On the south side of the street I saw a place called Cheers Tavern, with a sign outside that was about the same size as the set of the television sitcom. Since that successful show, there can be hardly a city, town, or village on the planet that does not have a bar called *Cheers*. I tend to stay out of these places, from the perhaps irrational fear that everybody will know my name. Can you imagine anything worse? Also the beer they served on *Cheers* looked pretty insipid. Did you ever notice that nobody ever seemed to get drunk at Mayday Malone's?

Turning back I passed a place I had missed going eastbound—The Bus Terminal Family Restaurant, which was a building that had very clearly once been part of a bus terminal. Had I been in the mood for a milk shake or a slice of cherry pie, I'd have been in there like my late cat Nosey on a dish of IAMS. I had my Girl Guide cookies, however, so I wasn't hungry. A neon sign in the window promised Molson Export on tap. I took this as divine warning, and I headed back to TKO's.

Sports bars always have lots of TV screens in operation, and TKO's was no exception. It also had some decent beer on tap, which is not always the case. So I sat at the bar with a pint of Conner's Dark Ale and watched a bit of US college football. This is something I do every couple of years or so, and it always strikes me that football is a game played with a ball that the majority of players never touch. Am I alone in finding this odd? Imagine a baseball player who never made contact with the ball. Okay, we could name a few of those, but at least they're trying. Another thing about American football is that there are guys whose job it is to catch footballs that have been kicked toward them, who then as often as not very pointedly don't catch it. I mean they deliberately don't catch it. They just stand there and let the ball bounce around until someone on the other team grabs it. Having then grabbed the ball, does the other team get to keep it? Of course not. And sometimes the team that's supposed to catch the ball catches it in the end zone and the guy then genuflects and everything stops, and it doesn't cost them a single point. I'll never understand the Americans.

Another thing I think about sometimes when I find myself gawking at a pub TV screen is sports uniforms. For the most part you can figure out how modern uniforms have evolved, although figure skating costumes seem to adhere to a set of rules that haven't been explained to the rest of us. Can you imagine leaving your house in figure skaters' clothes? Maybe it's something to do with ice, because I've never been able to understand hockey uniforms. These guys are wearing shorts. Shorts and tights. Ugly padded shorts and frequently striped tights. What sort of fashion statement is that?

The other thing about sports bars is that most of the time there's nothing of much importance going on. Sure, any night of the week you'll see live hockey or baseball games, and Saturday and Sunday afternoons there's usually at least a golf tournament or something. But the rest of the time can be pretty bleak for the stations that usually carry sports events. Maybe if I were a fisherman I'd take more pleasure in watching guys in a boat fondling the fish they've just caught, but I doubt it.

The absolute worst thing—and I've only seen this once—is turkey hunting. I once went into a Wal-Mart in rustic Pennsylvania during what I assume was wild turkey season, and there, by the gun section, was any amount of expensive stuff for turkey hunters, including every sort of camouflage and turkey caller you can imagine, and maybe a few things that you can't. All this to outsmart a turkey. I've always held that you can learn a lot from platitudes, and I've never heard anybody use expressions like "wily as a turkey" or "smart like a turkey". So to look up from a bar and see four TVs showing a couple of guys in full camouflage creeping through a field hoping to fool a turkey is not a life-affirming experience, especially when the other three sets are showing Golf Channel infomercials.

TKO's is a bar for Toronto Maple Leaf fans. This is made very clear. A sign behind the bar reads PLEASE BE ADVISED THIS BAR SUPPORTS.

THE TORONTO MAPLE LEAFS LEAF FANS RECEIVE PRIORITY SERVICE. Fair enough, you know where they stand. If you're hell-bent on the Anaheim Mighty Ducks, I'd advise you to try the Europe Planet Bar-Grill-Pub. Still, even though I was wearing no Leaf-abilia I was served hastily and pleasantly, and the Conner's wasn't too shabby.

Rather than get back on the subway and find another unknown destination, I started walking westbound, back toward what I tend to think of as civilization. Though I kind of liked the Coxwell-Danforth area. There were a couple of big chain things a little east of Coxwell, but it was mostly small local businesses of a frequently offbeat nature. I like that. There are no major universities in that part of town, but the Danforth Dance Studio is not far from the Danforth Karate Academy, so there is no shortage of opportunities for self-improvement.

I continued to walk westward because I had remembered an old watering hole on the way to Greenwood Avenue, a traditional old taproom called the Linsmore Tavern. Surely it could not have survived the last quarter-century of gentrification unscathed, but suddenly there it was, untouched. Ever wonder what happened to those old 6-ounce draught beer glasses? They're at the Linsmore, and for a mere eighty cents the kind of waiter I hadn't seen since the Morrissey Tavern locked its doors will bring you one filled with Labatt's 50 on tap. I haven't seen Labatt's 50 on tap since Christ left Cobourg. Labatt's 50 might have been what drove him out of Cobourg in the first place. He could turn water into wine, but there isn't much you can do with Labatt's 50.

I sat a spell in the Linsmore, watching a golf tournament on one of those early prototypes of large screen TVs, the kind that gives you a dim picture which disappears altogether if you're not directly face-on. The Linsmore still has old snowshoes nailed to the ceiling, and I was glad to see them. And I still had a few Girl Guide cookies left, so I wasn't tempted by the pickled eggs on offer.

Just west of Greenwood I found the apartment building I've long thought of as the ideal Toronto address for the stay-at-home drinker. Sure, Rosedale has its charms, and I know people who swear by Forest Hill, and the Annex has plenty of admirers, God knows. But the Adella Apartments at 1169 Danforth have a beer store immediately to their east and a liquor store immediately to their west. Only in the worst imaginable weather would you need anything more hardy than slippers. I must have walked past the Adella Apartments a hundred times in my life, but I've never seen an Apartment for Rent sign outside.

Adella Apartments

The drinking person is always on the lookout for a new little spot, some undiscovered gem your sophisticated friends don't know about, and I found just such a place west of Donlands on the north side of the Danforth. I had never even heard of The Only Café, and frankly I'm reluctant to tell you about it now. It's not a big place, longish and narrow, as city bars tend to be. The sign outside boasted 101 bottles and thirteen taps and I still had the taste of Labatt's 50 in my mouth, so I did what any right-minded drinking person would do: I walked in.

It's an odd kind of place, The Only Café, clearly not designed by some concept guy in an office several miles away. The concept guy would have demanded a more mainstream selection of beer, for starters. I mean, why scare the Coors Light drinkers away? And then there's the music. First we heard a bunch of songs by Woody Guthrie, and I don't recall ever hearing Woody Guthrie in a bar before. When that was over we got Frank Sinatra, in particularly good form. The old couple sitting near me at a table seemed to enjoy that especially, but the young tattooed guy next to me at the bar didn't seem to mind it either. The father-son duo at another table were too engrossed in their game of chess to notice.

I sat at the bar, supping my Kawartha Lakes Brewery Raspberry Wheat beer—an excellent lightish beer, perfect in summer; tastes like raspberries, but it tastes like beer too—and thinking warm thoughts about a bar that serves good beer and plays music for grownups. I was by now probably a good mile away from Coxwell and Danforth, but Patrick Kennedy's Subway Game had brought me to a great discovery. I would—I resolved then and there—return to The Only Café.

Canada's richest man, Kenneth Thomson ("Lord" to his friends), lives in Toronto's deluxe Rosedale area. The publishing mogul is worth an estimated twenty-four billion dollars, yet he lives an unhealthy mile-and-a-quarter from the nearest beer store. Frankly, the weight of a two-four could kill a man of his age over that sort of haul.

The official residence of the president of the University of Toronto is only slightly closer, but it has a difficult crossing of Mount Pleasant to negotiate. It would be treacherous with a case of beer under your arm. Fortunately the president is a younger man than Ken Thomson and, in any case, he's got Vice-Provosts and people of that ilk to fetch his beer.

Residents of the Adella Apartments on the Danforth may lack the niceties of life—like Vice-Provosts—but they don't need them. Door to door, they are a mere 33 paces to the beer store and only 19 to the liquor store. What price happiness?

(above) *Kenneth Thomson's deluxe Rosedale home.*

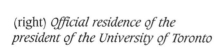

(right) *Official residence of the president of the University of Toronto*

While You're Up: What's My Poison?

I'm a fairly flexible drinker, but my specialty is beer. I liked beer back in the dark times of the sixties and seventies when consumer choice, particularly in North America, was declining dramatically. I like the taste of it—when it's good—and I like the strength of beer. You can feel drunkenness coming on when you're drinking beer, and you can decide how quickly you want to proceed toward that end. You can pace yourself with beer, unless you're a college student.

I made a decision at some point in my life to try to stop drinking bad beer. I've heard a Canadian beer expert say in public that there's no such thing as bad beer, but I'm not convinced. If I'm at a party where there's no good beer on offer, I drink wine. I have a better tolerance for uninteresting wine than dodgy beer.

My last Budweiser happened on July 4, 1983, and I think it likely I'll get to my grave without another one. Thank you, but no Bud, no Bud Light, no Coors, no Coors Light. In fact, I don't really want anything that's marketed as "Light" or even "Lite". The English brew beers of varying strengths, beginning at about three per cent alcohol by volume. The lighter beers are often called "session" beers because you can drink them over several hours without falling down. The notion of light beer confuses the English, and early in 2001 Anheuser-Busch announced that it was pulling Bud Light out of the UK because of poor sales.

The excellent Fuller's brewery in London makes three standard draught beers: Chiswick Bitter (3.5%), London Pride (4.1%), and ESB—or Extra Special Bitter—(5.5%). These could be characterized as ordinary bitter, best bitter, and strong ale, respectively. If you're going to be at it all day, you might at least start with Chiswick Bitter. If you were having a few, you'd be grateful for London Pride. And if you have only a short time before last orders, bring on the ESB. These are all wonderful beers, but I would never denigrate the Chiswick Bitter or the London Pride by calling them "light" beers. All three of these beers have been named Champion Beer of Britain at least once and they deserve to be drunk on their own merit, not because you're trying to beat the breathalyzer or save a few calories.

One of the wackier features of America is that you're not allowed to know how strong your beer is. A few American bars post the strengths of their beers, but you won't see it on a bottle or can. Why is this? Presumably because they're stupid. This is a country so full of lawyers that a bottle of tranquilizers will come with a warning: Caution. May cause drowsiness. Well, I should bloody hope so.

It was a decree of the Bureau of Alcohol, Tobacco and Firearms that made it illegal to advertise or even mention the strength of beer in America. This measure was presumably undertaken to keep breweries from plugging their extra-strength beers around the time they started making malt liquors like Colt 45. Ironically, not long thereafter, health-conscious beer drinkers began to look for lighter beers but were barred by federal law from finding out which beers contained less alcohol and exactly how much. In 1995 the Supreme Court struck down the law, but at last count the lawyers were still bickering. Meanwhile American drinkers are still in the dark.

How many Americans are charged with drunk driving every year? Oodles, that's how many. And has not one lawyer been able to defend a client with the argument that the poor sod had no idea how strong his beer was? Not one? I'm no lawyer (he said boastfully) but this defence seems a walk in the park. I have beside me a bottle of Old Crustacean barley wine from the Rogue brewery in Oregon. I know it's strong because it's a barley wine and because it comes in a small bottle. There are some odd numbers on the label, like 120 IBU, which I know stands for International Bitterness Units. It also claims 38° L and 73.1 M, and I'm out of my depth there. It does, however, cite a figure of 26° Plato, and I know that Plato is an obscure European measurement of beer strength. Doing my calculations, I reckon this beer is in the rough ballpark of 10-11 per cent alcohol by volume.

So I know roughly how strong this beer is (very!) because I'm at home with my reference materials, and I'm also reasonably sober. Now, take some American guy who stops in at a bar and decides he wants a change from the usual swill he drinks (but almost certainly doesn't know the strength of). Gimme something out of the ordinary, he tells the barkeep, who sees this as an opportunity to offload some of the Old Crustacean he brought in on a whim. Our guy takes a drink, recoils a bit, and asks the bartender how strong this stuff is. Beats me, says the barkeep, checking the label. It's either 26° Plato or 120 IBU, he reports. That's probably about normal, he says, unwilling to admit that he has no idea.

After a few Old Crustaceans our guy says Nood Gight to the bartender, walks outside, gets into his car, and kills a family of eight on its way to Bible class. Just before our new friend is put away for years, his lawyer points out that no one in America—including the judge, the jury, the DA, and the court reporter—knows how strong Old Crustacean is, least of all his client, and that he cannot possibly be held responsible. Acquitted of all charges, our man sues the bar, the bartender, the Rogue brewery, and the United States government, which has to sell off a couple of tanks to pay for the damages. It might have been such a case that led the Supreme Court to rule against the Alcohol, Tobacco and Firearms law.

There's no such thing as Old Crustacean Light, nor should there be. A beer, whatever its strength, should have its own integrity. The Canadian government, uncharacteristically wisely, requires that brewers print the strength of their bottled beers on the label, so I know that my Arkell Best Bitter from Wellington in Guelph weighs in at a cautious—but tasty—4 per cent, while my Trois Pistoles from Unibroue comes at me aggressively with the gusto of 9 per cent. I'm grateful for this information, so it seems churlish to ask if we could make them list their ingredients on the label as well. If you're putting it in your mouth, you ought to know what's in it, no? Oddly enough, our brewing friends resist this sensible suggestion, presumably because they'd rather not tell us how much corn syrup and other beer cheapeners they're using, not to mention assorted foam enhancing agents and the like. Canada's Food and Drug Act permits more than a hundred ingredients and chemicals and stabilizing agents and things in general in our beer, so we might start seeing much larger beer labels if they had to include all this information. Perhaps some of our brewers are afraid that consumers might be put off beer altogether if they saw what was in it. Remember that all you really need to make beer is malted grain, hops, yeast, and water.

So what's on tap in our pubs? For the most part the choice is dismal, even in the places with eighteen beer taps. One might almost say especially in the places with eighteen beer taps. You'll see the standard imports: Guinness (served too cold), Kilkenny, Boddington's, Smithwick's, and Stella Artois (the beer cleverly designed to fool the unwitting into thinking Belgium makes dull beer so the Belgians get to keep the good stuff for themselves). Then there are the standard domestic brands: Blue, Blue Light, Carlsberg, Carlsberg Light, Foster's, Keith's, Moosehead, Rickard's Red. Then, for the discerning drinker, what we call the premium beers: Creemore

Springs Lager, Amsterdam Nut Brown, Amsterdam Natural Blonde, Upper Canada Lager, and Sleeman Ale. You'll see slight variations from mainstream pub to mainstream pub, but those are your most likely choices.

There was a time not terribly long ago when we would have killed for this sort of beer selection, but we get jaded so quickly. The international picks are not inspiring. It isn't the publicans who insist on serving the Guinness so cold; it's Guinness. Nowadays they even offer an Extra-Cold Guinness to cater to people who want to be seen drinking Guinness but really don't want any taste at all. The domestic choices range from dull to execrable, and the premium brands run the gamut from over-rated to good but unsurprising.

There are no microbrewery beers in this list. (Please note that Rickard's Red is not a microbeer made by some reclusive artisan named Rickard. It's a Molson beer brewed in the same factories that produce the other stuff and marketed to seem to be a beer made by a reclusive artisan. There used to be rumours that it was Molson Export with food colouring, but I couldn't comment on anything as libellous as that.) Sleeman, which also owns and brews Upper Canada, is now a national player. Amsterdam and Creemore are fair-sized regional brewers and have left the micro world far behind them. Amsterdam is okay, but not exciting, so I usually wind up drinking Creemore as my default beer. It's good beer, all right (Michael Jackson, the beer demi-god, once called Creemore the best North American lager), but I wouldn't mind a bit of variety sometimes. A bartender recently said to me that it's good when the staff know your name, but it's better when they know your brand. I agreed quietly, but in fact I don't like to be that predictable. I'd like to go into an eighteen-tap bar and have to think about what I'm going to drink. Or what I'm going to drink first. That's when you know you've got a real choice: I'll start with one of those, move to one of those, and graduate to one of those.

Having done most of my drinking in Canada and England, I lean toward ale over lager. Canadian lager has, in my lifetime, been mostly insipid and characterless. The best you can say for it is that it's cold. If it isn't cold, you're in trouble. Not that the ale has always been much better. When the Big Three—now the Big Two—did all the brewing, one sought out the oddities in their lists: Molson Stock Ale ("The Original Blue"), Toby, Labatt's IPA. The IPA was so good they had to stop making it altogether to avoid embarrassing the other brands.

In 1993, worried about losing a tiny bit of market share to the burgeoning microbreweries, Molson launched its Signature series. These were beers that were brewed by craftsmen in traditional ways, or so we were told in a series of commercials that showed real craftsmen doing authentic artisanal things then switching to the genial, down-home Molson brewmaster making fine ale and lager. Molson was walking a very thin line in this campaign, trying to boast of making beer the proper way without coming right out and saying that everything else they made was crap.

Interestingly, the Signature beers—an ale and a lager—were pretty good, but the people who had switched to microbrewery beers didn't switch back, and the drinkers of Golden and Canadian were unwilling to pay the slightly higher price for better beer. Before long, the commercials stopped appearing and finally, without any fanfare, the Signature brands disappeared forever. Molson's experiment in brewing good beer had come to an end. In fact, of course, they probably sold more of the stuff than most microbreweries were selling, but that's not enough for a company as big as Molson.

The mass brewing scene in Canada is a minefield. The big brands are consumed largely by young folks, who are as fickle as all get-out. A new advertising campaign comes along, and they're off in hot pursuit. It's all about risk. There are fortunes to be made and lost. But you take a beer like Molson Stock Ale and you're dealing with easily predictable numbers. Molson knows, almost to the bottle, how many cases of Stock Ale it's going to sell every month. The only variable is if some old geezer dies carrying his case home. They brew in smaller batches, which is less cost-efficient, and they use better ingredients, which costs a bit more. On the other hand, they never have to advertise it and there's virtually no waste. Ergo, profit.

What would I like to see in a pub? Something surprising. Lately I've seen the occasional Continental beer on tap, a Hacker-Pschorr or a Pilsner Urquell, and I'm encouraged by that. But I see none of the great English beers on draught. The handful of English beers you see here are beers I would never drink in England. And on the rare occasions the good beers turn up, they're never in their real ale form. Sometimes I see them in New York, but never here. The names of Fuller, Adnam, Taylor, and Bateman are unknown in this barren land.

I've given up on the prospect of Molson and Labatt surprising me, but wouldn't it be nice to encounter something unexpected from the micros? I can think of only a handful of Toronto pubs that offer the excellent Raspberry Wheat Beer from the Kawartha Lakes Brewery. This is a beer that dazzles the punters every year at Toronto's Festival of Beer at Fort

York, but only the adventurous find it again until the next August. It's a splendid summer beer, a wheat beer with a perfectly balanced raspberry flavour. There are a lot of people who figure that beer shouldn't taste like raspberries, which is a pretty parochial view in my opinion. Beer shouldn't always taste like raspberries, no question, but every now and then there's nothing nicer. The Kawartha Lakes version has a nice fresh, tart taste that practically makes me purr with pleasure. To me it tastes like beer and like raspberries. Whenever I find it in a pub I almost always have a pint to encourage both the pub and the brewery.

I met an American guy one evening at the Victory Café in Toronto, a fellow called Matt who has been living in Toronto a handful of years. We were drinking Cameron's Auburn Ale, a pleasant enough beer from the Toronto area. Cameron's advertising material makes the point that their president is also their brewmaster, which is certainly not the case at most breweries you could name. Matt told me he had looked forward to coming to Canada and tasting the great microbeers of our land, but that he had been disappointed. He felt that Canada's mass-market breweries were better than Anheuser-Busch, Coors, and Miller's, but that our microbreweries were left in the shade by their American counterparts.

I wanted to disagree with him, but I wasn't sure I had any grounds. Most of our microbreweries are a mite timid, in that characteristic Canadian way. Nobody wants to give offence. The problem is that the market is already packed with beers that don't offend, beers that are bereft of personality. What's the point of going head-to-head with that market? And why would you go into brewing if you're just going to make another predictable beer?

If Quebec ever separates, many of Canada's most interesting beers will become imports. The brewers of Quebec put the rest of Canada to shame. The McAuslan Brewery of Montreal, founded in 1989, creates beers of an English nature, including the celebrated St. Ambroise Oatmeal Stout, perennially rated one of the country's finest beers. St. Ambroise is named for the Sulpician monk who was said to be the first brewer in New France. If his beer was as good as this, McAuslan was justified in elevating Frère Ambroise to sainthood.

The other superstar of Quebec brewing is a company called Unibroue, located in Chambly. Unibroue's inspiration is Belgian beer, and head brewer Gino Vantieghem produces a number of beers that could hold their heads up proudly in Brussels. Like their Belgian counterparts, Unibroue's beers start at 5 per cent alcohol by volume and climb sharply from there.

All the bottled beers are bottle-conditioned—i.e. they undergo a second fermentation in the bottle—so you'll find sediment in your beer. You have the choice of pouring carefully and getting a clear glass or getting the full bottle with some cloudiness and a little yeastier flavour. They're all pretty heady beers, so you'll want to pour carefully in any case. And if you're having a few don't make any serious travel plans.

Back in the early eighties a man named Ed McNally decided that Alberta was ready for some decent beer. Unfortunately the Albertan authorities were not ready, and McNally had to jump through hoops to get a licence for his Big Rock Brewery. This is a story that is repeated practically everywhere beer is made: a pioneer has to go in and get laws changed to allow someone whose name isn't Molson or Labatt to set up a brewery. These days we can get Big Rock Traditional Ale in a few places in Ontario, but I'd like to see more of McNally's Extra Ale, a strong ale more easily found in the western states than in Canada. Pity.

The microbrewery movement in Canada began in British Columbia. They had the first brewpub and the first microbrewery, and the rest of us must bow to them for that. So perhaps it's being uncharitable to question what they've done lately. Oregon and Washington state are hotbeds of imaginative brewing, but north of the border things have gone rather quiet. Is it possible that the good people of British Columbia have fallen under the sway of other drugs? When I first visited Vancouver, I don't recall seeing coffee shops on every corner. Nor, by all accounts, had the cultivation of hydroponic marijuana reached the advanced state I gather it has now attained. British Columbians are either in a state of frenetic caffeine-ridden activity or blissful cannabis-generated catatonia. Given these extremes, a pint of decent microbeer hardly stands a chance, I guess.

I live in Ontario. (Cue the abuse from all other parts of the country; when you've got that out of your system, I'll continue. There we are, thank you. Oh, sorry—you need more time?) Anyway, here in Ontario we have a number of breweries of various sizes. I've mentioned the Raspberry Wheat Beer from Kawartha Lakes. The words "yum" and "yum"—not necessarily in that order—spring to mind. The original Conners beers had a distinctive hoppy flavour that you don't find every day, and a hint of it remains through a few corporate changes—it was bought out by Brick in 1996, a departure from Brick's lager-based history. Not that you find a Conners beer every day, at least not in my neighbourhood.

A man called John Wiggins took over a hardware store in the town of Creemore, Ontario, and turned it into a brewery. Wiggins resolved to concentrate on one beer—a lager inspired by the outstanding Pilsner Urquell, from the Czech town of Pilsen. As noted above, I'm suspicious of Canadian lagers, but Creemore doesn't taste like those others. This is a proper beer, and is justifiably popular.

The Niagara Falls Brewery has created several noteworthy beers, including the bracing Gritstone, a hearty strong ale, and Eisbock, an annual brew made by freezing the wort and removing the ice (which after all is just water), a process that makes the concoction considerably stronger than it would have been. What a beer! (This is not to be confused with the so-called Ice beers brewed by the big guys, which are merely marketing plans in a bottle.) Niagara Falls used to make a Maple Wheat beer which changed flavour very noticeably as it warmed up, a pretty good Kriek (a cherry-flavoured beer of the Belgian school), and a very good stout—all of them now alas gone. (Mind you, if we'd all bought more of them, we'd still have these beers today.) I like their Best Bitter when I occasionally see it, but there is a fear that Niagara Falls has grown cautious. They now make a Saaz Pilsner and a German Weisse, but you'll be hard-pressed to find them outside the Niagara peninsula.

If I had to drink the products of just one Ontario brewery, I suspect they would be the beers of Wellington County, located in Guelph. Guelph, it must be noted, is Ontario's microbrewery capital. Our first modern brewery was Jim Brickman's Brick, and Philip Gosling was not far behind with Wellington. Where Brickman developed lagers, Gosling brewed ales. And not just any ales, but real ales, served as beer should be served: unpasteurized, free from artificial carbonation, and permitted a secondary fermentation in the cask.

Bartenders of my acquaintance have rolled their eyes at mention of Wellington County, complaining of unpredictable beers that didn't behave like other beers. Real ale needs special handling, that's for sure, but Wellington County Ale or Arkell Best Bitter—at their best and served via handpump in the traditional manner—are excellent beers. (I am beginning to see both these beers turn up in pubs in their non-real ale form; they're still decent beers, but a shadow of their optimum selves.) The Arkell is a very English beer with a mere four per cent alcohol kick. The County Ale at five per cent is a hearty beer with a slight nuttiness; in its real ale form it's something to savour.

Beer writer Jamie MacKinnon observes that "light" beer drinkers should cast aside their normal swill and turn to Arkell, which offers more flavour at four per cent that most beers have at five. MacKinnon's argument might convince more people if the beer were more readily available. If I could get it regularly in pubs, I'd drink barrelfuls of the stuff. The bottled version is widely available in beer stores, and comes with my recommendation. There's usually a bottle or two in my fridge, as there should be in yours.

(What else is in my fridge? Let's have a look. I've got a couple of Big Rock Traditional Ales in there, a Gale's Prize Old Ale, a Westmalle Trippel, a Mort Subite Kriek lambic, a 1997 Harvest Ale from J.W. Lees, a Black Chocolate Stout from the Brooklyn Brewery, a 2000 Christmas Ale from the Harvey Brewery, a Maredsous Abbey beer from Belgium, a Bell's Special Double Cream Stout from Kalamazoo, and a handsomely bottled Millennium Ale from the King and Barnes brewery in Sussex, which has been bought and closed down since this beer was made.)

But is my new friend Matt right? Do Canada's microbrews lack the excitement of their American counterparts? If you take Quebec out of the equation, then I have to concede, albeit grudgingly. We certainly lack the variety. I can't remember who brewed the hazelnut-flavoured beer I drank in Chicago in the late nineties, but I do recall going back for more. Imagine if I actually liked hazelnuts.

The character of the western hops used by most American breweries lends a flowery note to a lot of American beers, which some people like and others don't. The Americans have clearly been more adventurous than we have, experimenting with fruits and spices and a wider range of styles than we see in this country. They have a bigger country, of course, with a lot more thirsty people. They also—although this varies from state to state, county to county—tend to have more relaxed legislation governing the making and selling of beer. Canada is only now overcoming laws that prevented beer from being sold in a province in which the brewery did not operate. Moosehead Lager was a famous Canadian beer in the United States long before Canadians outside Nova Scotia ever got to taste it. My first Moosehead was in Detroit.

Compared to Anheuser-Busch practically everything's a microbrewery, but many of the American beers we may think of as micros are rather bigger than that: Anchor, the San Francisco brewery rescued by Fritz Maytag of the appliance family; the Boston Beer Company, creator of the Sam Adams line of beers; Sierra Nevada of Chico, California; and Pete's Brewing Company, maker of Pete's Wicked Ale among others. The Pete of Pete's Wicked became a homebrewer when he discovered that making beer was much quicker than making wine. You can't tour Pete's brewery for the good reason that he doesn't own one, having all his beers brewed under contract by other commercial breweries. The Sam Adams beers were once all brewed under contract until owner Jim Koch—stung by criticism from the likes of Anheuser-Busch (call yourself a craft brewer and you don't even have a brewery?)—took over a closed brewery and began making at least some of his own beer.

Okay, I hear you ask, but what's my favourite beer? It's the sort of question a beer enthusiast does all he or she can to avoid. One day it's going to be a nutty stout, next day it might be a tart cherry-flavoured lambic, and the day after that it'll be a big strong ale. But if the beer Nazis made me pick one beer to drink day in day out for the rest of my life (and promised to make unlimited supplies available, fresh and impeccably maintained), I'd hem and I'd haw a bit.

I'll go as far as to say—not that I expect a lot of contradiction—that the best beer made in Toronto is the Best Bitter Special from the Granite Brewery, and it must be pretty close to being the best in Canada. But I'd probably wind up narrowing down my selection to English draught beers, and then to Fuller's London Pride and Timothy Taylor Landlord. They're both delicious ales, both have been Champion Beer of England (Landlord has won a record four times), and any serious—or even frivolous—drinker would smile with unrestrained pleasure to be handed a pint of either. I've certainly had a good deal more Fuller's, only because the Timothy Taylor is hard to find.

Once on holiday in Dorset a few years back, we found ourselves in a very good pub with a fine selection of beers. I came back from the bar and handed Anne a pint of ale. She sipped it casually and said something not dissimilar to Wow, what is this? It was Timothy Taylor Landlord, and a week or so later it was named Beer of the Year at the Great British Beer Festival. Wow, indeed. So, with respect to Fuller's—not to mention Adnam, Harveys, Uley, Young, Black Sheep, Bateman, Hop Back, and all my other English favourites—make mine a pint of Landlord.

If You Ever Go Across the Sea to Ireland

There is an Irish pub in Chicago... No, let's start again. There's a place in Chicago called Fado—although the Irish probably pronounce it in some way the rest of us will never be able to replicate—that purports to be an Irish pub. Actually, it purports to be six Irish pubs in one. In which case it is probably the first Irish pub—or the first six Irish pubs—to offer valet parking. I have been to this alleged pub because nothing is too good for you, dear reader, and I encourage you to think of a multi-storey quaint Irish pub filled with possibly authentic bric-a-brac and a soundtrack of deafening American pop music. Jaysus, the missus and me exclaimed, let's get the Fado out of here. And so we did.

The Irish have become very sexy in recent years—well, perhaps not the actual Irish themselves, but the larger concept of Irishness—and there has been a lot of money to be made from the notion of Celtic wonderfulness. And rightly so, up to a point. Ireland truly is a grand place. I once spent a week in the West Cork town of Baltimore without ever finding out when closing time was, which was possibly due to the story we heard that the local Garda—the one local policeman—was retiring and perhaps didn't want any outstanding charges hanging over him.

I like Ireland, and now so does everybody. Across England perfectly decent pubs have been transformed into mock Irish pubs for the duration of the Celtic craze, presumably to be changed into German bierstüben or Greek tavernas or whatever becomes sexy once we all tire of celebrating the craic in fake Irish pubs. New York, of course, has long had Irish bars, frequently staffed by young Irish bartenders who have usually arrived that morning from Limerick. What New York Irish bars are going to do for staff now that young Irish people are all far too busy toiling in Silicon Bog and becoming dotcom millionaires I cannot imagine.

The irony of fake Irish pubs is that the true Irish pub is even less easy to typecast than the English pub. Many of them double as grocery shops, newsagents, or undertakers. Outside Dublin, many Irish pubs look like someone's living room, and they sometimes are. In Limerick with my friend Kieran Simpson—a native of that city—we were sat in a pub in his old neighbourhood when he exclaimed that we were sitting in what had once been the bedroom of an old boyhood friend.

And so to Fionn MacCool's, a large Irish pub on Toronto's Esplanade. Once an ignored, almost shunned, part of town, the area behind the Hummingbird Centre (as we must now call the O'Keefe Centre) has a number of old warehouses that now accommodate entertainment concepts. It began, I suppose, with the Old Spaghetti Factory, a lively barn of a place that brought "fun" to Italian food. Like spaghetti had always been deadly serious before this.

Fionn MacCool was, by all accounts, a legendary Irish hero and father of Ossian, but I suspect that the pub's name was chosen because it sounded, like, MacCool, you know? I am told that on St. Patrick's Day the young people start lining up in early afternoon for the evening's festivities, and good luck to them.

On one of the other 364 days of the drinking year, Fionn MacCool's was a little quieter, with only the insistent , if discreet, boompety-boom of the pop music without which no one would know if they were having fun or not. Otherwise it was just the craic, or what other people call conversation. The drinkers closest to me were talking about golf. Does that constitute craic, I wonder. I noticed that when the Celtic rage began (and before he got sent up for eight years for doing in Jez Quigley), *Coronation Street's* Jim McDonald started talking about the craic a lot more than he had, as in "What's the craic, boys?" Also, before Celtomania, we used to spell it crack, but that might have confused the users of the cocaine by-product. If Washington mayor Marion Barry had been smarter he would have claimed that it wasn't the crack cocaine he was after but a bit of the old traditional Irish craic. He might have got away with it too. Like O.J. Simpson, he could have vowed to spend the rest of his natural days seeking out the perpetrators of craic.

I wasn't hungry, but I did take a gander at Fionn MacCool's menu, because I know my readers care about these things. It boasted Celtic Fare like Bunratty Castle Caesar and Roast Beef Panini, presumably just like Granny used to make, saints preserve her. Sometimes it's a blessing not to be hungry. I did notice that the female servers—what we used to call waitresses in less enlightened times—were wearing those pert little tartan skirts, which I'm guessing are meant to suggest step dancing rather than private school girls. No doubt once the live music gets going in the evening the servers break into a sort of Riverdance routine. Unfortunately I couldn't stick around for that.

There's no shortage of Irish-style pubs for the local drinker, though most of them—it must be said—are not so much Irish as "Irishish". The James Joyce on Bloor Street West used to be a hamburger joint, but now it bears the proud Irish name of the writer who left Ireland as soon as possible and never went back. The sign outside carries the promise— Traditional Irish Pub—but I tried in vain to buy a pound of potatoes and the *Cork Examiner*. The only concession to Irish decor comes from a number of promotional items for assorted Irish beers, but there's a kind of Irish honesty to that as well. Real Irish pubs are very much as you find them, and if they have illustrations of Killarney on the walls you can bet they're pitching themselves at the tourist market. Likewise, there didn't seem to be anything Irish about Elizabeth Dooley's out in the west end, though I was tempted by the fish cakes on the menu.

Scruffy Murphy's, up on Eglinton Avenue East, seemed a nice enough place, with a lively bartender and a number of contented regulars, but the design spoke to me of the faux-genteel English suburban pub of the sixties, not like anything you'd see in Ireland. And I wonder how Irish people feel about this perpetual scruffy thing. In his fine book *McCarthy's Bar*, Pete McCarthy writes of seeing in Killarney a hotel bar called Scruffies, which employed a couple of large men to guarantee that no one scruffy got in.

This whole Irish pub business is presumably based on the notion that no one drinks like the Irish. As Spike Milligan notes in *Puckoon*, "Many people die of thirst but the Irish are born with one." A wonderful book that, by the way. I've read *Ulysses* and I've read *Puckoon*, but I bet I'll re-read *Puckoon* first. What's interesting about the Irish and drinking is that they settled pretty quickly on what they liked. There's whiskey or three kinds of beer: stout (usually Guinness), ale (inevitably Smithwicks), or lager (which was traditionally Harp). If you were close enough to Cork, you might get Murphy's or Beamish's Stout, by way of variety. Harp—the national lager—has given way to the global Carlsberg, and indeed if you find a drop of Harp in Ireland today it'll probably have been brewed in Canada. That's how mad the world is. Long the only ale choice in Ireland, Smithwicks has in recent years been joined by the likes of Kilkenny and Caffrey's, fine traditional ales of the 1990s, shot through and through with traditional Irish nitrogen. There is now even a Canadian guy brewing new and interesting beers in Dublin, practically in the shadow of Guinness's St. James Gate brewery, and so far living to tell the tale. You'll occasionally see his wares on Canadian liquor store beer shelves.

Bordering dangerously on being an Irish Concept pub is Dora Keogh, on the Danforth. Opened in 1997, Dora Keogh is a handsome room with that vaguely Georgian look of the Dublin pub, all high ceilings and right angles, but with the hard, un-upholstered furnishings of the country pub. What it also had for me was a surprise. I didn't expect to meet Fionn MacCool at his eponymous pub, or James Joyce at his, and I'd have been surprised to meet Elizabeth Dooley at all out in the west end. And I'm not sure I'd have wanted to encounter Scruffy Murphy.

But there really is a Dora Keogh. She's an attractive redhead and I met her, just standing there at the bar, so she was. She told me that her mother was very proud of her, having her name on a pub and all, and quite rightly too. I'm sure the Duke of York's mother is similarly proud of her son whenever she comes to town.

Not being an investigative journalist, I never quite established Ms. Keogh's role in the operation, but I had a nice chat with John Maxwell, who actually owns the place. Maxwell—who also owns Allen's next door and P.J. O'Brien downtown—is a slight former New Yorker who has been in the hospitality lark since 1964 and clearly knows what he's about. Running places like Dora Keogh, he says, is about "passion", and he wants his places to be not only where someone like me might be comfortable but also places his deceased father and elderly mother could be proud of. It was getting a bit late when he mentioned that he hoped he died before I did because he didn't want to be in this business when the likes of me were no longer around. Maxwell does not cater particularly to young people, which is a blessed change in this youth-crazed marketplace. Looking worriedly around, he confides that he doesn't even like young people, referring darkly to "feral youth", an expression I liked so much I made a point of writing it down on a paper napkin.

One of the key things in today's hospitality biz is catering to groups, and Maxwell has thought of this in his design for Dora Keogh. The pub has a self-contained snug with its own access to the bar, which is a nice touch, and a kitchen in the back that can be booked for a group of eight to fourteen for a private dinner. And private it is, with your own Irish server and plates stacked high with roast lamb (it's always been the lamb when I've been there) and vegetables and two kinds of potatoes. It's like having a big family dinner without actually having any of your family there. You can decide for yourself whether that's a good thing.

If it's authenticity you're looking for, the toilets at Dora Keogh are labelled *Fir* and *Mna*, a couple of Gaelic words not in common use in these parts. My wife got caught by this confusing dilemma in Limerick once, so we've learned the hard way which is which. You might think that F and M might correspond to Female and Male, and *Mna* is clearly an anagram of Man, but you'd be barking up the wrong tree in this case. I wonder how often in an average evening the staff are called upon to usher non-Irish drinkers to the correct loo.

Probably the most Irish pub in Toronto is McVeigh's, at Church and Richmond. It's been there forever, or at least since 1961—which, in the drinking life of this town, is pretty close to forever. It's a dark room, with the odd Irish mural you can't see terribly well in the gloom. I was served one day recently by Mr. McVeigh himself, a gentleman of a certain age. I felt sheepish asking for a receipt—listen, when you write this sort of book, you keep receipts—and I got the feeling I was the first customer who had asked for a receipt in his forty years on the premises. I got the receipt, but he didn't talk to me again.

Luckily for me, other people did. Fair enough, they weren't Irish, but we can't all be. They were at least Scottish, which is not far off. Patrick was over from Motherwell to visit family, particularly his uncle Jimmy, who hadn't been well. Jimmy looked pretty good that afternoon, with teeth that occurred enthusiastically if sporadically. Patrick is a train engineer back in Scotland. Although he acknowledges that driving a train is a lifetime dream for some people, it's just a job for him. What he likes is something going wrong, something he can fix. That's the job satisfaction for him. I wasn't sure if I'd want to be on Patrick's train, knowing that the guy up front was aching for some misadventure.

When I arrived the conversation—craic, if you like—was about Billy Connolly, the Scottish comedian who apparently drops into McVeigh's whenever he's in town. Mr. McVeigh was hearing no ill of Billy Connolly, whom he described as a "humble man" who could, after all, drink anywhere at all. Jimmy and Patrick acknowledged that he could indeed drink anywhere at all, but felt nonetheless that he had forgotten his roots. As Patrick said, "His personal remarks about Scotland do not sit well with me, Mr. McVeigh." There was unlikely to be a lasting consensus about Billy Connolly, and Mr. McVeigh went off to serve other customers.

We were joined by Ian, another expatriate Scot, who likes darts and jokes. Patrick told a variation on a Superman joke of which I am very fond, and Ian followed with the story of a long-married couple, the wife of which finds her husband drinking intoxicating beverages early one morning, clearly in an upset state. When asked what was the matter, he reminded her of the time she was sixteen and pregnant and her father had told him that if he didn't marry her he—the father—would have him—the husband—charged with rape and that he'd serve twenty years for it. "You're not still bothered about that", the wife says. He shakes his head sadly. "I'd have been a free man today," he says.

We had a good laugh over that, and Jimmy's teeth—well, you couldn't take your eyes off them—were much in evidence. Ian followed with the other Superman joke I know, also well received, and Jimmy joined in with a Newfie joke. Patrick made it clear that he didn't appreciate racist humour, but Jimmy would not be gainsaid.

Patrick told me that, as a Celt, he cared most about family—he was not in Canada to see the sights—and having a sociable time in a pub. The English, he said, looking at me a bit accusingly, I thought, were more concerned with their houses. I'd have stayed longer, but I had to go and see a guy about getting a conservatory added on to the library in the west wing.

I forgot to go to the gents' and check the place for condom machines. In Ireland in the summer of 1993 I recall seeing such a public convenience in a public convenience and thinking what a revolutionary sight this was in a country that not long previously had banned any sort of birth control, even for respectable married couples. There was no mistaking this machine for anything else. It used strong words like "ribbed" that had not been seen in Ireland since St. Patrick drove the snakes out. No doubt some people were made uneasy by this blatant display of the prophylactic arts, and a few days later in a different pub I saw a plain white metal box attached to the wall of a corridor leading to the facilities. It gave no hint of its contents, but a small sign beside a coin-collecting device asked the passerby to insert two one-punt coins. Perhaps it dispensed condoms, perhaps small tokens of absolution. There was no evidence that the machine issued receipts, so I didn't take the chance. And now I'll never know.

If you ever go across the sea to Ireland—and if you haven't you should—it's important to keep your wits about you. Certainly it seemed to be the case that the barmen of West Cork greeted their customers with the words "Y'all right?" Which, to a polite Canadian, deserved the response, "Yes, we're fine, thank you very much." Whereupon the barman turned away with a quizzical look and went back to preparing the perfect pint of stout for the fellow down the bar. What we slowly discovered was that "Y'all right?" was a short form for "Do you need a beverage of some sort given that you've come all this way, so?" It still seemed presumptuous to

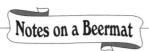

respond straightaway with a drink order, so we settled upon a Canadian compromise: "Yes, thank you, we're fine altogether except for the lack of a drink so perhaps we could trouble you for a couple of pints of Smithwicks, thank you very much."

I am Canadian (But I Also Like The Taste of Beer)

The people of Canada have a pretty mixed bag of drinking choices. A lot of it is luck. Maritimers, of course, have a lively drinking life but no decent beer to drink (except of course for the wonderful Granite Brewery in Halifax). I'm sorry, but it has to be said.

But at least they have a lively drinking life. In early 1990 I was in Ottawa for a spot of business, and late in the day I found myself downtown, thirsty, and with an hour or so to kill before I headed for the airport. I was aware of the reputation Canada's capital city had enjoyed vis-à-vis fun back in the past, but I was confident that things had changed. I walked into one bar, and about five minutes later I walked into a second bar. Friends, I heard the words "last call" spoken in earnest twice before seven o'clock. I was never so glad to get on a plane bound for Toronto, which suddenly took on the aura of Sin City.

People who know Ottawa tell me I was just in the wrong place. (It was worse than that: I was in two wrong places.) I am assured that there are pubs in Ottawa that stay open as late as eight or nine, and if I'd had a couple more hours before my flight I might have found them.

Here I am perpetuating the notion that Ottawa is a dull place. When my friend John Jackson was an undergraduate at Carleton in the mid-sixties, I went to visit him. This was, of course, still the era when you were required to be significantly older than we were to drink in Ontario, so we—like practically everyone else in Ottawa—drove to Hull to raise a little heck. In Hull—it being Quebec and all—all that was required was that you had the cash to pay for your beer. That was exactly the kind of ID I was carrying, and I had a wonderful time, though my recollections are admittedly fuzzy. I vaguely remember singing along with the Beatles' *Act Naturally*, a popular hit of the time.

Those were my first several beers in Quebec, but not my last. The Québécois, of course, laughed at us Ontario types and our absurd drinking laws. Our bars closed at midnight, if they opened at all. We were repressed; they had joie de vivre. In Ontario, joie de vivre was an indecency. Practicing joie de vivre in the presence of minors constituted a major violation of the Criminal Code. When I got to Montreal, I was like wow, as the young people delight in saying. They had joie de vivre and style as well, which put them two up on us. It was at Expo 67 that I first got drunk twice in one day. It was my attempt at joie de vivre, if not necessarily style. Mind you, it's easier when you're young, isn't it? You recover from lunchtime and off you go again. Those were the days.

For all their superiority, it must be said that there were a couple of questionable traits to Québécois drinking life. I mean, what was with these tavernes, for Pete's sake? They seemed to close at midnight, just like our bars, and didn't allow women. I think drinking with women is fun. In the early eighties I tried to take my wife to Toe Blake's celebrated bar in Montreal. Nothing doing. That chromosomal thing was a problem. Did she just sit back and take it? Of course she didn't. She went shopping, leaving me to drink at Toe Blake's. What a woman.

Although it was the extremes of the country—Vancouver (Horseshoe Bay and Granville Island Brewing) and Halifax (the Granite Brewery)—that got good beer going in Canada, it was Quebec that took it to new heights. Are there better beers being brewed on a commercial scale in this country than those produced by Unibroue of Chambly or Brasserie McAuslan of Montreal? Of course there aren't. Unibroue took its inspiration from the Belgians, and it brews a number of exotic beers of disturbingly high alcohol content. Its motto—Boire Moins, Boire Mieux—is altogether appropriate when your beer weighs in at nine per cent alcohol by volume. I am indebted to Stephen Beaumont for pointing out that Unibroue in 2000 began offering a twelve-pack of their beers in some Ontario beer stores, a fine selection of beers only a few of which had ever been seen in Ontario before. They actually make a 6.5 per cent beer for the St. Hubert chicken restaurant chain in Quebec; it's in the twelve-pack.

As you cross this great country you encounter all sorts of interesting local customs. In the summer of 1972 ("Didn't it rain, children? Lord, didn't it rain!") I was hitchhiking in an easterly direction across the Prairies, whenever the rain let up enough. The rains of 1972 verged on the biblical. This particular day was a cool day, with a sinister wind at my back. I was on the outskirts of a town called Lloydminster that straddles the Alberta-Saskatchewan border. I might have been there a day or two at this point. Every hour or two a car passed me by, pointedly speeding up as they approached.

Suddenly a Volkswagen van stopped. The pulse rates of hitchhikers of that era were known to accelerate at the sight of Volkswagen vans, such was the hitchhiker-pick-up quotient of their drivers. Unfortunately this particular Volkswagen van was on the other side of the Trans-Canada Highway and pointed in a westerly direction, but it was nice to see that vehicles in the Prairies actually did have brakes. I hadn't seen much evidence of any slowing-down mechanism so far. Anyway, what the hell, maybe I'd go back westward. Eastward was no great shakes.

You know what they say about Canada, that it's a very small population strung out (and I do mean strung out) across a huge land mass. So we should not be surprised to run into our friends in a place like Lloydminster. I'd never been to Lloydminster before, so I was surprised. I wouldn't be now. Yes, the Volkswagen van carried three old pals from Toronto who were driving westward to Victoria.

We decided to call it a day, travel-wise, and we booked into a campsite somewhere in the greater Lloydminster area. Settled in, someone proposed a beer. By a narrow four-nil vote the measure was passed, so we made our way into downtown and found a bar. I don't remember what it was called—possibly the Palace or the Paramount or something like that—but we walked toward it with resolution. These were four young fellows who liked a drink. As we arrived we saw a sign on the front door, a sign that stopped us big city guys in our tracks. The sign read: "Please use door." Our bravado left us. What kind of place was this that drinkers had to be informed to use the door? How did they usually get in? Would we look like a pack of wussy eastern bastards if we didn't come bursting through the wall like everybody else? At the risk of standing out, we used the door. And we were just fine. Funny what you remember about a place.

I stand by my theory that you can learn a lot by hanging out in bars. I got drunk in Dawson City one evening with a guy who was AWOL from the Dempster Highway building project. It took them twenty years to build a 450-mile road through country that didn't take to road building, and every now and then one of the guys would get a little stir crazy and hitch a ride into town for the purpose of sitting in a bar and getting shit-faced. I, for one, would not blame such a man.

This particular man was well into the aforementioned process by the time we fell into conversation, and it became clear to me that this was a man with a dream. The dream in question was to build and operate a sort of lodge somewhere on the Dempster Highway, catering to the many travellers who would surely make their way up that gravel road once it finally got done. What he needed—and this was where I came in—was a partner. Was I such a person? Frankly, I didn't think so. My lack of capital was matched by the absence of any relevant lodge-building skills, and an aversion to remoteness and an antipathy to black flies and mosquitoes wouldn't have helped much either.

I hope his dream came true, and that enough people drive up the Dempster Highway to make such a dream viable. If you haven't been up there, I can tell you—having done it all via the hitchhiker's thumb—that it's a hell of a long way from practically anywhere. To get to the Alaska Highway you need to get to the top of British Columbia. Then you drive a very long way north-by-northwest into the Yukon. When you get to Whitehorse you leave the Alaska Highway and head farther north again. Quite some time later, when you've gone farther north than most North Americans of European origins ever go, you're at the very beginning of the Dempster Highway. No wonder people get thirsty.

As a resident of Toronto, I am a bit reluctant to write about Vancouver. Torontonians and Vancouverites don't get along very well, even though it is only the regular infusion of Torontonians that keeps Vancouver from losing its status as a city. Scratch a Vancouverite—not that it's a practice I advocate—and chances are you'll find an expatriate Hogtowner. Like religious converts, these newfound westerners are the most wild-eyed believers in the mythology, the most likely to promulgate the idea that Vancouverites routinely go skiing in the morning and sailing in the afternoon. There is no recorded instance of anyone actually skiing and sailing in the same day, but the belief that it can be done holds a lot of people in thrall. In fact Vancouver's traffic nowadays makes such a practice unlikely, and in any case Vancouverites don't have the time for it, having to work like Torontonians to make the payments on their leaky condos.

What the residents of these two cities have in common is an irrational smugness, an utterly unfounded belief that they are living in the best city in the world. We grasp desperately at warm comments from visitors, keen to be noticed by outsiders. The best of all is when we get acknowledged by international studies that rank the cities of the world. These surveys invariably come up with widely divergent results, and sometimes Toronto does well and other times it's Vancouver.

Early in 2001 we learned—and don't think there wasn't a bit of teeth-gnashing in Toronto—that Vancouver had been named the best city in the world for "quality of life", and for the second year running. (We'd have been more upset in Toronto by this news had we not been preoccupied by the impending arrival of the International Olympic Committee, coming to judge our Olympic bid. We were desperate to host the Games, if only to annoy the hell out of Vancouver.) The point, of course, is who's conducting these studies. If the Campaign for Real Ale names Vancouver the best city in the world, I'll be on the next plane. If Mick Jagger or John Updike or Jane Jacobs tells me Vancouver's the best city in the world, I'll take at least pay attention. It is worth noting that Vancouver was actually tied for first with that most exciting of cities, Zurich, justifiably famous for its discreet banks and not a lot else.

Who decreed that Vancouver is the best city in the world? Does the name William M. Mercer mean anything to you? William M. Mercer, it turns out, is not so much a guy as a bunch of guys. A bunch of accountants and actuaries, if you must know. (No wonder they also liked Zurich.) Frankly, being named the best city in the world by a firm of accountants and actuaries is not the highest possible recommendation. I doubt they're losing sleep in Paris and New York. (And if you like you can label this sour grapes from a resident of Toronto—tied for nineteenth with Montreal.)

What I remember about drinking in Vancouver the first time I got there was the funny licensing hours. Someone explained to me that bars could be open for any consecutive twelve hours. The obvious twelve were noon to midnight, but I remember a Granville Street bar that opened at 9 a.m. It had to close early, sure enough, but it got a bustling breakfast crowd. And I mean bustling.

British Columbia was in the vanguard of interesting drinking in Canada. It had the first microbrewery and the first brewpub. By all that's right and decent, it should be far and away the pub capital of the country. So where did it all go wrong?

I went to a conference in Vancouver in the latter half of the nineties. I looked forward to it, I really did. It had been a decade since I had been out to lotus land, and I looked forward to supping some of these celebrated BC microbeers in the new pubs that had surely popped up all over town. I got into Vancouver in mid-afternoon, made my way to my hotel, and at about five o'clock I strolled out for a refreshing pint. I was centrally located, so I foresaw no difficulties. At 7:30 I sat down and celebrated the first of the day. I seemed to have covered miles. I had a couple of pints, listened to an alarmingly redneck conversation going on at the next two barstools, and got a definite whiff from the barkeep that the place was about to close. When I say whiff, I mean he said it was going to close, which might have been his way of getting me out of there before the guys next to me noticed

I had a beard. It was still light. I went to a nearby liquor store, bought a six-pack of decent beer, and headed back to my hotel room.

While I was in Vancouver I tried to find out where I had gone wrong. I kept meeting local residents and I made a point of asking them where they drank. Many of them weren't sure, which I took as a bad sign. A number of them had to think about it for a long time, which wasn't encouraging either. The handful who were able to come up with a name all came up with the same name. Where else would that happen? Ask twenty New Yorkers where they drink and you'll get at least eighteen different answers. Ask twenty Torontonians and you'll get at least ten. The only bar Vancouverites could think of was the Yaletown Brewing Company, and that was probably because the conference had held its opening night party there.

(To be fair, I am given to understand that there are now a few more places to drink in Vancouver than when I was last there, though to this day no one I speak to seems to know about them. Stephen Beaumont lists five brewpubs in Vancouver, but on a per capita basis Victoria surely puts the rest of the country to shame, brewpub-wise.)

(All right, while I'm being fair to British Columbia—and it goes against the grain, I have to say—it is worth noting that Stephen Beaumont, in his *Great Canadian Beer Guide*, awards three or more stars to 75 beers across Canada. Of these, 24 are B.C. beers, compared to 21 Quebec beers and a mere 20 Ontario brews—the Prairies muster 6 and the Atlantic Provinces 4, by the way—so I'll shut up now. Well, actually, I probably won't. If B.C. has all those fine beers, it's all the more criminal that you can't find anywhere to drink them.)

Coffee you can get in Vancouver. This was just before designer java hit Toronto in a huge way, and it was a novelty to see coffee shops on every corner. But novelty takes you only so far. My theory is that Vancouverites are so laid-back that only caffeine keeps them from sinking into total torpor. As a hypertense central Canadian, I need the calming effect of the depressants to simmer me down a bit. You can keep your stimulants, thanks very much; the last thing I want is to stay awake through all of this.

It turns out, of course, that there were at least two decent places to drink in Vancouver. A friend at the same conference went to a ballgame at the old Nat Bailey Stadium and reported a fine environment and a choice of decent beers, which is more than can be said for attending a game in Toronto. Mind you, Vancouver's baseball team has since left town (and gone to Zurich, for all I know), so I can't vouch for anything of the sort now.

My beer discovery was even less predictable. By a quirk of scheduling for which I can't take the credit, I had a free day before the conference began. This was a booksellers' conference, so I had some bookstores I needed to see, one of which was the University of British Columbia Bookstore, a considerable bus ride from downtown. I had a good look around and contemplated my next move. It was the sort of day the rest of Canada assumes never happens in Vancouver. We hope it doesn't, anyway, unless we're actually there. It was warm and sunny and perfect in every way. An afternoon at the beach seemed called for. Sadly I hadn't thought to bring swimwear; happily I happened to know that the beach nearest to the UBC Bookstore had no dress code. More of an undress code, if the truth be told.

I had been to Wreck Beach—Canada's most celebrated (and possibly first) nude beach—half a lifetime before, on just such a day, and I made the long trek down the hill in a fury of nostalgia. I hadn't kept my boyish figure, but I thought it unlikely I'd run into anyone I knew, and I didn't. Though heaven knows the place was busy. Wreck Beach had retained its raffish, sixties feel, but it had changed a bit. For all I know, the people were the same people I had seen a quarter century before, or possibly their sons and daughters, but there were no LIP grants or anything of the sort to sustain today's residents.

The people of Wreck Beach had to support themselves now, and they seemed to be doing so excellently. There was hardly anything you couldn't get or have done at Wreck Beach. You could rent a hammock or an umbrella, have your hair braided (not likely in my case—see author photo), get a henna tattoo, or buy fresh baked goods. A young man in a fez and a change belt flogged turkish coffee, an admirable young woman sold shot glasses of Southern Comfort, and several vendors did the rounds with coolers full of beer. It wasn't clear to me how all this commercial activity was being carried out. I assume some Mr. Big was bringing the beer in by boat, but it was always cold and there were some palatable microbrewery beers available.

For all my obnoxious Toronto-centric prejudices, I had to admit that, with a snow-capped peak off in the distance across the water, I couldn't think of any watering hole back home that offered such a view or such a relaxed dress code. (I've often wondered, for instance, if you'd be served at a Shoeless Joe's franchise if you turned up barefoot.) Where Vancouverites drink in bad weather I still don't know, and I never did get to the Yaletown Brewing Company.

The Walk to the Ballpark

I hate to go on about how primitive drinking conditions in Toronto used to be, but it is a recorded fact that in 1977 there was one major league ballpark on the planet that catered expressly to abstainers, and it existed in Toronto. Not that it was much of a ballpark. Tucked into one corner of a concrete football stadium, the baseball part of Exhibition Stadium was a cold, windy spot where most of the seats faced somewhere other than the makeshift baseball diamond. Frankly, sitting on a cold metal seat, absorbing a cold wind off Lake Ontario, did not always make one cry out for an equally cold beer.

Still, it was the principle of the thing. There is something in human nature that hates to be told we're not allowed to do something. Our political leaders in this part of the world have never liked to trust us—the drinking public—to do the right thing. Older readers may recall a series of television ads in the eighties which were designed to encourage us to behave sensibly. You Are Your Own Liquor Control Board, we were told. Hallelujah, we Ontario drinkers cried. Power to the people! Alas, we learned the next day that the Liquor Control Board of Ontario had not been disbanded. The government had not, in fact, relinquished control over us and our nasty habits. It wanted merely to get us to do its work for it. We were our own liquor control boards but, just in case we didn't manage it properly, we could be overruled by the government.

It was that kind of thinking that determined that beer in the ballpark was a bad idea. People might actually drink it, and then where would we be? (Not long afterwards the province of Ontario permitted bars to sell drinks cheap at certain times of day. Happy Hour proved to be wildly popular, so it was quickly banned. It would have been fine had no one taken advantage of it.) Eventually, of course, the forces of progress took over and beer drinking was allowed at Exhibition Stadium. It turned out to be all right, needless to say, because the beer was so bad and so expensive that only a fool or a lawyer would want or could afford to abuse it.

The idea, then as now, is to have a drink before you get there. That was definitely the case in 1977. Watching the early Blue Jays sober was a mug's game. One July day I decided to go see the locals in action. I knew that a little advance drinking was needed, so I started at noon. I would have started earlier, but noon was when the bars opened in 1977. I like to walk, so I went to a second bar, then a third. I know for a fact that the Blue Jays were playing the Minnesota Twins, but don't ask me who won.

Thus the Walk to the Ballpark was born. Drinking alone from noon until game time could be interpreted as evidence of a drinking problem. Or possibly a social problem. In any case, the Walk to the Ballpark needed more people. Terry Shoffner, a genial graphic artist from Arkansas, was persuaded that this combination of walking and drinking was a good thing, and he and I constituted the second Walk, with sporadic help from friends along the way. I don't even remember who was playing.

With the passing years the Walk to the Ballpark grew in popularity. Otherwise responsible people—some of them with mortgages, then cell phones and eventually Palm Pilots —took the day off work to tour the bars and pubs of Toronto in congenial company. And, at least in the early years, we actually went to the baseball game. We went to baseball games even though the Blue Jays were becoming more competitive and more of a draw. We sat way out beyond the right field fence one year and couldn't see the ball, sitting in seats that faced practically nothing at all but an empty football field. I vaguely recall being cranky that year. I recall it because people regularly remind me of it. I believe it was the last time the Walk to the Ballpark went to the Ballpark.

The following year—this might have been about 1982—Walk day was cold and raw. We sat in the old Palace Hotel at King and Strachan, the last bar before the ballpark, and the younger, keener participants were beginning to whine about it being close to game time. I wouldn't have sent a dog out on an evening like that, let alone fifteen or twenty people who had been drinking for more than seven hours, but tradition seemed to call for some sort of action.

Just then a vision appeared in the form of a man called Bill Martin, who does something in advertising. I believe it's something creative. Bill had missed the Walk so far, but suddenly here he was, standing in the doorway with our waiter, a man in the mandatory white shirt and black pants of the day and holding a tray filled with glasses of beer. As the proprietor of the Walk to the Ballpark I had to make a snap decision. We stayed exactly where we were. Hypothermia, after all, is a dreadful thing, and I didn't like to think of the legal repercussions of sending people off to a freezing cold ballpark. In any case, since then the ballpark has been more a metaphor than a destination.

1982 might also have been the year of The Only Punch Ever Thrown (To Date) On The Walk to the Ballpark. We discuss it to this day. Was Russ Hughes justified in introducing his fist to the general region of Jon Comerford's nose? History has yet to pass its definitive judgement. What we know is this: Russ Hughes was sitting in a chair, while Jon Comerford stood behind him, behaving in what Russ saw as an annoying manner. I believe I'm right in reporting that the words "Cut it out" had escaped Russ's lips at least once, which is possibly fair warning. Did young Comerford cut it out? He did not. Finally—and I have run this episode through on my internal VCR a hundred times—Russ, without leaving his seat, turned around and delivered a blow to the Comerford beak. This caught us all by surprise, but especially Jon Comerford. The power with which Russ connected from a seated position, his back to the punchee, was impressive.

Apart from the Hughes-Comerford dustup, the Walk has been violence-free if you discount the occasional food fight. Well, okay, there was the time that Michael Lee was removed from the Wheat Sheaf for defending the honour of his sister-in-law, but no punches were thrown. What is far more likely is the spectacle of people falling in love, or something that might pass for it. Sometimes this attraction is ill-fated, if not altogether inappropriate, but it is not completely unknown for people to get lucky on the Walk. (See chapter on Drinking and Sex, with particular reference to the possible debilitating effects of large quantities of beer.)

It seems extraordinary now, but in our early days we used to get to some thirteen bars and still get to the ball game by 7:30. Nowadays we get to ten bars over about fourteen hours, which is thoroughly manageable. It's all about pacing, eating whenever possible, and taking on water as if one were running a marathon. Even so, we still see the occasional sprinter on the Walk, and the consequences are usually dire. In the early eighties a young man called Ray—I won't embarrass him by mentioning his last name (Chong)—was regularly the first drinker with an empty glass at each stop, egging the rest of us on to drink up and keep moving. At the El Mocambo he stood up, informed us that we were crazy, and vanished. Two years later he attempted to do the Walk on a diet of nothing but Black Russians. This was a spectacularly bad idea, though he did get two bars farther this time, not crashing out until the Rex Hotel. I wonder what Ray's up to these days.

It's a mixed group of people who make up the Walk to the Ballpark. We usually have at least two lawyers (when what we really need is doctors), some riff-raff from the book trade, a philosopher, an importer of hi-fi equipment (or whatever we call it these days), the odd teacher, an accountant, a comedian, a politician, a landscape architect, a historian, one or two guys who seem to do things with computers, several people who work in offices, and a bunch of people who may or may not have jobs of any sort. The beauty of the Walk is that the constant change of venue encourages one to consort with different people along the way. If you stay long enough you'll talk to everybody.

The Walk takes in a variety of watering holes, from neo-English pubs to barely transformed taprooms, from a campus hangout to a biker bar. It takes in two of Toronto's oldest bars and one of our funniest waitresses. It's usually a Friday, usually in June. If you encounter a pub crawl on a Friday in June, say hello. Or, better yet, join us.

The Agenda (more or less):

11 a.m.: Meet at the Madison, second floor. Drinkers straggle in, get the first of the day under their belts. Old friendships renewed, new ones inaugurated. Greet the engaging Igor Martin, who not only turns up every year but who walks from his home in suburban Etobicoke just to warm up for the event.

Noon: Short stroll to the Ferret and Firkin, formerly the Sticky Wicket. Lunch is ordered and eaten, then massive undertaking of figuring out the bill follows. Generally one or two new faces who find it difficult to get up before noon, plus a few cheerleaders who turn up for lunch then go back to work.

1:45 p.m.: Congenial hike down Spadina Avenue to the Graduate Students' Union pub. Good beer, pleasing ambience, not much incentive to leave. But reality calls, and we're off again.

3:15 p.m.: We cross College Street, passing from midtown to downtown and getting serious at last. Crowds beginning to gather in the street to cheer us on. And into Grossman's, historic if grungy old bar famed for blues and other musical events, also venue for Milton Acorn's being named The People's Poet in 1970. Toilets upgraded slightly in about 1998 after generations of acknowledgement as Ontario's worst. Lousy beer, dim surroundings, but Dawn the waitress is the funniest in town.

4:05 p.m.: Begin the longest trek of the Walk, zig-zagging (deliberately) in a southeasterly direction through Chinatown and Grange Park to the

Rex Hotel, a great Toronto watering hole. Usually pick up a few new drinkers fresh from the workplace. I always hate to leave the Rex, but...

5:40 p.m.: A short walk to the Beverley. Now that we're on Queen Street, the walks between bars become shorter. It's men-and-boys, sheep-and-goats time, i.e. telling one from the other. Weather permitting we climb to the rooftop patio of the Bev, the pleasing urban vista offering some consolation for the appalling choice of draught beer. More post-work stragglers show their dreary, duty-obsessed faces.

7:00 p.m.: On to the Black Bull, one of Toronto's oldest taverns and a favourite of the motorcycle community. My notes by now are becoming more difficult to read, so not sure what it's really like. Never been there sober. Might have been here that Walk veteran John Jackson had his shoelaces tied together by lawyer B.C. Keith, with the predictable consequences.

8:00 p.m.: We're west of Spadina now, and it must be the Duke of Connaught. Not the sort of place you'd take the Queen if she passed through town, unless she came on the Walk. Mediocre beers, dark and grim setting; we usually sit out on the patio in the back, enjoying the smells from the Kentucky Fried Chicken across the street.

9:10 p.m.: Make our way down to the venerable Wheat Sheaf, formerly Toronto's oldest continuously operating bar until it closed down for a couple of years in the early nineties. Still, dating back to 1849, it's got a history. Blue Jay Charlie Moore was once hit by a bit of falling ceiling here, the site appropriately indicated. We eat dinner, some of it becoming airborne in utterly unnecessary food fights.

11:00 p.m.: Along the street to the Toad in the Hole, the closest we actually get to the ballpark. Used to finish at the Spadina Hotel, now gone. Have on occasion gone for a final pint at place next door to the Toad, but Walk perennial Igor Martin was refused service in 1999, so they will have to live without our munificence.

1 a.m. (or so): Final notes are scrawled into official notebook, and remaining drinkers are sent home to their beds (or beds of others, where appropriate—or inappropriate). Hey, taxi!

Patrick Kennedy's Subway Game, Westbound

Having given Patrick's Subway Game a try, I went back to the source to try to fine-tune the rules. It turned out there weren't many rules, which is jake with me. Patrick insists on the sacredness of using the subway to get to your destination, and that's as it should be, though he has no objection to using any means at your disposal to get away from it. In some suburban locations you might find yourself far from the subway by the time you find your beer.

Upon reflection, Patrick did manage to come up with another rule: the Subway Game must be played solo. And I think he's right. The point of the game, after all, is to discover new parts of town and take a look at what goes on there. If you're with friends or loved ones, you're just going to talk about whatever you usually talk about and forget about where you are. It's human nature. I'm sorry, but these are the rules. I don't make them up. If you've got a problem with the rules, talk to Patrick.

As an avid supporter of Brighton and Hove Albion Football Club, I'm used to games having a competitive thrust. (All right, not all that competitive a thrust, and I'm used to losing more than winning.) I began thinking of ways of making the Subway Game conform to traditional gamesmanship. Player A, say, could send Player B off to one subway station, while Player A would go to a destination of Player B's choosing, points awarded on the basis of how quickly beer is found, with possibly points added or subtracted according to the quality of the beer found. Or the whole city could be handicapped by a knowledgeable drinker and transit user, with points awarded on the basis of difficulty. So finding a beer at Yonge and Eglinton would be worth maybe half a point—only George W. Bush could fail to find a beer at Yonge and Eg—while High Park Station might be worth ten points.

Patrick listened to this sort of talk with the patience of a man who has worked a long time in the hospitality industry, a man who has heard everything at least once. He's not a big sports guy, Patrick, and I could see he didn't think much of my idle speculation. The Subway Game would remain as it was. I don't see it becoming an Olympic sport any time soon.

Having sampled the east end, I turned my attention to the west. Unlike most people, I actually know of about three pubs in Etobicoke, so there were a couple of subway stops at the western end of the line that were disqualified on the basis of prior knowledge. There was no question that I could find drinking spots as far west as Dufferin, and I didn't feel up to trying Lansdowne. When he first told me about the Subway Game, Patrick mentioned getting off at Lansdowne once and finding a place that seemed to be filled with drug dealers who didn't much like the cut of Patrick's jib. I've always found Patrick's jib to be well tailored, and I thought that if these guys didn't like his jib they probably wouldn't like mine either, so I decided to save Lansdowne for another day.

I could vaguely picture the area of the Jane Street subway station but couldn't imagine any drinking spots around it. I didn't know of anything between Bert and Ernie's at Runnymede and the Whatsit and Firkin just short of Islington. Right then, Jane Street it would be, knowing I could always walk east to Runnymede in a pinch.

Jane Street, I guess, marks the western limits of Bloor Street West Village, a cheery, upmarket stretch of boutiques and specialty food stores. I know that part of town only because I've had to visit a funeral home along there a couple of times. What the living did in Bloor Street West Village was anybody's guess. I do know that heading home from one of these funerals my wife and I had had the devil of a time finding a drink. So Jane Street seemed as if it might represent the sort of challenge the Subway Game thrives on.

I don't care where you're coming from, it's a long ride to Jane Street, and I emerged from the subway with the sort of thirst you associate with the genre of cartoon that usually features two guys crawling through a desert looking for an oasis. It takes a couple of minutes to hit Bloor Street from the station, but as soon as you get there the first thing you see across the street is a place called Bryden's, very obviously a licensed establishment. I was beginning to wonder if there was any challenge to the Subway Game at all.

Once again, I strolled about the neighbourhood to see if there were any alternatives to Bryden's. What I found was Billy Bob's Bistro and Saloon. Now, I like the ring of "saloon". This town can boast of lots of neo-quasi-English pubs and more sports bars than I care to think about, but saloons are thin on the ground. P.J. Clarke's on Third Avenue in New York is a saloon. Billy Bob's, from where I stood, did not look like a saloon. So I went back to Bryden's.

Bryden's was a bit upmarket, with couches and armchairs for those who like to lounge while they drink. I headed for the bar toward the back of the place and cast my jaundiced eye along the row of beer taps. The choice was noticeably lager-heavy, I couldn't help noticing, the only ales being imports of the "smooth" variety. This smooth business is a mite tiresome, I have to say. You take what might once have been a decent enough beer then you shoot it full of nitrogen. This gives it that "smooth" quality and simultaneously removes any discernable flavour. It is important to remember that, although lots of people drink beer, not many people actually like the taste of beer, so brewers are constantly finding new ways of taking the taste out. Remember when "dry" beers became all the rage? Remember the proud "no aftertaste" boast? Why would you... oh, don't get me started.

I had a pint of Tetley's bitter, ruined by the patented Smooth-Flow process, and studied the menu. With delight I spotted the entry for Caeser Salad. Very few menus spell "Caesar" right, but this was a new twist. It quite perked me up, it did.

The music was a bit more eclectic than most piped-in pub music. It featured some jazz with even some recognizable people like Ella Fitzgerald, not the annoying generic lite jazz you get sometimes. Still, Bryden's was not going to hold me for long. I headed eastward, keen to see if the trendy Village had gained a drinking spot. And it had. A Dark Horse—not, please note, The Dark Horse—was a new pub from the Empire Freehouse chain. It was bright and modern and offered Muskoka Cream Ale on tap, which you don't see every day. With a pint of Muskoka in front of me, I was well placed to listen to the piped-in music, which was Adult Contemporary Crap Pop.

Soon I was off again. Across from Bert and Ernie's at Runnymede was a new spot called the Yellow Griffin, which seemed to serve only imports on tap for some reason. The people of Bloor Street West Village have my sympathy. The area used to be dry by law, but the publicans of this town have not come storming in.

Walking along, I came to the High Park subway station. Here is a challenge for the Subway Game. Not much in the way of intoxicating beverages around here. The resourceful might step into the park and walk briskly for ten minutes due south, knowing the Grenadier Restaurant was there. Let me advise you to preserve your strength. If you want to drink in High Park, you'd better bring something with you.

East of the Keele Street station there was finally something to celebrate. Whelan's Gate was a splendid pub, sporting plaques by the bar commending both the bar's record of selling Guinness and keeping it in good condition. The Gate is a small pub with an upstairs bar that opens in the evening. The piped-in music is of the Irish variety, ranging from the *Whack Foll the Daddy-Oh* variety to U2. I know it was U2 because I looked at the CD case.

Whelan's Gate filled me with that warm sense of contentment that a good pub can generate, and the locals who cheerfully filled the room seemed happy as clams. Once again Patrick Kennedy's Subway Game had delivered me indirectly to a fine local watering hole.

The Belgians, Beer, and God

One morning in the late sixties, I found myself strolling through the streets of Antwerp. That's what the late sixties were like: somebody handed you a dodgy-looking cigarette, and the next thing you knew you were in Antwerp.

As I strolled I came upon a young man attempting to push his car along a major Antwerp street, holding up a fair chunk of Antwerp traffic in the process. Having been raised to help out in times of need, and estimating that the car in question couldn't weigh much more than a standard toaster, I pitched in. In no time we had this fellow's car safely stowed on a side street and out of harm's way.

Astonished, the young man asked where I was from, quickly adding that no Belgian would have helped him out. Obviously no Belgian had helped him out, so he was right on that score. Keep that in mind next time your car breaks down in Antwerp. Look for a Canadian.

Clearly the young man was eternally in my debt. I can't stress enough how effusive he was about this. Belgians must really be a mingy bunch of bastards if one small act of consideration can turn into a deed of Mother Teresa-esque proportions. Would I accept a beer or two as an expression of Belgian gratitude? Well, of course I would. Belgium might be one of those countries in which rejection of hospitality is a hanging offence. You can't be too careful.

By a stroke of luck, we were perilously close to a watering hole dear to the heart of my new friend and his fellow students, and in we went. I was introduced around the table as the sort of saint that was seldom seen these days on the streets of Antwerp, and beer was quickly ordered. There I remained for some hours, as I vaguely recall.

All these years later, I wish I could tell you that we opened with a couple of interesting lambics—possibly a gueuze and a kriek—and followed with a characteristic spicy white beer, from which we moved on to some of Belgium's great red and brown beers, making our way through one or two strong ales before settling in with a choice of the great Trappist beers. But I cannot. I was young and stupid, and beer was beer. I have no idea what I was drinking, just as I had no idea at the time that I was in the most interesting brewing country in the world.

Belgium is, in some ways, the Canada of Europe: an uneasily bilingual country widely regarded as intensely, almost aggressively, boring. This is partly because the French have routinely stolen all the best Belgian stuff and claimed it as their own. Jacques Brel, for instance. What we call French fries are actually Belgian, and are served with mayonnaise or other tasty toppings in the streets of any Belgian town. But the French have yet to produce a beer that could crack the Belgian top twenty. (Admittedly the French have made the odd decent wine, which confirms my theory that countries can produce good beer or good wine, but seldom both. There are, sadly, countries that do neither.)

Most people, if pressed to name a Belgian beer, would eventually come up with Stella Artois, just about the only boring beer in the country. This is not surprising: the most famous beers of most countries tend to be the dullest. Think of Budweiser or Heineken, for starters. For years, the most famous beer of England was Watney's Red Barrel, which says it all. But get beyond Stella Artois, and you're into a stunning range of beers of all sorts and colours. The Belgians actually brew a kind of beer that's left in an uncovered vat in a room with open windows, where it attracts wind-borne yeasts that drift in and ferment the stuff. Imagine Molson leaving beer to chance.

Belgium hasn't yet become as sexy as Ireland, but one can drink Belgian beer in many jurisdictions these days without having to push anybody's car. The trend may have begun in London with a chain of restaurants called Belgo that must account for hundreds of thousands of mussels a week. Just off the Danforth in Toronto, you will find Café Brussel, a handsome Belgian bistro that looks just the ticket. There's a small bar and, although I was told that they didn't encourage boozehounds during the dinner hours, I was allowed to sit there and take aboard a glass or two of the national product. Perhaps they recognized me from Antwerp. (There may be something to this karma thing after all.) They seemed very nice, and I really do mean to get there for a meal some time.

There's no trouble getting a drink at the Esplanade Bier Markt, down on Concept Bar Parkway. Owned by Prime Pubs Inc., proprietors of Fionn MacCool's next door, the Bier Markt is a big, labyrinthine place where mussels go to die. I'm more impressed by the Bier Markt than by its mock-Irish neighbour. The design actually turns a barn-like room into manageable, almost intimate, areas, and there's a nice long bar for someone who wants to have a beer or two without murdering any molluscs.

The proprietors of the Bier Markt wisely procured the services of beer expert Stephen Beaumont to advise them on their beer offerings, so you get an excellent choice of draught and bottled beers from around the world, highlighted by five Belgian beers. These are exactly the same five you'll find at the Café Brussel, which leads me to believe that these are the five Belgian beers Interbrew makes available over here. Ten years ago no one had ever heard of Interbrew, the Mr. Big of Belgian brewing, but now they're the second biggest brewing force on the planet after the entirely unnecessary Anheuser-Busch. They're buying up breweries right and left, which seems uncharacteristically aggressive for Belgians. Interbrew snaffled up Labatt in the early nineties, becoming in the process the unwitting owners of the Toronto Blue Jays. I'm a Belgium booster, but no one's going to suggest that they know beans about baseball, and the Interbrew ownership years will not go down as a golden age in the Blue Jays' history. Remember that Flemish third baseman they had for a spell? Absolute rubbish. More important, did the Interbrew years mean an improvement in the quality of beer served down at the Big White Thing? They did not. Could you get proper Belgian frites served with a big dollop of garlic-flavoured mayo? You could not.

But where was I? Ah yes, the Bier Markt. Five draught beers from Belgium is, frankly, not a whole lot, especially in a place that celebrates its Belgianness. Five beers is barely scratching the surface. It's a bit like offering a choice of five French wines in a fancypants restaurant, three white and two red. Especially when one of the five beers in question is the ubiquitous Stella Artois.

Hoegaarden is a white beer whose recipe dates back to the fifteenth century—actually, it's pale yellow with a white head—and is flavoured with coriander and Curaçao orange peel. Other choices are a blonde and a brune from what was once the Trappist brewery of Leffe—now brewed by Interbrew under licence—and the excellent Belle Vue Kriek, a beer made with cherries and full of flavour. Part of the pleasure of drinking Belgian is visual, and all the beers have their own appropriate glasses and beer mats, and I wish only that we could have more and more of it. If you sit at the bar at the Bier Markt, try to land a spot near the authentic Belgian beer dispenser, a nice piece of technology that has its own built-in glass washer.

And don't blame the bar staff for the numerous misspellings of the simple word *its* in the Bier Markt menu. I assume it's not their fault. I'm sure they all know that *it's* means *it is* and can never be used as the possessive pronoun. At least they stopped short of the breathtaking *its'* which makes the end of the world seem a highly desirable prospect.

Speaking of the end of the world, Belgian beers are famed for their strength. They tend to begin at about 5% alcohol by volume and head sharply upwards from there. If you think the end of the world has arrived, it might be simply the impact of the Belgian beer. Cease intake at once, seek out a couple of Aspirin, and lie down for a good long spell.

Perhaps the saddest fact of modern Belgian life is that fewer monks are active in brewing strong Belgian beer than at any time within the last eight or nine centuries. There's something very appealing about the thought of monks doing God's work, whether it's brewing beer or making odd liqueurs. Saint Bridget (born 439 AD) is reported to have transformed water into beer for the benefit of the unhappy lepers she was administering to. We should all get such nursing care. And sixth-century Irish-born Saint Columbanus exercised the power of prayer to double his supply of bread and beer while toiling among the heathens of Germania. Neither of these saints became the patron saint of brewers and brewing, an honour that fell to one Gambrinus, about whom we know unfortunately little.

It's very Catholic, this pro-alcohol line. Having said that, of course, I recall the accounts of Pope John Paul II's first triumphant visit home to his native Poland. Addressing a crowd of a million souls, he berated his fellow Poles for their excessive drinking. According to the newspaper reports, his audience responded spontaneously by crying out at once, "We swear we will be teetotallers!" I've always been suspicious of this story. Any time you read about a crowd crying out as one, it's always people speaking a foreign language (unless it's a stadium full of English football supporters). And it's usually reported by an English-speaking journalist. I don't know how you say "We swear we will be teetotallers!" in Polish. Perhaps it's a well-known catchphrase that comes naturally to Poles, though I doubt it. In any case, I doubt that the annual intake of alcohol has seriously diminished since that moment of delirium. Poland, after all, is the only country I know of that has a Beer Lovers' Party represented in its government.

Although the Anglicans are generally pretty good on the subject of the demon drink, you don't hear about Anglican monks operating breweries and making perilously strong ales. Mind you, for many years my parents' Anglican church in Etobicoke, of all places, held an annual pub night in the church basement, though the beer fell short of Trappist standards. (Most beers do.) And there's a Cornish pub called the Seven Stars in

Falmouth whose licensee is the Rev. Barrington-Bennett, with whom I once had a pleasant chat about Bill Bryson. I've never talked religion with Bill, but I suspect he'd like the Seven Stars. The Rev. Barrington-Bennett certainly liked Bill Bryson.

No, it's the Protestants—and when it comes to drinking the Anglicans are definitely not Protestant—who rail against drinking. And it all seems so arbitrary. As Housman writes, "And malt does more than Milton can/ To justify God's ways to man." Some years ago, Anne and I attended a Presbyterian wedding. It was not Presbyterian simply in the sense that the bride and groom were both Presbyterians, which they were, or even in the sense that the bride and groom were both Presbyterian clergypersons, which they were. No, practically everybody in the room was a Presbyterian clergyperson, or was married to one.

We had been warned ahead of time that drink would not be forthcoming at this wedding, and we were grateful for the tip-off. Fair enough, we're open-minded people who can adjust to different cultures. Our friends—the aforementioned b. and g.—were not teetotallers themselves, and have in fact attended the Walk to the Ballpark, which comes up somewhere else in this book. What rankled, however, were the repeated references throughout the service—and there had to have been at least three or four such references—to the wedding feast at Cana. You'll recall the story, in which the founder of Christianity saved a wedding party at which the wine had run out by transforming a vat of water into wine. And not just any wine, either, but clearly a grand cru from a fine chateau. Don't wedding-feast-at-Cana me, I thought to myself. Any chance of lightning striking twice, I asked my wife. Don't torture yourself, she replied. The bartender at the Duke of Gloucester very likely never saw two such thirsty faces as he did later that afternoon.

The anti-booze activists of the church tend to waffle a bit when you bring up the wedding feast at Cana. It's a metaphor for something else, they might say, or they come up with biblical quotes to justify their stance, most of which come from that Saint Paul chap, as far as I can figure out. Look, I'm sure Saint Paul was a decent fellow and good to his mother, but he was not a barrel of fun. Old Miseryguts—as I'm sure his former friends called him after his conversion—was against practically everything that makes this vale of tears at all palatable. You will look in vain for a joke of any sort in either of the Epistles to the Corinthians, and the Thessalonians don't get off much lighter.

I picture a couple of Thessalonians running into each other in town.

What's happening, says Thessalonian One. Just had a letter, says Thessalonian Two. Oh, says Thessalonian One, who from? Paul, says Thessalonian Two, and it's addressed to all of us. The fellow who used to be Saul, inquires Thessalonian One. That's the fellow, says Thessalonian Two. What's he on about, asks Thessalonian One. This and that, replies Thessalonian Two, oh, and you'd better put that beer down.

(Oddly enough, particularly given the important role beer has played in human history, there is no reference to beer in the Bible. Not in the King James Version, at any rate. The New International Version, on the other hand, offers no fewer than nine beer entries, all in the Old Testament and all appearing in verses where the King James Version uses the words "strong drink". Take Proverbs 20. King James says, "Wine is a mocker, strong drink is raging," while the NIV prefers "Wine is a mocker and beer a brawler." Or Proverbs 31: "Give strong drink unto him that is ready to perish, and wine unto those that be of heavy hearts." (KJV) "Give beer to those who are perishing, wine to those who are in anguish." (NIV)

Interesting, that. Most of us don't think of beer as "strong drink". There's a movie in which John Wayne goes into a saloon and asks for a beer. Told he can't have one because there's no drinking allowed on election day, Wayne moans to the bartender, "Awww, beer ain't drinkin'!" But, when you think of it, what other strong drink did they have? I don't think the Israelites had the benefits of distillation, so most of what we would consider strong drink today would not have been available to them. I just thought I'd bring it up.

For that matter, while I'm still in parentheses here, there is another theory that all those Old Testament references to wine are the product of inadequate translation, that in fact they were far more likely to have been drinking beer. Now I really must get out of these brackets and into something more comfortable.)

And it's not just the Judeao-Christians. A few years ago I was in an Afghani restaurant and found myself having a look at the bottled beer selection behind the bar. There was a label I didn't recognize. Is that an Afghani beer, I naively asked the barkeep. No sir, he replied, if you make beer in Afghanistan they kill you.

I used to work with an Iranian who came into my office one day looking for advice. Quite honestly, more people offer me unsolicited advice than seek it from me, so I put on my best Ann Landers face and vowed to do my best for the poor wretch who had been reduced to seeking me out. He had, he said, a problem with kidney stones. Ah yes, I said, nodding sympathetically but not sure how I could help. His doctor, it seemed, had called for plenty of fluids, but especially beer. Nothing would help like beer. A good Muslim, Ala had never bought beer before; what should he buy? I was happy to help, but I couldn't help thinking that if he'd been brought up Catholic, he probably would never have suffered from kidney stones in the first place.

The last word on divinity and alcohol belongs to Benjamin Franklin, though I'd not be surprised if he'd been drinking when he said it: "Beer is living proof that God loves us and wants us to be happy."

Mind The Gap: The Subway Game in London

It stands to reason that a city with a bigger subway system offers more scope for players of Patrick Kennedy's Subway Game, and they don't come a lot bigger than the London Underground. That said, it should be noted that much of the Underground—once you leave central London—is in fact Overground, so not strictly speaking in keeping with the spirit of the game. (The same applies to the New York subway, which is elevated over much of Queens and Brooklyn.)

The real difficulty in playing the Subway Game in London is in fact the London Underground itself. There's a lot to be said for the Tube: those dizzyingly long escalator rides, the racy lingerie ads, the cute rounded trains built to fit the cute rounded tunnels, the recorded exhortations to Mind The Gap, that distinctive London Underground smell. I love it all. Unfortunately no money—public or private—has been spent on the system since about the time of the Crimean War, so it's inclined to be falling apart.

On my last visit to London I resolved to see if Patrick's game travelled well, and I picked up my London Transport one-day Travelcard for zones 1 and 2, determined to find out. And, of course, I have to admit to lying to you in the last paragraph. Money has been spent on the Tube, most of it by the long-suffering user of the system. But in recent years an extension to the Jubilee Line was built to take workers to the newly-developed Docklands area and tourists to the Millennium Dome in Greenwich. Apparently some of the new stations on this line are quite impressive. Unfortunately I have to take their word for it.

I had decided to have a look at the Canada Water tube station in Rotherhithe, which had a nice ring to it. Would I find an ancient dock workers' pub or something modern for whomever now works in Rotherhithe? I took the Northern Line down to Waterloo and followed the signs to the Jubilee Line, stopping only when I heard the announcement that it was shut down until further notice. I read the next day that Prime Minister Tony Blair had also been inconvenienced that day while attempting a morale-boosting visit to the wildly unsuccessful Dome. Part of the boost to morale—though possibly not for him—was to be a Tube ride. Presumably the sight of the prime minister waving cheerfully as he entered the Underground station would lift the hearts of the working masses. Sadly, the Jubilee Line—in its democratic way—was working for neither the prime minister nor me that day.

Thinking quickly, I changed my plans. Checking the map, I determined that the farthest I could go on my Zone 1-2 ticket was North Acton, so I took the Northern Line back to Tottenham Court Road then transferred to the Central Line westbound. It worked. Well, it worked inasmuch as I got to North Acton. Somewhere around White City the Central Line emerges into the daylight, and you get a very good view of Wormwood Scrubs, the venerable prison with the excellent name. This is the highlight of the trip. At North Acton the train is in daylight but sunk in a sort of trench. Unable to see anything, I decided that the fundamental rules of the Subway Game had not been violated.

The North Acton station is not the most prepossessing of sights. There are ramps leading left and right, the only directional indications being signs for buses that promise to take you away from North Acton. I picked right—as opposed to left, not wrong—and came out on what was a very good impression of a superhighway. North Acton appeared to be something that got in the way of motorists and caused them to slow down, though not much. Most of the traffic took the form of very large trucks, or lorries as they say there.

I may have been the first tourist North Acton has ever seen, or at least the first tourist who wasn't utterly lost, who had gone there on purpose. There's a BBC building in North Acton and an Elizabeth Arden building. There is something called the Victoria Industrial Estate, which has probably won some sort of award from the British Tourist Authority for being the part of England least like a quaint Cotswold village. There's a sandwich bar and a caff, and most important there is the Castle. This is not a castle in the sense of Edinburgh Castle or Leeds Castle or any castle you may have heard of. It is a pub, and a fairly big pub too, with a kind of fifties design to it.

What made my heart soar was the discovery that the Castle was owned by Fuller, Smith and Turner, the great brewery of west London. In the first 23 years of the Campaign for Real Ale's Champion Beer of Britain competition, Fuller's beers won five times. I am more than partial to Fuller's beers. I love Fuller's beers. There, I've said it. After my adventure south of the Thames, it was 11:30 a.m. when I arrived at the Castle, apparently the first customer of the day. I took my pint of London Pride to a table and listened to the Christmas fare on the sound system, to a backbeat of massive great lorries thundering by outside. If you've ever been to England at Christmas, you will be familiar with the roughly four popular Christmas songs that get played over and over in pubs and shops. There's that Band-Aid song of some years ago, there's one by Paul the Beatle, one by John the Beatle, and one by a band called Slade, apparently called *Merry Christmas Everybody*. It was the latter that was playing as I sat down. I knew the others would not be far behind.

Another customer came in shortly thereafter, only he turned out to be someone looking for work. The next real customers appeared at 12:15, around the time I was leaving. They may have been there for the Food of the World menu, which ambitiously features the cuisine of England, Scotland, the USA, Mexico, Thailand, and India. It's comforting to know that you can get beef enchiladas in North Acton these days, but I was already thinking about my next stop.

If you're ever in London and want to cheat on the Subway Game, take the District Line to Parsons Green. Turn right from the station and walk about half a block until you see the White Horse. Parsons Green used to be west of Chelsea, but Chelsea continues to expand westward as property values rise, and Parsons Green is very much part of Chelsea now. Every time I go to the White Horse its clientele gets posher and the lunch gets fancier. The beer, however, persists in being wonderful. The 1994 Champion Beer of the Britain was a hard-to-find Suffolk ale called Adnam's Extra, which very quickly ran out on the first day of the Great British Beer Festival. That afternoon I took a bus down to the White Horse where they offered Adnam's Extra on tap, as a matter of course. At that point the pub accounted for some sixty percent of the output of that fine beer (it has since been discontinued by the brewery). That's the sort of pub the White Horse is. There's no music in the White Horse, unless you count the snippets of popular classics that announce incoming cellphone calls.

From there I decided to try the east end and settled on Bethnal Green as a destination. Once again the challenge lay in actually getting there. The sign in the Tube station suggested one thing, the train that eventually appeared suggested something else, and they were both wrong. After what seemed a lifetime I got to Mile End station. I was close to Bethnal Green—only one stop away on a different line—but I was by now desperate to get off the system altogether so I changed my plan. Mile End was my new destination.

The area around Mile End station featured another very busy road, but—unlike North Acton—there were actually people around on foot. I was a long way from Chelsea, I quickly discovered. The locals were not as successful as the denizens of the White Horse, and they—or probably their parents, for their accents were mostly London—were once from somewhere else. Again, you don't get a big tourist trade around Mile End.

Getting off the Underground you have no sense of direction, and the dim light of London in December gives you little hint of where the sun might be setting. In one direction seemed to lie acres of housing estates. There was something that looked like a prison, with loads of barbed wire keeping people either out or in, and I encountered two pubs that offered no real ale at all that I could see. I'm pickier than Patrick Kennedy about what I drink, so I held on for a pub called the Matter of Time—formerly the Flautist and Firkin—and a pint of Greene King IPA. Novelist Graham Greene was a member of the Greene brewing family, and indeed the brewery issued a celebratory bottled beer to mark the writer's eightieth birthday.

The Matter of Time was an okay pub, and I was happy to have found it (not that it was difficult; it was right there on the very busy road), but it was starting to get dark. Actually it had been starting to get dark since about noon, which was roughly when it had stopped getting light. The days are short in England in December, especially when it's overcast, which is most of the time. The sun—if "sun" isn't too strong a word for it—rises in the south and then, not long afterwards, sets in the south. But I knew that Anne's day of shopping would be drawing to a close and that I needed to get home to be husbandly. So I caught the Tube—reasonably uneventfully this time—and went to Euston station for a quick Christmas ale at the excellent Head of Steam, a railway-themed pub. An interesting day, all in all, and good value for my £3.90 Travelcard.

How Your Granddad Drank: Canadian Drinking as It Was

When I arrived in Canada, back in my boyhood, Toronto was still being labelled the Belfast of North America. This, I think, was not intended as a compliment. It spoke of a grey dourness, of uneasy relationships between Protestants and Catholics. It was the tail-end of an era in which membership in the Orange Order was a prerequisite for becoming mayor or, for that matter, anything at all of any importance.

At least Belfast had pubs, which set it apart from Toronto. Even after warring factions started blowing up Belfast pubs from the late sixties on, it still had more than we did. The paucity of drinking establishments in Toronto was actually a fairly recent development. In 1837 there were fifty taverns in the tiny quadrant bordered by King and Front Streets and Yonge and Church, according to *Tavern in the Town*, the definitive study of early pub life in Ontario by Margaret McBurney and Mary Byers. Alcohol was cheap and plentiful, and there was no shortage of places selling it. Booze is an integral part of the development of Toronto. Bloor Street is named for brewer Joseph Bloor, and Finch, Steeles, and Sheppard Avenues are all named for innkeepers who kept premises at the intersections of those streets and Yonge Street.

As in England, Canadian inns sprang up along coaching routes. Horses and passengers needed rest and refreshment, and before long there was no shortage of places offering such services. By the time the traveller up Yonge Street got to Holland Landing, he could be in quite a state. Given that tavern-keepers usually treated coach drivers to free drinks in return for bringing passengers their way, the driver might be in even worse shape.

Nor was the early Canadian drinker certain of what was in his drink. McBurney and Byers offer a few recipes of the day. Wisely they note: "These old recipes are presented for interest only; they should not be used." I'll say. Their recipe for port calls for 28 gallons of cider, 9 gallons of whiskey, 15 pounds of white sugar, as well as cinnamon, cloves, orange peel, ground cochineal, carbonate of potash, and – if necessary – two ounces of ground alum. I don't think that's the way they make it in Portugal. There are no grapes, for starters. I'm trying to imagine how I'd feel the next day. Now I'm trying to *stop* imagining how I'd feel the next day.

Inns were in many instances the only buildings around big enough to hold large groups of people, so they became town halls, Sunday Schools, courtrooms, and concert halls. Jordan's Hotel on King Street hosted a session of the legislature of Upper Canada in 1814 after American forces had torched the original building. The Wheat Sheaf at King and Bathurst and the Black Bull on Queen Street continue to serve intoxicating beverages more than a century and a half after they first opened their doors. The Jolly Miller on Yonge Street south of York Mills was built in the late 1850s and survived in greatly altered form until quite recently.

We complain of life in Canada today, but mid-nineteenth-century Canada must have been a daily series of adventures. No wonder they drank. When I say they drank, I guess I mean that the men drank and they drank like bejesus, to use a technical term. Men, after all, are weak creatures and need the aid of intoxicants to get through a day. It was only a matter of time before somebody started a temperance movement, and in the nineteenth century somebody did. The first temperance society in Upper Canada was established in 1828 in the appropriately named Bastard Township. Temperance, to begin with, is not necessarily the same thing as abstinence. The initial idea was to encourage more temperate rates of drinking, but as always the hotheads of the movement gained the upper hand and soon the drive was for zero tolerance. Some witty Upper Canadian publicans favoured abstinence for their customers, but only in the sense of abstaining from unpaid tabs.

I blush to admit it, but I have sung in a temperance choir. Strictly for historical reasons, you understand. I have stood before paying audiences—fair enough, they weren't paying much—and sung songs with such titles as *"I'll Drink No More Rum Punch"* and *"The Teetotallers Are Coming (With the Cold Water Pledge)"*. My fingers were crossed behind my back all the while. We frequently retired to a pub after our gigs. We were being ironic. Our audiences didn't always pick up on the irony, however, particularly an audience we wowed in Kitchener, Ontario, which missed all our postmodern signals and invited us afterwards to perform at the annual general meeting of the Women's Christian Temperance Union. Personally I'd have done it, but our leader begged off on grounds of insincerity.

The best of the temperance songs invariably involve drunken fathers who persist in not coming home from the tavern, even though either a wife or a child is quite obviously dying at home. In *"Come Home, Father"* a child turns up at the tavern at one, then two, and finally three, pleading with her father to return home before poor little Benny succumbs to Fatal Absent Father Syndrome. *"Has Father Been Here?"* has yet another wretched child seeking a father from Mr. Barkeeper, Mr. Policeman, and Mr. Jailer, trying to free his old dad with the words: "Oh 'twas not my father who did the bad deed, /'Twas drinking that maddened his brain..." In *"Father's a Drunkard and Mother is Dead"* a barefoot and tired child observes that "We were so happy till Father drank rum/ Then all our sorrow and trouble begun." The song ends, "God pity Bessie, the Drunkard's lone child." Not a dry seat in the house, as my mother-in-law is fond of saying.

With songs this powerful, the temperance movement was bound to make a dent, and it did all of that and more. As always it's the people who have time to hold meetings who change the world, and the non-drinkers tend to have plenty of time. If you're ever in Westerville, Ohio, you can visit the Anti-Saloon League Museum, Monday to Friday, 10 a.m. to 6 p.m. Well, what else is there to do in Westerville? I imagine they do good business while people are waiting for the town bar to open.

By the turn of the century, the temperance movement was hitting its peak. In 1900 the government of Prince Edward Island banned the sale of alcohol. The First World War – a time of madness on a global scale – seemed an opportunity to criminalize alcohol as a patriotic measure, and one by one the provinces climbed on board. Quebec, not surprisingly, resisted the longest, and eventually barred the sale of distilled alcohol briefly in 1919. Soldiers returning from the trenches presumably found it difficult to believe what had been going on in their absence, and the Canadian experiment with Prohibition gradually ended. (Very gradually: PEI finally broke down in 1948, long after the rest of Canada.) The Americans, of course, clung to Prohibition until the end of 1933, a position that made happy millionaires out of Canadian distillers and smugglers.

The end of Canadian Prohibition didn't mean a return to the days of anarchy and cheap booze, however. As provinces repealed their bans on booze, they placed strict government controls on its manufacture and sale, putting in place the systems that survive across much of the country to this day. There was also the local option legislation (the Canada Temperance Act of 1878) that gave local jurisdictions the power to ban the sale of alcohol in their areas. Even today the unlucky drinker is apt to find himself in such a spot. The last dry part of Toronto disappeared only in 2000, which is a good stick with which to beat obnoxious Torontonians who see themselves as the zenith of sophistication.

In 1947 the cocktail lounge was decriminalized in Toronto, and the Silver Rail became the *ne plus ultra* of cosmopolitanism. It remained a decent place to drink until 1998, when the by now venerable old bar was evicted. The space was required for an upmarket outdoorsy store, which lasted for about a year and a half, by which time it was too late to give us back the Silver Rail.

In the early sixties, an American actor called William Redfield came to Toronto to play Guildenstern in the celebrated Richard Burton/John Gielgud production of *Hamlet*. In his account of the experience, a fine book called *Letters From an Actor*, he writes of trying to make himself at home in a strange town during the rehearsal period. Lacking the necessities of life, he went out in search of a corkscrew and a cocktail shaker. He went to Eaton's, he went to Simpson's, all in vain. Finally, in Aikenhead's hardware store he found the goods he needed. As a bonus he was given a special reduced price, given that the items in question had been sitting in the store, unsold, for so very long.

The Toronto of my young adulthood was a city of taprooms, places of bad beer served up in small glasses by hefty beerslingers who expected the worst of their clientele and were seldom disappointed. Their customers sat at small Formica-topped tables and drank beer, usually on draught. Bottled beer was available but more expensive. Men without women sat in a men-only room that was usually undecorated to the point that it could be hosed down after an evening's drinking. Fights were not uncommon. The idea of these places was to get drunk, and few failed to meet this target. The streets after closing time were thick with drunkards. For all I know they still are, but closing time is much later now and I seldom see it any more.

By 1976 we began to develop more sophisticated drinking spots, places in which one could, if one chose, drink standing up. This had formerly been a crime. The Duke of York on Prince Arthur was the first of what would become a good many mock-English pubs. Eventually we started to grow American-style sports bars as well. Almost overnight our public drinking life began to change. Entrepreneurs could suddenly get liquor licenses without having to be a close friend of a cabinet minister. The days of the Ontario taproom were numbered.

Most of the old beverage rooms of one's youth are gone: the Morrissey, the Embassy, the Babloor, the Place Pigalle. A handful linger on. The Linsmore, as we go to press, remains, still selling lousy beer in six-ounce glasses. Even the pickled eggs are probably the same ones I first saw decades ago.

In my university days I was not an habitué of the Brunswick House, the fabled student hangout of Bloor Street. In those days, if you succeeded in persuading one bar's set of waiters that you were of legal age (and hardly anyone was of legal age in those days), you were reluctant to break in another team. Still, alone of the University of Toronto bars of my day, the Brunswick survives. The resident dwarf of the sixties and seventies, mind you, is long gone. Or short gone, if you're a stickler for accuracy.

A couple of years ago the Brunswick was the site of a minor kerfuffle during Orientation week, when a troupe of Victoria College freshpersons were brought to this bustling bar on what turned out to be Show Us Your Tattoo Night. Unfortunately—but possibly not coincidentally—this coincided with Smirnoff vodka night. I gather people today have tattoos in fairly remarkable places, and some of the more delicate freshpersons complained that their education was not scheduled to begin until the following week. A spokesperson for the Brunswick noted afterwards that no genital regions had been exposed during this event because, after all, the place had a reputation to uphold. It was widely agreed that the Brunswick's reputation had been upheld admirably.

People over the age of twenty-two are most likely to visit the Brunswick – if they visit it at all – on Saturday afternoons between four and seven to listen to a band called Holiday Ranch. It's a darn good band, and people have a lot of fun. They might have even more fun if the Brunswick sold better beer, but Toronto is still not entirely bullish on fun and you've got to set limits.

There are Toronto taprooms that have adjusted slightly to the modern era, offering marginally better beer in pint glasses while continuing to maintain the grim, authoritarian feeling of the sixties. Others have adapted very well to a new age. The Rex Hotel on Queen Street used to be a standard Toronto taproom, manned by the standard waiters in white shirts and black pants, their change holders suspended before them like Ontario sporrans. Somehow the Rex has transformed itself without sacrificing its blue-collar appeal. One of the city's prime live jazz venues by night, the Rex continues by day to be a thoroughly decent Toronto beverage room, its beverages a lot better than they used to be. And it still doesn't take credit cards.

And then there's the Paddock, at Queen and Bathurst. The Paddock was never, in my experience, much of a bar. It wasn't the sort of place you'd take your mother to, unless your mother was a tough old bird who liked to drink draught beer out of little glasses. Well, the Paddock has changed. It's smaller now, with a handsome retro cocktail lounge look to it, though probably a bit ironically retro. It's hard to know because I'm the least hip person in the place. That's all right. These things are relative. I was the hippest person at the Linsmore. Practically anybody I know would be the hippest person at the Linsmore.

I'm probably also the oldest person at the Paddock, but the staff don't seem to mind. On one of my visits, a pretty bartender moves a candle closer to me so I can read my book more comfortably, and I don't know many bars where that would happen. (I can think of bars where they'd move the candle closer in the hopes of setting you on fire.) She stops short of calling me Gramps, bless her. The Paddock also offers a decent choice of beers, although the kids seem mostly to be drinking martinis of various flavours. (I'm old enough to remember when martinis had one flavour, maybe two if you were liberal about these things.) On my first visit I even quite like the music; even if it's retro, I listen to it non-ironically.

The trick about the Paddock is that it doesn't open until late in the afternoon, so the really ideal hours for enjoying the place are not available. It would be perfect about three p.m., the place mostly empty, a bit of Old Blue Eyes in the air. By prime time in the evening the place is often uncomfortably busy and noisy, but that late afternoon/early evening lacuna is pretty good. I'm a bit dubious about turning old drinking establishments into trendy nightspots, but even I have to admit they've done a pretty good job at the Paddock.

The Campaign for Real Ale, or Whatever Happened to Watney's?

When I worked at the Argyll Arms in London in the late sixties, we offered several draught beer choices to our many customers. Having come of beer drinking age in Canada, however, the subtleties were lost on me, I blush to admit. One day while it was quiet, an older gent seated at the bar took it upon himself to point out to me that only one of our selections was worth allowing down one's gullet. That beer was Bass. It was served from a handpump, and I was informed that this was proper English beer served in the way it should be served. Right, Gramps, I thought to myself, but his words stuck in my mind. He didn't call it real ale, as the expression hadn't been invented, but real ale was what he was talking about.

At the time, traditional English ale was an endangered species, being rapidly supplanted by mass-produced beer made in gigantic beer factories and shipped the length and breadth of the country. The new beer—pasteurized keg ales and lagers—had an indefinite shelf life and promised greater profits for the new megabrewers that were busily taking over smaller regional breweries. It wasn't as good as the old beer, but advertising made it highly attractive to a new generation that didn't want to drink the tired old beer of its father's day.

You can't stand in the way of progress, we are often told, but a small group of English beer lovers on holiday in the west of Ireland in 1971 thought otherwise. They might have been drinking at the time. They created something they called the Campaign for the Revitalization of Ale, which by 1973 had become the Campaign for Real Ale. Real ale, as these visionaries saw it, was unpasteurized ale allowed a secondary fermentation in either cask or bottle and served without artificial carbonation. In other words, traditional English ale as it had been served for centuries. It wasn't broke, it didn't need fixing.

The campaign received a boost in the early seventies when the annual report of Young's, a family-owned brewery in southwest London, revealed that the company was making a better profit per pint of beer than the big guys while offering its ales to the consumer at a lower price. (It didn't need to be pointed out that the beer was better too.) The trumpeted efficiency of mass brewing was obviously a lie. Bigger was not necessarily better or even more profitable. The big brewers were not helped by the energy crisis that arose at the same time. If you've ever rented a car in Britain you will have gasped at the price of gas, or petrol as they like to call it. Suddenly the efficiency of hauling kegs of beer from Reading to Hartlepool made less sense.

Still, the real ale guys were swimming against the tide, but if progress always had its way we'd all be eating our cheese out of plastic tubes by now. Sorry, perhaps you do. The founders of CAMRA struck a nerve with a public that slowly began to realize that it was being gulled by brewers who cared for neither the beer they made nor the punters who were expected to drink it. Wisely CAMRA picked out a villain, someone we could all isolate as the guys in the black hats: Watney's.

In the late sixties Watney's owned an alarming number of pubs, having taken over and closed down countless breweries in order to pillage their pub holdings. England was being overrun by pubs painted red and black with little red barrels hanging over their doorways. The barrels referred to Watney's Red Barrel, the new-style beer on which Watney's had staked its future. "What We Want is Watney's" cried the advertising material, but CAMRA's campaign led the public to think twice about what they really wanted. As the campaign advanced, Watney's (or Grotney's, as CAMRA preferred to call it) became something of a laughing stock among astute consumers. Being seen going into a Watney's pub was a risk to one's social standing.

CAMRA's first *Good Beer Guide* in 1974 rashly used the words "avoid like the plague" in connection with Watney's beer. The printer, fearing legal action, forced a change to "avoid at all costs", but the direction was clear. Watney's responded to the increasingly successful campaign by painting its pubs green, then by taking its name off its pubs altogether. Sometimes it even tried painting its pubs the same colours as its more successful and more honourable local competitors, but people continued to stay away. By the eighties it started labelling its pubs with the posher name of Watney Combe Reid, presumably hoping to sound like a law firm. The egregious Red Barrel was by now long gone, utterly unsellable in the UK. By 1990 Watney's had stopped brewing beer entirely, though some might argue that they'd stopped brewing beer long before.

The Campaign for Real Ale marches on all these years later, publishing its annual *Good Beer Guide*, organizing the Great British Beer Festival every August, and lobbying to improve the drinking lives of decent people everywhere. It lobbies against brewery closings, for more civilized licensing hours, for lower taxes on beer, for full measures, and for practically everything that is good. Watney's is gone, but new enemies crop up all the time. They win some, they lose some, but CAMRA's still at it. As a regular visitor to the UK, I keep my membership up to date. They're working for me, too.

If You Can Make it Here: The Subway Game in Gotham

I'll make it clear from the start: I heart symbol New York. I've heart symbolled New York since the first time I saw it early one morning in 1967 as I tumbled off an all-night Greyhound bus. Even then the Bronx was up and the Battery was down. And in 2001, in a Broadway theatre, I sat two rows behind Betty Comden and Adolph Green, the songwriting team that wrote those words in 1942. That's the kind of place New York is, and it's why I heart symbol it.

It wasn't always a good beer drinking town. Well into the 1980s America's biggest city was awash in Budweiser, and even today it's easy to wind up in a place that hasn't heard of anything more enterprising. There have always been good bars in New York, but until recently you had to drink hard liquor if you took drinking at all seriously. It's a competitive town, of course, and rents are crazy, so even a semi-regular tourist sees good bars come and go.

There used to be an Irish bar called O'Lunney's on West 44th Street, attached to a fleapit hotel called the Mansfield. In the early 90s the Mansfield reinvented itself as a hip and expensive (and presumably fumigated) hostelry, and O'Lunney's was evicted, too dowdy and old-fashioned for the hotel's new demographic. Some time later Mr. O'Lunney resurfaced on the south side of 43rd Street, hopeful of a long tenure just off Times Square. But the Disneyfication of 42nd Street was underway, and the pub sat in a space that was needed for Garth Drabinsky's new theatre. O'Lunney's closed its doors again, and the pub-minded mourned once more. Still, he's nothing if not determined, is Mr. O'Lunney, and in March 2000 he opened yet another eponymous establishment on 46th Street, a few steps east of 7th Avenue, and he got it open two days before St. Patrick's Day. Bless Mr. O'Lunney and his intrepid family, and I hope they get to stay where they are for a while. The beer choice could be better, but the O'Lunneys run a nice bar.

If you're apt to go to the theatre as Anne and I do, you get to know the places to drink near Times Square: O'Lunney's, McHale's, Virgil's BBQ, the St. Andrew, and Langan's. They have all saved our lives a time or two. I heart symbol the Blind Tiger and Chumley's in the Village, and d.b.a. and McSorley's (crummy beer but good atmosphere and two good cats) in the Lower East Side.

And I like the Waterfront Ale House on the East Side. I was there late on Oscar Night 2001 drinking Stoudt's Maibock when the best actress category rolled around. Our bartender was a woman of strong views, and she had it on good authority that Julia Roberts was not only not the nicest person on the planet but that she hardly scraped into the top twenty. For her money, it was Anybody but Julia Roberts for the little gold statue. I don't go to a lot of movies (they cut into pub time something fierce), but I learned long ago not to argue with a good bartender. As the moment drew closer, the barkeep issued those of us at the bar with beermats (Brooklyn Brewery, as I recall), with instructions to whip them at the screen if Ms. Roberts came up trumps, as of course she did. The TV screen suddenly filled with several dozen unnaturally shiny teeth, and we barflies let rip. For a moment or two the teeth vanished behind a sea of beermats. Yeah, I kind of like the Waterfront Ale House.

That said, I wasn't about to take the subway to 2nd Avenue at 30th Street to play the Subway Game, New York version. For starters, the subway doesn't go there, and anyway there wouldn't be any surprise. Playing the Subway Game in New York offers an embarrassment of choices. There must be hundreds of stations, from Van Cortlandt Park in the Bronx to Mott Avenue in Far Rockaway. All within reach for a buck and a half (2001 prices). There's a Prospect Avenue station in the Bronx and another Prospect Avenue station in Brooklyn. There's a 71st Street in Brooklyn, a 72nd Street in Manhattan, a 74th Street in Queens, and a 75th Street in Jamaica. From Mosholu Parkway to Sheepshead Bay, there's almost nowhere you can't get to on the New York subway. Except the Waterfront Ale House.

I settled on Coney Island. Born in an English seaside town, I have a grim affection for out-of-season resort spots. In England, of course, out-of-season can be any time of year. This was late March, on a day that smacked more of late or even mid-February, and I felt that Coney Island would represent that sort of mortification of the flesh we all need from time to time. Or at least writers of this sort of book do. You know you wouldn't be happy if I'd taken the subway to Columbus Circle and stepped straight into some swank bar. Nothing's too good for you.

I caught the N train at 49th Street, along with a number of other people. The N train was popular, at least in midtown Manhattan. By the time we travelled under the East River we had lost most of our pilgrims. Clearly not many other people were playing the Subway Game that morning, or if they were they were taking easier options. It took me an hour and five minutes to reach the end of the line, by which time I was the only passenger on my car. This answered my question as to whether Coney Island had an off-season clientele.

Not that it's any of your business, but I actually lived in Brooklyn for a spell in the early seventies. Even so, I'm not so sure I ever got to Coney Island. None of it looked familiar to me. The station gives the impression of having seen no fiscal investment since about WWII, but maybe it looks more cheerful on a sunny day when it's filled with festive New Yorkers. The exit to Surf Avenue looks pretty permanently sealed off, so you come out of the station on Stillwell Avenue, which is not a particularly prepossessing street, it must be said. As you look left, however, you see the bright lights of Nathan's, Coney Island's original fast food extravaganza. Off-season, even Nathan's looks kind of frumpy, and smaller than one expects.

What I don't see right away are any bars, but an area that caters to millions of heat-escaping Gothamites on a summer day must have all the mod cons, right? The forecast is for rain, but it hasn't quite started yet so I head for the beach. I walk past a number of boarded up fast food places, all presumably waiting for warmer weather, and the Coney Island Batting Cage, which is open. There's even a young guy in there taking his cuts. The boardwalk is quiet but not entirely deserted. One of the fast food spots is even open, and I buy a potato knish. When I lived in Brooklyn I was no stranger to the knish, but either I've moved on or they're not making knishes the way they used to.

I could have had a cold beer to take away with the knish, but at this point I still have my heart set on a beer indoors, somewhere out of the wind. I go out on the sand and look around, I go back to the boardwalk and look around. There's a fun fair and a big old wooden roller coaster, all sitting abandoned but for a handful of workers who seem to be making a less than fully committed effort to get it all in working order. They seem no more convinced than I that summer is a realistic prospect.

I move back inland where it's less breezy, and I walk along the apparently bar-free Surf Avenue. I turn right on the bar-free Stillwell Avenue, then left on what proves to be a pretty bar-free Mermaid Avenue.

Don't get any naïve aesthetic notions about Mermaid Avenue; it's not as nice as it sounds. The ubiquitous security measures suggest a level of insecurity among the locals. Clearly the gentry have not swarmed to this seaside paradise, elevating property values. I see a couple of restaurants along the way, established presumably in the hope that tourists will tire of the beach and will make their way a block inland in search of fine dining. On a cold March day, this seems a trifle optimistic.

Still no bars. What I do see are corner variety stores, most of them billing themselves—a little grandly, I think—as delis. Deli is a fairly elastic term. These places sell food, all right? Eventually Mermaid Avenue loses its charm and I turn left again, back toward Surf Avenue. I am slowly and reluctantly concluding that there are no bars in the greater Coney Island area, so I let myself be seduced by the Express Deli Supermarket, which looks a little bigger than the other delis I've seen. Not that bigger is necessarily better, you understand, but I'm hoping that bigger might possibly mean a bigger beer cooler and possibly more choice.

I realize that I haven't fully absorbed the rules of the Subway Game. Get on a subway—check. Go somewhere you don't know—check. Have a beer. Does that mean a sit-down beer in a bona fide bar? I'm a long way from Patrick at this point, and I have to make a decision. The only sit-down beer I've seen has been Nathan's. I could sit down at Nathan's with a cold mug of Bud, surrounded by the other pathetic people who find themselves at Coney Island in March, all needing somewhere warm to go. No, Nathan's is too depressing.

The beer cooler at the Express Deli Supermarket has the stuff you'd expect—Miller, Bud, and all of that—but it actually holds a few surprises. I'm all set to pick up a chilled Sam Adams Cherry Wheat when I notice a bottle I've never seen before. A moment or two later I've put back the Sam Adams and I'm headed for the cash with a bottle of Riga Strong Beer, a product of Rigas Alus, Latvia. Contrary to the dictates of the Bureau of Alcohol, Firearms and Tobacco, the label on this bottle actually tells me that Riga Strong Beer packs a wallop of seven per cent alcohol by volume, which is the kind of oomph I need on a day like this. For a mere US$1.25 I leave the Express Deli Supermarket with my booty cleverly concealed in one of those distinctly American paper bags that cover the entire bottle except for the mouth. The young man behind the counter kindly removes the bottle top, and I'm free to go.

I return to the boardwalk, marvelling that I've just bought the first Latvian beer of my life from a Puerto Rican deli on Coney Island. The wind is up and the rain is starting, but I'm packing a strong beer from Riga and I feel all right. They know a bit about bad weather in Riga, I reckon, and they make a beer that's designed to help Rigans (Rigaites?) deal with it. And it's not bad either, though I'm drinking it in less than optimum tasting conditions. I walk by a ballpark under construction—home of the brand new Brooklyn Cyclones, bringing baseball back to that much-maligned borough—and I think that maybe summer will come again. Soon I've done a big figure-eight of downtown Coney Island and I'm feeling the warmth of my Riga Strong Beer. I get back on the subway and head back for the bright lights and high prices of Manhattan. I don't know if swigging a beer from a paper bag meets the letter of the Subway Game's laws, but it certainly captures the spirit.

16 Not Bad Places to Drink in Toronto

As one of those glass-half-empty people, I thought this was going to be the toughest section of the book to fill. Could I manage a Top Ten list of Toronto watering holes, I asked myself. Indeed I could, and few more besides, and I'd still be leaving out places I think highly of. For reasons of geography and sociability, I am frequently to be seen at the Duke of York (the one on Prince Arthur, not Queen Street East) and Paupers. I am very attached to these pubs, and Paupers almost made the list simply on the strength of not playing music at me. I value Paupers highly for that tender mercy. The Duke of York nearly made the list on the strength of its manager, a hard-working and charming woman called Kim Bartley. If the beer list had been more exciting and if Kim didn't make us listen to bland music...

I nearly put the Graduate Students' Union Pub on my list, because by day it is a not unblissful place to be for those on or near the U of T campus. By night, however, the GSU is a bit noisy and crowded for the over-25 set, of which I am a member. Sometimes I feel I'm a founding member. The Artful Dodger is a decent pub, filled—it often seems to me—with crotchety men with a lot of opinions. It's possibly the hit-and-miss service that makes them crotchety. The Imperial Public Library deserves consideration on the strength of its jukebox, a fount of wonderful jazz since 1950. McVeigh's New Windsor Tavern is an old-fashioned Irish bar that manages to encourage conversation. That might seem a simple enough thing to do, but many bars don't pull it off. The Rotterdam offers an opportunity to taste the Amsterdam Brewery beers fresh out of the kettles, which is much more a good thing than a bad thing.

What are my criteria? I want interesting stuff to drink and an interesting environment in which to drink it, and I don't think I'm asking a lot. These experiences—to state the bleeding obvious—are subjective, and one can be lucky or unlucky in one's encounters with bar staff, ambient noise, other customers, and other such variable factors. I freely admit that I avoid noisy large places whose purpose is to get young people drunk and horny, largely because the doorpersons won't let me in. And I don't get to the sort of karaoke bars and suburban nightclubs where people go to kill each other, if my reading of the papers is at all accurate.

I often don't eat in pubs, so this list should not be seen as an endorsement of the food served in the following establishments (though if I have any information of that sort I may just pass it on). It's also possible I've missed some wonderful pub whose regulars have succeeded in keeping under wraps. It's the risk you take when you compile a Best Of list.

West of Bathurst

I have been grateful in the past to find pubs in Etobicoke. These days I have no business in that far-flung borough, but I was happy to find the Shamrock and Thistle on Dundas Street West and the Rose and Thorne, tucked away in a little mall on Islington Avenue south of Bloor. But the westernmost pub to make my Most Interesting Places list is **Whelan's Gate** at 1663 Bloor Street West, east of Keele. Having made a fuss about interesting beer choices, I have to acknowledge that Whelan's offers a fairly Irish selection, i.e. not much beyond Guinness and Smithwick's. (Guinness drinkers will wonder what else is needed.) Still, it's a friendly place with a good feeling to it, high on those pub intangibles. (See also page 13.)

The **Munster Hall Pub**, at 751 Queen Street West, is a quirky spot with a quirky landlord who has a bit of a louche air about him. (I mention this only because in my line of work I seldom find an opportunity to use the word "louche", but it's altogether appropriate in this case.) Every time I'm there the beer selection has changed dramatically, but there's usually something offbeat and interesting, like the St. Ambroise Oatmeal Stout from Montreal. The big TV is there mostly for Sunday afternoon showings of *Coronation Street*, and who could argue with that? John the proprietor says the pub offers a "quiet alternative" to the sorts of places you're likely to find on that stretch of Queen Street, which are inclined to be of the head-banging variety.

The **Victory Café** at 581 Markham Street, a block south of Bloor, gets the nod over nearby Paupers and Kilgour's Bar Meets Grill on the strength of its beer selection, which is likely to include Raspberry Wheat and Nut Brown from Kawartha Lakes and Cameron's Auburn Ale. Yes, they make you listen to music, but some of it is palpably jazz. I've never heard Celine

Dion or the Eagles or Phil Collins or Whitney Houston or really any of that crowd. The main room at ground level is decorated with Toronto theatre posters and is pretty good to look at, though there is a signed photograph of Liona Boyd behind the bar. Liona Boyd went to my high school, though I didn't really know her, and when she wrote her memoir I immediately had a look to see what she had to say about her teen years. I didn't expect her to write about me, even if I had been her student council president when she was in Grade Eleven, but I also didn't count on seeing the following line: "The boys in Kipling Collegiate held minimal attraction for me." For starters, surely that "in" should be either "at" or "of", but apart from that I could name you several guys who were babe magnets, and I don't count myself in their number.

Anyway, if you don't want to look at Liona Boyd, the Victory Café has an odd little semi-private room off the corridor inside the entrance. I've seldom seen anyone in it, but it looks rather nice. There's another large room upstairs which hosts musical events, literary readings, private parties, and the like. The Victory seems proud of its burgers, and the one I had was darned good. They also offer a choice of thin fries or thick ones, which can't be bad. Both seem to have their devotees.

As we go to print, it's too early to put the new and improved Gladstone Hotel in bold type, but it's worth mentioning that the venerable old watering hole's new owners have embarked on a live jazz program in collaboration with the Rex Hotel (see below). Built in 1889, the Gladstone is possibly Toronto's oldest operating hotel. Not only older than the Royal York and the King Edward, its top price of $55 a night is considerably cheaper, though I haven't inspected the rooms. There's plenty of scope to turn the Gladstone into a very impressive bar without, I hope, evicting the friendly locals. I watch its ongoing refurbishment with interest.

Uptown

We all have our blind spots, and the country above the escarpment that runs along the north side of Davenport Avenue is something of a mystery to me. In prehistoric times—before the Leafs were good, let alone before they were bad—most of what we now call Toronto was under water, hidden beneath the waves of Lake Iroquois. There are many Canadians today who wish that golden age would return. To them I say: tough. The shoreline of that old lake was at the top of the hill that makes the trek up Bathurst or Avenue Road such an ordeal. If Casa Loma had been around in those days it would have been a lakefront property.

For a long time the north country of Toronto was a barren spot for drinking folk. Was there anything at all between the old Ports of Call and the Jolly Miller? It kept a pretty low profile, if so. Things have improved, I'm happy to say, and the prospect of a glass of beer at those heady altitudes is no longer unrealistic. The 1970s saw a boom of apartment and condo building in the Yonge and Eglinton area, with a predictable influx of young, fun-seeking people. They needed bars and, as sure as supply follows demand, they got them. Many of these places have opened, closed, and re-opened many times since then, but a couple of places have become entrenched centres of excellence.

On the east side of Mount Pleasant, just south of Eglinton, you'll find the **Granite Brewery**, a local institution since 1991. I write about the Granite on page 24, but some of it is worth repeating. This was not Toronto's first brewpub, but it was the first to produce a dry-hopped Best Bitter Special, a beer that could hold its head up at the Great British Beer Festival. The two main rooms with their large windows are bright and cheery by day, while the dining room in the back offers a view of the brewery. Owner Ron Keefe holds occasional beer-related events which you can learn about by submitting an e-mail address to ron@granitebrewery.ca and getting on the e-mailing list.

Yes, the music's inclined to be the standard crap-pop, but I'll forgive a lot for the sight of a hand reaching for the handpump to pour me another pint of Toronto's best beer. In 2000, Keefe opened a second location—Beer Street—on the Danforth, offering the same fine ales.

There's nothing terribly fancy about the **Duke of Kent** on Yonge Street, north of Eglinton, but it somehow feels the most English pub in town. As long as they continue to sell Wellington County Ale and Arkell Best Bitter on tap, served from the handpump, they'll have the beer to back up their English pretension. It's not a big place, but who needs a big place? It's big enough to accommodate a crowd of loyal regulars; if I could stand the rarified air up there, I'd be one of them.

I wondered about including the **Bow and Arrow**, farther south on Yonge Street, north of Davisville. The music is really annoying. But the beer! This is part of a loose chain of pubs across southern Ontario—Guelph, Peterborough, and Ottawa are also represented, and they all manage to squeeze the word "arrow" into their name, albeit clumsily at times—that very militantly sells a wide range of Ontario microbrewery beers and Ontario cuisine. Okay, I acknowledge that Ontario cuisine is a difficult-to-define concept, but they do a pretty good job of being convincing about it. And they also sell Wellington County and Arkell Best Bitter on handpumps.

No longer uptown—but I don't know where else to put it—is the **Rebel House**, at 1068 Yonge Street, on the fringes of Rosedale. After all, the highfalutin folk of Rosedale need a pub too, though whether they deserve a pub as good as the Rebel House is up to you and your political views. You might also wonder what they're rebelling against—probably paying taxes.

The rebels in question are, I assume, the rebels of 1837 who marched down Yonge Street from Montgomery's Tavern with the idea in mind of raising a little hell. Some were hanged for their impertinence. Had the Rebel House been in place at the time, I could imagine the rebels dropping in on their way, as indeed Anne and I did on the big anti-megacity march of 1998, a march that followed much of the route taken by William Lyon Mackenzie and his supporters. We found that by marching near the front of the pack we could nip into the Rebel House for a quick pint and easily get out in time to rejoin the end of the column. As demonstrations go, it was a full pint in length.

There's not a lot of room in the Rebel House, though there's a very nice patio out back, shielded by an open parachute. Space on the patio on a warm summer evening is as rare as socialists in Rosedale, but you never know your luck. The menu is full of possibly authentic historic Ontario fare, and the beer list is pretty darn good. When Creemore is the most mainstream beer on tap, you know you're on to something. The Rebel House is apt to close on long weekends, so call first.

East of the Don

I refuse to be drawn into the debate over whether the part of eastern Toronto out past the old racetrack is the Beach or the Beaches. I have to admit that I never heard it called the Beach until some time in the seventies, but I've never lived there so I can't swear that the locals haven't been saying "Beach" since time began. Part of me suspects the usage sprang up as a reaction to the growing popularity of the area, around the time the last parking space was swallowed up by a tourist from downtown. I think I'll just call it the "B".

In appearance and temperament, the B is the part of Toronto most like Vancouver, and for a long time it shared Vancouver's shortage of watering holes. I can recall going out there and finding nowhere to drink but the old

Orchard Park Tavern, a taproom that existed mostly to refresh patrons of the Greenwood racetrack. Now the track is gone, the Orchard Park has become a Days Inn, and Queen Street East between Coxwell and Victoria Park is dotted with pubs and bars of all sorts, including the quirky Castro's Lounge and the small but friendly Kitty O'Shea's. Probably my favourite of the Queen Street bars is Quigley's, a decent spot with Sunday afternoon live jazz and a beer choice that's just good enough to make a person think a moment before ordering.

Kingston Road is less picturesque but less given to tourism. I have stopped in at Paddy O'Farrell's with no regrets, but I was on my way to the **Feathers** at 962 Kingston Road, and with good reason. Opened in 1981, the Feathers offers five home-brewed beers (actually, under the terms of a strange Ontario law governing so-called brewpubs, they are brewed elsewhere, but "fermented, filterered, carbonated and kegged" on the premises), one of which is a real ale. I keep being told that the real ale they used to make was excellent, but the Auld Reekie is possibly an acquired taste that few are bothering to acquire. The staff will happily give you a sample taste before you commit to a pint. I want to like Auld Reekie more than I do.

The first time I went to the Feathers I ran into my old friend Charlie Dougall. This was not surprising. I have run into Charlie at Pat McGinty's in Buffalo, so encountering him a few blocks from his home was almost inevitable. A product of the west end, Charlie has been living in what he calls the Beaches for a couple of decades. (He says there's more than one beach, so it's the Beaches. When he found me at the Feathers I was well into a pint of the pub's Beaches Best Bitter. Look, I'm just reporting what I see; I'm not judging.)

A bit surprised to find me drinking so far from home, out in the B, Charlie approved of my choice of venue. Up on Kingston Road, he told me, is where the geezers drink. We worked our way through the homebrew choices of the Feathers, then we made our way to Quigley's and Lion on the Beach before Charlie was required elsewhere. At some point at Quigley's he expressed regret that we baby boomers had not changed the world as we had promised to do. He was a bit harsh on us, I thought, but you expect that when you drink with Charlie.

Anyway, the other key thing you need to know about the Feathers is its remarkable selection of single malts, some 270 of them if the menu is to be believed. The pub is decked out with high-quality photographs of the British Isles and, unless I've just been lucky when I've been there, it doesn't play music at you. Except on Saturday nights, when the music is live. I can't vouch for it. One December afternoon I saw a notice of the pub's forthcoming New Year's Eve party. It was ticket-only, but the tickets were free and were for regulars only, which I reckon is fair enough.

On page 121 I write about discovering the **Only Café** at 972 Danforth Avenue, just west of Donlands. It's a quirky place with a good beer selection, including an exotic display of bottled beers in the "Hall of Foam". It's an excellent neighbourhood bar with lots of surprises. I don't mind being surprised in a pub, as long as the surprise doesn't involve vermin or loud music. As mentioned elsewhere, I had put in a lot of man-hours in pubs in many lands before I ever heard Woody Guthrie being played, and it was the Only Café that pulled it off. If you're going to make me listen to music, make it something out of the ordinary. Most things at the Only Café are out of the ordinary.

Just east of Pape I'm happy to find **Beer Street**, the sister pub of the Granite Brewery. Whenever I've been there it's been pretty quiet, which I can stand, but I assume they're busy at other times. I hope so, because I wouldn't want that Best Bitter Special sitting too long.

Heading westward you find a spate—almost a passel—of pubs, including the Court Jester, Brass Taps, the Auld Spot, Allen's, Dora Keogh, the Black Swan, and the Old Nick, each serving its own constituency. It would take a trained anthropologist to uncover why some drinkers are loyal to, say, Brass Taps over the Court Jester or the Auld Spot over the Old Nick, but we've all got our own intangibles. Allen's is the most celebrated of the lot, although it always seems more of a restaurant to me than a pub. I've been happy sitting at the bar, but you can't count on finding an empty stool whenever Allen's is busy, like during opening hours. Dora Keogh is more pub-like (and it has a fireplace too), but it doesn't have as rich a beer selection. I wish them all well.

Central Toronto

For a very long time, public drinking in Cabbagetown was restricted to sidewalks and the Winchester. Parliament Street remains a very mixed community, but it boasts a range of dining and drinking opportunities these days. The Winchester survives, tarted up a bit since its more ragged days which began in 1888, and on a recent pub crawl we were served well by a young waitperson called Shelley. The Ben Wicks Pub seemed a little down at heels, the Brass Taps was deafening, and a place called Winny's had a friendly, if unexceptional, feel to it. The cream of Cabbagetown—in the view of three seasoned pubgoers—was the **House on Parliament**, at 456 Parliament Street.

It turned out we slightly knew the couple who run the place from their days at the Duke of York, and I was delighted with what they've done. My happiness level started to rise as we walked into the House on Parliament and it stayed high. This is a pub with all the best intangibles, as evidenced by the fact that the place was packed on a Wednesday evening. The music was more interesting than I'm used to, my liver and onions were good, the waiter (identified on the bill only as Server 0020002, so possibly a highly developed cyborg) was terrific, and my pint (or so) of Gritstone (which had been replaced by Black Oak Nut Brown Ale the next time I got there) went down a treat.

In the late nineties (the late nineties, not his late nineties), my dentist moved into the Gooderham Building, also known as the Flatiron Building. He's at the sharp end, not the blunt end, and he's right at the top. Apart from enjoying a bit of local heritage whenever I go for a bout of blood-letting (where else do you find not only an antique elevator but an actual—albeit not antique—elevator operator?), I have the pleasure of taking aboard a bit of general anaesthetic afterwards at **C'est What**, at 67 Front Street East.

C'est What is the sort of place that makes me almost look forward to a dental encounter. It's even better if you go there when you're not in pain. Opened in 1988, it offers the city's biggest range of Canadian (mostly Ontario) microbrewed beers, along with a few house-fermented beers (including a hemp beer, a rye beer, and a coffee porter, none of which you see every day in most places). You get your choice of twenty-nine almost entirely interesting taps, and the place even makes its own wines as well. There are always at least three or four real ales available, and just writing about it makes me wish I were there right now. It's a pub that does beer tastings, wine tastings, port tastings, single malt tastings, and vodka tastings, plus a few tastings I've no doubt forgotten.

The pub's other passion is music, and its music room (now called Nia) offers up entertainment seven nights a week, with traditional jazz on Saturdays from four to seven. C'est What's monthly schedule offers helpful tips along with the names of the mostly up-and-coming musicians, such as "soulful swing pop", "funky folk", or "brooding pop". And you can get the monthly newsletter by e- or snail mail. C'est What's food gets mixed reviews but my gums are usually too tender to eat, so I couldn't tell you.

Not far from C'est What is the **Esplanade Bier Markt** (56 The Esplanade), described in some detail on page 157. It's got beer, it's got food, and it can hold all of us at one time. It's corporate as all get-out, but any place that employs Stephen Beaumont as its beer consultant deserves to be taken seriously.

On the strength of its beer rather than its ambience or abysmal music, **Denison's** at 75 Victoria Street warrants mention in this section. Denison's operates three drinking establishments under one roof, but only one brewery. It makes nothing but German-style beers, both light and dark. You'll find seasonal specials—a Märzen or Bock, for instance – but the most dramatic beer in the place has to be the Weizen, a cloudy, spicy wheat beer that is packed with flavour, much of it banana-esque. It's way too scary for the average drinker, and the bartender told me that their biggest seller was the Bavarian Hell, a pale lager. I'd say go for the sampler pack, then order a Weizen.

One of the quirkiest places in town is **Smokeless Joe**, a little downstairs room at 125 John Street, between Richmond and Adelaide. Imagine going to your bank manager with this business plan: I want to open a downtown bar that opens at 4 p.m., so to hell with the lunchtime trade. I'm going to sell mostly beer, but nothing that most people have ever heard of. The music policy is Blues, and nothing but the Blues. No hamburgers or conventional pub food. (The menu also stipulates: "This is not the alarmingly creative food served around town these days.") Oh, and no one's allowed to smoke, even on the sidewalk patio outside.

In a part of town noted for enormous warehouse spaces transformed into playgrounds for Corona-swilling youth, Smokeless Joe has given us a dim little room with unusual beverage choices and a strict nicotine ban. You go to Joe's place, you live by Joe's rules. Joe doesn't like to see coats draped over the backs of his chairs, so a member of the staff will be there to hang your coat up. You will be asked your first name, you will be given a couple of pieces of bread and butter, you will be given small samples of Joe's current draught beer choices, none of which you will have seen advertised on television, and you will be handed the menu, most of which comprises a list of something like 250 bottled beers from around the world. Actually the sign outside reads: 250 Famous Beers, as if there are 250 famous beers, given that Joe doesn't sell Bud or Coors or Molson or Labatt. Welcome to Smokeless Joe.

While other Toronto publicans sweat to provide no-smoking areas to appease the authorities, Joe offers nothing but. You'll find some really obscure beers you don't see everywhere—try ordering a mulled *Glühkriek* at the Brunswick which you can use to wash down the fresh oysters that Joe keeps on ice behind the bar. In 2000 Joe started offering a real ale, generally from the Durham brewery. Joe isn't cheap, but Joe is interesting. On Stephen Beaumont's advice, I had a bottle of XO from France, a beer that has 25-year-old cognac added to it during the fermentation process. It's expensive but unforgettable.

I wasn't going to include music bars that levy a cover charge, but I can't in all conscience leave the **Rex Hotel** (194 Queen Street West) off my list. I first set foot in the Rex in October, 1972, when it was a run-down but friendly old taproom. Two taprooms really, because although the old Ladies and Escorts rule had been repealed the Rex maintained two separate rooms, and it was easy to see which had been which. In those days the hotel rooms upstairs were still being used, primarily as far as I could tell on a very short-term basis. The people I saw going upstairs seemed to be consenting adults, and that was good enough for me.

Under the management of the ever-boyish Bob Ross, who took over from his father in 1965, the Rex has re-invented itself to keep pace with bustling Queen Street. Ross long ago took down the wall between the two rooms, improved the menu, brought in some decent beers, and turned the Rex into one of the city's prime live jazz venues. And he's done it all without changing the basic nature of the place. He's certainly done it without changing the men's toilet. By day the Rex remains a friendly, unpretentious bar. By night it hums with a constantly changing lineup of jazz bands of all sorts.

I love the Rex Hotel. It's a Toronto landmark with its own distinctive integrity. Chicago has Andy's Jazz Club, we have the Rex. Lucky us.

So This Fellow Walks Into a Bar

This fellow walks into a bar in Red Deer, sits right at the end of the bar all by himself and orders three pints. The bartender says he'd be happy to keep them coming, that there's no need to order them all at the same time, but the fellow says no, he'd like them all at once, thank you very much. He sits there quietly, drinks the three pints, and leaves. Same thing the next night. On the third night, the bartender's curiosity gets the better of him and he asks about the fellow's strange drinking habits.

"Oh that," says the fellow amicably. "When I lived in Vegreville I used to meet after work with my two brothers and we'd have a pint together. Now that I'm in Red Deer, this makes me feel I'm still with my brothers."

The bartender is happy with this explanation, and he passes the word on to the other regulars, who had been finding it a bit odd themselves. And so it went through most of the winter.

Then one evening in March the fellow walks in and asks for two pints. The bar falls silent. The bartender pours the two pints and drops them in front of the fellow. A naturally empathetic man, like so many of his profession, the bartender wipes his hands on a towel and says, "Listen, it's none of my business, but I'd just like to say how sorry I am about your brother…"

The fellow looks up, a bit confused, then says, "Oh, I see what you're saying. No, my brothers are fine. It's just that I've given up drinking for Lent."

★ A fellow walks into a bar in St. John's, takes a stool, and has a pint with a whisky chaser. After the second of these he strikes up a conversation with the guy at the next stool. "You from around here?" he asks.

"Born and bred no more than a mile from here," the man replies.

"Get out," says the first fellow. "What school did you go to?"

"St. Michael's," is the reply. "How about you?"

"The very same," says the fellow. "What year did you graduate?"

"Sixty-two," the man responds.

"Extraordinary," says the fellow. "Same as me. What street did you live in?"

"Anderson Terrace," is the answer. "What about you?"

"Anderson Terrace myself," the fellow says, "just north of the bakery."

"Just north of the bakery!" exclaims the second man. "What are the odds against that?!"

At this point another fellow walks into the bar, takes a stool, and says to the bartender, "So, anything happening around here today?"

"Naah," says the barkeep, "just the McGillivary twins getting drunk again."

★ A fellow walks into a bar in Williams Lake, carrying a small dog. The bartender tells him that dogs aren't allowed, to which the fellow replies that the dog won't be any trouble because he has no legs. Hearing this sad news, the bartender relents. "What's the dog's name?" he asks.

"Doesn't have one," says the fellow.

"Cute dog like this?" says the bartender. "Why don't you give him a name?"

"What's the use?" says the fellow. "Damn dog never comes when I call it."

★ This fellow walks into a bar in Toronto, actually the rooftop bar at the old Park Plaza Hotel. He sits at the bar, next to a guy in a suit. The other guy says to him, "How's it going? You from around here?"

"No," says the fellow, "I'm from Vancouver. I'm in town for the booksellers' convention."

"Ah," says the guy in the suit. "So you probably came up here to look at the literary stuff. You see the caricatures over here? Peggy Atwood, Bob Fulford..."

"Who's the guy with the funny ears?"

"Him? That's Doug Marshall."

"You don't say. No, that's not why I came up here."

"I see," says the guy in the suit. "You came up here because you heard about the unusual wind patterns around this place."

"Uh, no," says the fellow. "I never heard anything about that."

"Really?" says the guy in the suit. "This place is famous for it. You can jump off the balcony over there and just before you hit the ground there's this incredible up-draught that lands you soft as a feather on Bloor Street."

"Now that I don't believe," says the fellow, who wasn't born yesterday.

"Come over here," says the guy in the suit, leading him to the balcony. "If you jump from right here, you come to no harm. Give it a try."

"No way," says the fellow. "That's impossible."

"Impossible?" says the guy in the suit. "Hundred bucks says I can do it."

So the fellow pulls out a hundred bucks, and the guy in the suit jumps over the balcony. Sure enough, just before he hits the ground he slows down and lands gracefully on his feet. He looks up, smiles at the fellow from Vancouver, and re-enters the building. A couple of minutes later he steps off the elevator and, with a big smile, takes the fellow's hundred dollars. "Tell you what," he says, "I'll give you a chance to win back your money. Double or nothing if you do it yourself."

People in the book trade can't afford to lose that sort of money, so the fellow from Vancouver peels off his last hundred dollars, slaps it down on the bar, and walks back out on to the balcony. "Where's the right spot?" he asks.

"Right down there," says the guy in the suit. "Aim for that manhole cover. You'll be fine."

The fellow from Vancouver climbs over the ledge and jumps, aiming for the manhole cover. He hits it going a terrible speed. He'll never see the Yaletown Brewing Company again. The guy in the suit returns to the bar, picking up the late Vancouverite's money. Just then Harold, possibly the best waiter in the world, walks by. "Jesus," says Harold, "get a couple of drinks into you, Superman, and you turn into a real shit."

★ A fellow walks into a bar in Moncton and gets into conversation with another guy. They start talking about holidays they've had. The second guy mentions having had a holiday in the Gaspé.

"Jeez," says the first fellow. "Nothin' ever came out of the Gaspé except whores and hockey players."

"That so?" says the other guy. "My wife comes from the Gaspé."

"You don't say," says the fellow. "What team did she play for?"

★ A fellow walks into a bar in North Battleford with his golden retriever. The bartender says, "Sorry, pal, no dogs in here."

Thinking quickly, the fellow looks just slightly to one side of the bartender and says, "But this is my seeing-eye dog."

Abashed, the bartender apologizes, and serves the fellow a drink. When he's had his pint, the fellow leaves. Just outside he encounters another fellow about to enter the bar with a chihuahua. "Watch your step," he tells the second fellow. "Seeing-eye dogs only in this place."

So the second guy walks in and is told by the bartender that dogs are not allowed in the bar. "But it's my seeing-eye dog!" he replies.

"Seeing-eye dog?" says the bartender. "That's a chihuahua!"

"What?" says the fellow. "They gave me a chihuahua?!"

★ A fellow walks into a bar in Winnipeg and tells the bartender to set up one of each of his single malts. The barkeep pours them out, one by one, and sets them on the bar, all twenty-four of them. The fellow thanks him and starts downing them, one by one. The bartender watches, and within ten minutes most of the glasses are empty.

"You're in a hurry," says the bartender.

"You would be too," says the fellow, downing the last one, "if you had what I've got."

"Jeez," says the bartender. "What have you got?"

"About a dollar eighty."

★ A fellow walks into a bar in Victoria and sits down next to an attractive woman. He doesn't say anything to her, just starts checking his obviously high-tech watch. She watches for a bit and finally says, "That's a fancy watch you've got there."

"Fancy," he says. "That's an understatement. This watch does things no other watch can do. It tells me things that are going on around me. Like right now it's telling me I'm sitting next to the most beautiful woman in the place."

"Uh-huh," she says. "What else does it tell you?"

"Hang on a moment," he says. "It says you're not wearing any underwear."

"Not such a smart watch," she says. "I'm wearing underwear."

"Damn," he says. "The thing's running an hour fast."

★ A seal walks into a bar. The bartender says, "What'll you have?"

The seal says, "Anything but Canadian Club."

★ A fellow walks into a bar in Calgary. After he's had a beer he says to the waiter, "Listen, I know this great joke about the Canadian Alliance."

The bartender leans forward and says, "Look buster, you oughta know that I'm a member of the Canadian Alliance. That big guy sitting next to you, he's the local treasurer of the Alliance. The huge guy standing behind you with the tattoos, he's our local Alliance candidate. You still sure you want to tell this joke?"

"Hell no," says the fellow, "not if I'm going to have to explain it three times."

★ Three brewers walk into a pub during the Guelph Beer Festival, and the bartender asks them what they'll have. The fellow from Molson orders a pint of Golden. The fellow from Labatt thinks for a moment and orders a pint of Blue. Ron Keefe, from the Granite Brewery, pauses and asks for an orange juice. "Hell," he says, "if these guys aren't going to have a beer I won't either."

★ So this dyslexic walks into a bra.

★ A fellow from Quebec walks into a bar in Toronto and finds there's this competition going on. The bartender explains that anyone who can drink twenty pints of Molson Canadian not only gets it for free but wins a hundred bucks as well. "Well, I don't know," says the guy from Quebec, who then walks out.

The competition goes on, with no winner in sight. Finally the guy from Quebec comes back in and says, "Okay, let's go."

The twenty pints are put in front of him and he makes his way through them, finishing the last pint after about twenty-five minutes. He gets a round of applause and five crisp twenty-dollar bills. "Congratulations," says the bartender. "But I have to know why you disappeared for twenty minutes before you came back and won the contest."

"Oh, dat," says the guy from Quebec, who only now has put on an accent, "I 'ad to go to the place next door first to see if I could do it."

★ A fellow walks into a bar and says to the bartender, "Quick, give me a pint before the trouble starts."

The bartender serves him a pint, which goes down pretty quickly. The historic comic rule of three applies, so we know that the same thing is going to happen a second time—a pint before the trouble starts—without comment, and finally a third time. Having served this fellow his third pint, the barkeep asks if the fellow is considering paying for these beers.

"Uh-oh," says the fellow. "Here's where the trouble starts."

★ Three fellows walk into a bar in New Liskeard. They all order a pint of beer, and—wouldn't you know it?—each pint has a fly paddling like crazy in the foam. The fellow from Vancouver puts his beer to one side and orders a fresh one. The fellow from Halifax deftly pulls the fly out of his glass and drinks the beer. The fellow from Toronto takes the fly out of his glass and squeezes it over his beer, crying, "Spit it out, you little bastard!"

★ A fellow walks into a bar on Granville Island, sits down, and from a bag takes out a small wooden box. He opens the box and out steps a little man in a tiny tuxedo, who runs down the length of the bar and jumps over to the piano, where he plays a few warm-up scales before dazzling the bar with a Bach fugue and a Scott Joplin rag. A guy sitting next to the fellow with the little wooden box is impressed, and he says so.

"Oh, you see a lot of surprising things in here," says the fellow. "You see that old lamp down at the end of the bar? There's a genie in that lamp and he'll give you a wish, but you want to be careful."

Without another word, the guy approaches the lamp, rubs it a bit, and out comes the genie. The fellow with the little wooden box watches as the guy speaks softly to the genie. "Speak up!" cries the fellow with the little wooden box, but it's too late. A moment later the bar is filled with ducks.

The guy returns to his seat, fighting his way past all these ducks. "Man," he says, "that genie is deaf. I asked for a million bucks, but I got a million ducks."

"Tell me about it," says the fellow with the little wooden box. "You think I asked for a twelve-inch pianist?"

★ Superman walks into a bar. It's the sort of bar that superheroes go to when they've had a long day of fighting evil. Rubberman is already at the bar, and he can see that Superman is not at his best. His tights are scuffed and there's a rip in his cape. "What happened to you?" asks Rubberman.

"What a day," says the bedraggled superhero. "There wasn't much going on today, and I was just flying around keeping an eye on things. Anyway, I found myself flying over that building that Wonderwoman lives in. You know the place?"

"Sure," says Rubberman, "I been to a couple of parties at her place."

"So you know she's got that terrace outside. Well, I'm flying overhead at about 8,000 feet, and I look down and there's Wonderwoman out on her terrace and she's got nothing on."

"Wow," says Rubberman. "Wish I could fly."

"So I bank left, decelerate, reduce altitude, go over again at about 4,000 feet, and I can see she's definitely naked. And she seems to be writhing."

"Oh man," says Rubberman. "What did you do then?"

"Bank left again, decelerate further, reduce altitude again, so I'm flying immediately overhead. All previous conclusions verified. Wonderwoman is clearly in a state of sexual excitement."

"So what the hell did you do, Supe?" asks Rubberman, who is by now in a bit of a state himself.

"Do?" asks Superman.. "What could I do? I'm only superhuman, after all. I swooped."

"You swooped?"

"I swooped straight down on Wonderwoman."

Rubberman pauses to visualize the moment. "I bet Wonderwoman was surprised."

Superman rubbed his powerful chin. "She was surprised, all right. But not half as surprised as the Invisible Man."

★ A grasshopper goes into a bar in Saskatoon and orders a beer. The bartender says, "Say, did you know we've got a drink named after you?"

The surprised grasshopper replies, "Really? You've got a drink called Nigel?"

★ The original animal-walks-into-a-bar joke: This alligator (1) walks into a bar and orders a beer (2). The bartender pours the beer (3) and says to the alligator, "That'll be $13.50." (4) The alligator pays up and drinks the beer, then prepares to leave. "Say," says the bartender, "we don't get a lot of alligators in here."

"At these prices," replies the alligator, "I'm not surprised." (5)

(1) This joke has encompassed practically the entire animal kingdom over the years. Sometimes it's a bear, an emu, various breeds of dog, you name it. I use the alligator myself, because it's the way I first heard it, and I like the visual image.

(2) It is a given of the animal-walks-into-a-bar joke that the animal can both speak and comprehend English.

(3) It is also a given that the bartender is of the I've-seen-everything school and will serve the animal without asking for ID or checking the local bylaws.

(4) The joke—feeble as it is—hinges upon the animal being overcharged for its beer. It has never been clear to me if this is simply an expensive bar or if the bartender is deliberately bilking the animal, assuming that an alligator, say, will not know the going price of a beer. If the latter, it reflects poorly on the bartender.

(5) The punch line is one you can see coming a mile away, but it becomes clear why this has to be an animal. See the definitive study by Smithers (University of Oshawa Press, 1984) on the comic incongruity of animals in bars. It wouldn't work if it were, say, a Nova Scotian or a Jehovah's Witness or a bookseller.

A Wee Bibliography

Books and pubs go together like port and Stilton; they're terrific on their own but sensational together. You could make an argument for matching authors and beers, much as wine (and beer) writers match beverages to particular foods. If you're reading, say, early Evelyn Waugh, you might want a beer with a biting hop character. A spunky American IPA would do the trick. Carol Shields might call for something with an air of surprise to it – something made a bit perky through the addition of cherries or raspberries, for instance. The Russians, on the other hand, need a beer that's big and solemn, a beer to get you through a Moscow winter: a big Belgian knock-you-down kind of beer.

Or you could simply read books about drinking. Ray Oldenburg's *The Great Good Place* – mentioned in my introduction – cries out for a place that is neither home nor the workplace, a democratic third place where men and women can gather as equals and speak freely. In most cultures the third place is some sort of bar or pub; elsewhere it might exist to serve coffee. I know which I prefer.

I have taken much inspiration from *The Faber Book of Drink, Drinkers and Drinking*, an eclectic collection of drink-related poetry and prose edited by Simon Rae. (A barkeep of my acquaintance asked me what I was reading one day, and I showed him this book. "It combines all my interests," I told him.) This invaluable compilation draws on such writers as Shakespeare, Marco Polo, Dorothy Parker, and Homer – a quartet that would make up an admirable dinner party.

Anything by Michael Jackson (and I mean the bearded Englishman, not the odd American fellow who looks like Diana Ross) is worthy of your attention. He is all-wise and all-knowing. As well as excellent beer guides, Jackson regularly produces eye-catching coffee table books filled with wonderful, thirst-inducing images. Jackson's Canadian equivalent is Stephen Beaumont, whose *Great Canadian Beer Guide* (2nd edition, 2001) is compulsory reading for anyone who even considers drinking a beer in that country. His *Premium Beer Drinker's Guide* (2000) steers the drinking person to "the world's strongest, boldest and most unusual beers." It's a journey worth taking. In 1997 Jamie MacKinnon produced *The Great*

Lakes Beer Guide (Eastern Region), a fine book that could stand to be updated in this fast-changing world. It is not for nothing that the Campaign for Real Ale updates its outstanding *Good Beer Guide* annually for the pleasure and edification of beer lovers in the UK. I wouldn't go to Britain without it, though I often take *The Quiet Pint* and *The Good Pub Guide* as well.

Literate drinking folk in my neck of the woods can learn plenty from *Tavern in the Town: Early Inns and Taverns of Ontario* by Margaret McBurney and Mary Byers, published by University of Toronto Press. It's out of print, but the resourceful reader can track one down on abebooks.com.

Finally, if you've always wondered what drinking and hanging about in pubs is like but you've been too timid to try it yourself, read practically anything by Kingsley Amis. Amis is the most frequently cited contributor to Simon Rae's aforementioned collection, and for good reason. He knew whereof he wrote.

Acknowledgements

Peter and Diane Waldock plied me with intoxicating beverages and made me write this book, so the lion's share of the blame must rest on their shoulders. My great friends Charlie Owen and Linda Jenetti, on some otherwise unremembered birthday in the seventies, gave me a second-hand typewriter, an instrument that started me on the slippery slope that led to this book, so some of the blame accrues to them as well.

In fact, there are few innocent parties in this sorry tale. Anyone I have passed time with in a pub is in some small way guilty of aiding and abetting, and it's a very long list. I must single out John Jackson as a singularly egregious influence. (To his long-suffering wife Mary I can simply apologize for having allowed John to burn down their kitchen one memorable evening. I had no idea that macramé was so dramatically inflammable, and I bet John didn't either.)

Drinkers tend to travel in packs, and I'm happy to acknowledge members of the Sunday afternoon baseball/Artful Dodger crowd, the estimable Morrissey Tavern set, and the august denizens of the Duke of York, not to mention habitués at various times of the Embassy Tavern, the Chez Moi, the Rex Hotel, the Sticky Wicket, the GSU, and other such palaces of pleasure. Veterans of the Walk to the Ballpark are worthy of attention, if only for their ability to drink and walk on the same day, sometimes at the same time.

I thank Kevin Harper and his colleagues at North 49 Books for their enthusiasm toward this project, Fortunato Aglialoro for making it all look good, and tireless publicist Pat Cairns for bringing this book to your attention. Thank you, Patrick Kennedy, for the Subway Game. When I told Patrick I was stealing his idea, he bought me a pint. Surely this should have been the other way around, and I really mean to rectify this oversight. Thanks also to Glen "I'll have wings with that" Sutherland, who bravely came along on a couple of fact-finding missions to pubs unknown. I am grateful to Bill Bryson, that wonderfully funny and insightful writer, for graciously contributing his foreword. There can be no nicer guy on or off the bestseller lists. I must also grovel to my workmates at the

University of Toronto Bookstore for enduring me at the best of times, let alone when I'm attempting to write a book in my spare time.

I salute the quality brewers of the world, those men and women who persist in making good beer when it's cheaper and clearly more profitable to make bad beer, and to those publicans who bring their own distinct verve to their establishments, valuing character over formula.

There's a song in *Les Miserables* about empty chairs and empty tables, and as we get older we lose some of our companions. I could wish for another pint with the likes of Michael Lee, Winston Nelson, Tom Monohan, and Sky Jones, all taken from us far too soon.

Finally, at the head of the Without Whom column is my wife Anne, the Evergreen Bride, whose loving support continues to dazzle me. During the writing of this book she awarded me more than one Compassionate Litter Leave, cleaning up after cats even when it wasn't her turn, and she behaved with remarkable forbearance even when I came home late, stinking of research. To her, countless thanks.

The Last Word

A writer goes into a bar and orders a beer. The bartender, drawing the pint, says, "You seem pretty chipper tonight."

"Indeed I am," replies the writer. "I just finished my book."

"Hey, me too," says the bartender, handing over the beverage.

"Really?" says the writer.

"Yeah," says the bartender, "just before I started my shift. Look, you can borrow it if you like. It's by Tom Clancy."